John Williams is an academic at the University of Leicester who has written widely about football and football culture.

Ramón Llopis is an academic at the University of Valencia who has been involved in recent research comparing football and football cultures in England and Spain.

RAFA

LIVERPOOL FC, BENÍTEZ AND
THE NEW SPANISH FURY

JOHN WILLIAMS
AND **RAMÓN LLOPIS**

MAINSTREAM
PUBLISHING

EDINBURGH AND LONDON

This edition, 2007

First published (under the title *Groove Armada*)
in Great Britain in 2006 by
MAINSTREAM PUBLISHING COMPANY
(EDINBURGH) LTD
7 Albany Street
Edinburgh EH1 3UG

ISBN 9781845962050

A catalogue record for this book is available from the British Library

Typeset in Ehrhardt and Folio

Printed in Great Britain by
Cox & Wyman Ltd, Reading

John Williams:

For the new arrivals Amelia (Millie) and Sasha.

Ramón Llopis:

For Maria, Guillermo, Alvaro and Nicolas.

Contents

Prologue

Cardiff 2006 and Athens 2007

UEFA bungles in Athens; England versus Spain and the new European game; Steven Gerrard breaks Alan Pardew's will in Wales; Rafael Benítez and Liverpool Football Club; downed by Pippo Inzaghi and Jorge Valdano.

THE MADNESS OF ATHENS: 23 MAY 2007

Welcome to Planet Football – to Athens on Wednesday, 23 May 2007. What has happened to the Aegean weather? It is positively throwing it down in Syntagma Square in the centre of the city on the late morning of the day of the 2007 UEFA Champions League final. The match will be staged in this sprawling, chaotic city in just a few hours' time. Not that this unseasonable rain at all bothers UEFA's elite. They are holed up in the impressively expensive Hotel Grande Bretagne on the edge of the square. Nor does the rain seem to dismay the thousands of dishevelled, replica-kitted Liverpool fans – hundreds without match tickets – who are gathered outside these hotel windows and who have now shaped an impromptu standing Kop on the stone steps that rise just behind the nearby subway exit. They continue to sing their football litany in the driving rain: songs in praise of their new hero, their meticulous strategist manager Rafael Benítez. He is the man who is most feted by them, a man who has brought their club back to near the pinnacle of the European game. These fans have faith in Rafa. They willingly perform their acts of devotion for the locals and for the world's media, and parade their wonderfully preposterous flags and banners all around Syntagma: 'I Love Liverpool, But Not In A Gay Way'; 'Strange Brilliance'; 'We've Got More Euros Than The Post Office'; and, with a philosophically local nod to Plato, 'This City Is What It Is, Because Our Citizens Are What They Are'. The Liverpool FC European fan roadshow is back in town.

In the five-star Grande Bretagne Hotel (where a double room costs three hundred and six euros a night) the echoes of this mass football singing are strangely reassuring. Tom Hicks, one of Liverpool's new American owners, later says, 'We know we are lucky to be here. We had dinner with our families on the roof of the hotel, and we could see the lighted Parthenon in the distance, and we could hear our fans singing below us, and we said, "This is as good as it gets."' Note that 'we' are 'his' fans already; we come as valued collateral with this football club. (Does he have any spare tickets?) Maybe these hard-nosed US businessmen have a feel for the values and cultural resonance of British sport after all. But right now the brilliant men from UEFA have other things on their minds. They are busily tending to the needs of hundreds of top corporate guests. We can see coach loads of them arriving, carelessly squishing through the gathering troughs and puddles, spraying the T-shirted Liverpudlians on the roads around Syntagma. We will see examples of these key UEFA invitees all over the city later today, wearing their summer slacks and their tans and their expensive watches and their priceless and provocative 'Grand Fan' UEFA arena ID around their necks. They had better watch out, these football innocents, for there are squads of Scouse ticket snatchers roaming the city today, all of them still urgently seeking access. We see them everywhere.

These UEFA guests – the global football smoochers, the great accredited uncommitted – are the type of customers that are a common feature at all major sporting events today. They are the clients and friends of Coca Cola executives from Brussels, the Heineken marketers from Dusseldorf, and the Ford and Mastercard deal makers from Paris and all points south. They, and their companies, have all helped build the Champions League into the amazing commercial and cultural success it has become over the past decade, so this final is also partly 'their' day. They certainly seem to have no obvious guilt about their own presence: 'I have worked hard for this day out.' (If not in dedicated fan hours.) And we might say the same thing in their position – take our own chances for sporting perks if and when they arise.

These global companies, in turn, live off the shimmering, seductive power of big-time sport. They spread valued access to global sporting contests to their favoured clients and customers, to politicians and company spouses and friends, as a signal both of their proprietary gratitude and as a marker of their international influence. This booming market in corporate sport – the global football–sponsorship synergy – is now part of the core of the new international machismo of business. The quality and number of tickets you have access to for the best sporting events today reflects nothing less than the relative size of your corporate dick. So, with most Liverpool supporters here in Greece knowing loved ones and friends – real fans – who have no ticket for the final, they view these arriving sponsored coaches into the centre of Athens with something approaching contempt. A message comes out strongly from the drenched Red ranks in the Syntagma rain. It is this: *they* have *our* tickets, these prized UEFA guests and money men.

The Olympic Stadium, which was refurbished for the 2004 Olympic Games, will hold a reported 63,800 fans tonight – it has already, shamefully, been shorn of around 9,000 of its seats simply to accommodate the necessary advertising space for UEFA's family of sponsors. Only 34,000 tickets have been allocated to the competing clubs. This means that once each deals with their own demand from corporate fans, sponsors, players and staff, as well as shareholders and other hangers on, this allocation will dwindle – in Liverpool's case at least – to around 11,000 tickets (out of a total of 17,000) for fans. Four thousand of these will automatically go to those supporters who have seen seven European matches this season, at least one abroad. Which means that there are a paltry 7,000 European Cup-final tickets available for distribution via the general Liverpool fan ballot. Better to have no tickets at all than this pittance. How do you possibly meet the demand and keep fans sane? Liverpool FC alone has around 28,000 season-ticket holders and a waiting list to match. Before this trip to Greece, Rick Parry and the Liverpool club board had been bitterly accused by Reds fans and even by fan organisations in England of showing a lack of transparency in ticket sales. Some even accused them of rigging the Liverpool ballot, the final ticket allocation for those at the very end of the line: the fans. Some Liverpool followers are walking around Athens today wearing badges that argue for more tickets for real fans and not for sponsors. Fair enough. There are even a couple of explicitly anti-Parry Liverpool banners showing through the rain. Getting to this final again should have been a real pleasure for the Liverpool club staff, but, instead, it has turned into a horrible, horrible nightmare of abuse, accusations and recriminations. The Anfield ticket office has even been physically attacked.

Frankly, the ticket charge against Parry and his staff was always a daft one – one borne out of anger and wretched disappointment rather than one based on the facts. It should have been a warning about what was now likely to happen in Greece. The ticket famine was really a case of UEFA falling irresponsibly short of Liverpool's desperate demand. Possibly up to four times that number of eleven thousand Liverpool fans are said to have travelled to Athens for today's events. Who could doubt it after Istanbul? These supporters want to be part of this fantastic event, and they feel, perhaps wrongly, but who can blame them, that they have a right to be here. More of a right at least than the coach loads of UEFA corporate guests. No Liverpool Red wants to risk missing out on another Istanbul. Some have paid £1,000 or more for the privilege of just getting to Greece with no match ticket – and with precious little prospect of buying one. Others have bummed onto trains and hitched rides and have got here at little personal cost. Many made their travel arrangements well before the grave ticket situation became clear, trusting that something would turn up. They were not dissuaded, of course, by the greedy travel companies that instantly conjured up flights to Athens, thinking little of how their customers might get match tickets or even get home. A huge marquee has been set up over grass at the new Athens airport to hold Liverpool fans overnight – like cattle. Anything else eats into profit margins.

Many other Reds fans have flooded into Athens today from the Greek islands, or else via obscure flight connections. Most of them have nowhere to stay tonight and no way of leaving. Everything they have is staked on the slim possibility of buying a ticket or else somehow getting into the stadium. They will find friends' hotel rooms or shop doorways and park benches to doss in tonight. They will deal with that problem later: now it is all about tickets. Notwithstanding UEFA's advance internet ticket sales and their local allocation to Greek fans – much of which will, of course, end up on the black market and be sold at up to ten times their face value, mainly to Liverpool supporters – probably close to around 25,000 of the original capacity of this stadium has, in some way, been used to satisfy UEFA's own requirements: to deal with the various demands of its gorging 'family' of sponsors, workers, officials and guests.

This combination of UEFA's (mis)allocation of tickets and the unwillingness of Liverpool supporters to accept that what is done is done and that they should stay at home if they have no ticket is storing up trouble. And do you want to know the really stupid thing about all this? You want to know why all of this is especially dumb? It is that everyone involved in this event expects – in fact *wants* – at least 30,000 or even 40,000 Liverpool fans to get into the Olympic Stadium tonight. Indeed, UEFA positively crave their attendance in order that these 'true fans' might add the necessary atmosphere and the authenticity to their big show – to light up the event for the TV millions. Just as they did in Istanbul. So, all of this is just a little absurd, don't you think? That the organising body itself should collude in its policies in shaping a white-hot illicit ticket market and then, via internet scallies and British touts, local people, and sponsors who don't really care about football, effectively inject it with tickets, hoping that these might eventually end up in the hands of the real fans? But at what cost and risk: we would soon find out.

With Liverpool in town in such numbers and with UEFA at least nominally at the helm, the other thing you can absolutely count upon tonight, as well as the inflated street prices, is a massive market in ticket forgeries. Just consider the profit margins: £54 tickets selling well on Athens streets today for £500 or more. Do the maths: ten tickets moved on in an hour would potentially earn the ticket touts about £5,000, most of it profit. The real beauty is that in this dirty business your customers are actually thanking you for doing them a favour, because no one wants to believe they have bought a dud ticket. We have already come across guys in Syntagma today who fear they might have purchased fakes. One has faithfully paid £1,000. What is their response to the possibility that they may have been ripped off and that they will be locked out tonight despite their outlay? It is something we will hear a lot today: 'Fuck it. We'll get in anyway. We have paid. It is UEFA that have cocked this up.'

There *are* some Reds here today, of course, who might, in other circumstances, have accepted this bleak ticket situation. These are people who just wanted to be in Athens tonight to soak up the atmosphere, to maybe have a drink up and then watch the game on a big screen at a fan festival with thousands of other Scousers. They could then join in the (testing fate here) celebrations later, just like tens of thousands of England fans did peacefully in Germany for the World Cup finals in 2006. Then, fans without tickets laughed at the touts and their huge mark-ups because they knew that the big screen was a good crack, loads of ale and no real loss of face. All right, it is a different situation here, but a big screen and a fan park with bars in the centre of Athens would definitely offer another focus for the ticketless; it would be a very good reason not to take the metro all the way north to the Olympic Stadium at Irini. But for this final, and with the determined, ticket-free Red hordes already massing in Athens, UEFA and the Greek organisers have unaccountably decided not to advertise or promote a big screen showing of the match for what they call 'security' reasons. This is a critical mistake – one among many.

So, now we do have a major problem brewing: you can sense it on these Athens streets. There are, of course, a small number of Reds here who will always see bunking into matches abroad and major finals as a masculinity and ingenuity test – as a badge of honour. They are there at most Liverpool matches in Europe, checking for soft spots. Let's not try to defend this. It is a simple, selfish and dangerous case of fuck Hillsborough and the 96 and everyone else's safety and also the club's reputation. The antics of these guys, the irregulars and adventurers, the professional scallies of European-wide reputation, will make up most of UEFA's later report on the alleged bad behaviour of Liverpool supporters all over Europe. It is UEFA's handy get-out clause tonight: 'Unfortunately, in Britain, it is the way,' says William Gaillard, UEFA's director of communications. 'Liverpool are the worst offenders.' Suddenly, Liverpool fans are not the heroic figures they were gratefully painted to be by UEFA in Istanbul in 2005 and, indeed, just before this 2007 final. They are instead disreputable, unwanted disruptives. This is UEFA's handy little secret, revealed only when the wheels come off, as they will do later. But even if this charge was true – and it seems absurd – it would actually make UEFA doubly culpable for the stupidity of tonight's arrangements. Do you prepare least well for your most trying test at your most prestigious fixture? Do you, as a result of your arrangements, effectively encourage *worse* behaviour from the fans you purport to fear the most?

So, this accusation about Liverpool seems a craven response, even if UEFA does have a slightly different point to make. It is this: no platoons of marauding AC Milan fans will turn up tonight with plans to bunk in, less still to break down fences. But this cunning little Liverpool football militia, the one that has definite designs in this area, is usually a manageable problem, and UEFA is responsible, after all, for dealing with a range of different European football cultures. What will make this issue less manageable tonight will not be the hard core and their ugly ambitions. It is that now we will also have in the ticket checking battles the decent, desperate Liverpool fans, those who have paid through the nose for crap forgeries. We will also have those ticketless tourists who might well have happily watched proceedings unfold on a big screen somewhere in town. There could even have been a screen erected on the stage where Pete Wylie will perform tonight in front of a mere handful of Reds fans within the Olympic complex. This might have helped siphon off at least some of the frustrated and the defrauded. But none of this has been properly thought through, despite prior warnings from Liverpool FC about the dangers of getting services and security wrong for this match. Instead, the Athens metro heading north tonight will now be full of conspiracies and self-justifications, housing a growing, typically English – and profoundly Liverpudlian – discontent and bloody-minded determination to get access to the final, come what may. You can hear the plans hatching already: 'Hang around outside. We'll *all* get in.'

Because of the UEFA ticketing fiasco and the vast sums of fan money already spent – and the scallies and the bad forgeries, and soon the chaotic arrangements outside the stadium – even usually sensible Reds fans, those people who have consciences and tickets, will also begin to sympathise with some of those planning their strategies to slip through these childlike security systems. It's wrong, of course it is, but it happens: we all *believe* we have a right. What takes hold now is a sort of crude street morality, a real sense that fans are somehow justified in undermining Liverpool's and UEFA's alleged elitist ticket policies. This determination for illicit entry is converted in the collective fan mind into a crude political act of defiance. Some ticketless Reds even chant 'Justice' as they get inside, which is also a rather grotesque and oblique Hillsborough reference, of course.

The anything goes sentiment only grows stronger now because of what we see in the short space between the Irini metro station and the venue. It is a display of utterly inept Greek and UEFA security around the Olympic Stadium. This includes a shambolic three-cordon ticket 'checking' system which completely breaks down. In fact, there are no means whatsoever of systematically checking match tickets outside the stadium and then weeding out and removing the ticketless or those with obvious forgeries. Forged tickets are simply returned to the ticket holder who then has license to try elsewhere. Many do. Michael Howard, ex-Tory party leader and Liverpool fan, who is at the match tonight, describes the ticket checks outside as 'a joke'. In a long political career it is possibly the only thing he has ever been right about.

There are also some darkly hilarious instructions at police security checkpoints at the very height of the scrum outside: 'Hold your ticket in the air.' Why? So you can try to check it in the dark through a visor? So someone can nick it? This sort of idiocy may work for well-healed, mixed-sex and sober crowds in the summer sunshine at the Olympic Games – for sports tourists – but it will not do among thousands of the desperate and the dispossessed tonight. These are people who, having got this close, would sell their own grandmother for this ticket, for this opportunity. Some tickets waved skywards in this way, or ones just taken out of pockets, are indeed stolen – Red on Red. This behaviour is brutal and inexcusable – but also wholly predictable in this sort of frantic, chaotic climate. It is part of another Greek police tragedy.

When the Greek police finally begin telling Liverpool fans outside who have tickets that no more people can be allowed into the stadium because of a combination of the absence of any effective stewarding or stadium organisation and the sheer opportunist recklessness of others, what, exactly, do they expect the reaction of the great excluded to be? Do they expect these Liverpool fans who suddenly find themselves locked outside the very event they have scrimped and saved for weeks to attend to thank them for their good work? To quietly disperse? Would you? Instead, there is a kind of enraged and righteous panic; a mass surge towards police lines with some making it through, followed by the liberal use of police batons, shields and tear gas to try to turn back the angry Red wave. This aggrieved, bubbling mass includes a reported couple of thousand Reds fans who have real match tickets and who will now be debarred entry from a stadium that is already dangerously overfilled with people with forged tickets, or no tickets, or with fag packets or scraps of blue paper they have successfully passed off as tickets ('Hold your tickets in the air'). Two Norwegian Reds who have paid over £2,000 for packages, including match tickets, are refused entry and attacked by the police for no reason. It is sheer, miserable chaos.

A lucky few of these abused ticket holders will eventually get inside near half-time, some crawling, with the ticketless, under police vans to do so, others apparently randomly allowed access to the stadium by the Greek police. Still others, frightened and dispirited and shedding tears of frustration and tear gas, will simply return to town and consider their legal options. These legitimate ticket holders, these people with a (very expensive) contract with an inept and buck-passing UEFA – the same body that sanctioned the staging of the 2005 Champions League final in a hideously facilities-free, near inaccessible field some 40 kilometres outside Istanbul – have been treated like criminals or, worse, animals. They are the innocent victims of all this righteous selfishness and especially the gross ineptitude of the European football officials in whom they had to place their trust. We know already, of course, that in any official inquiry into this debacle – into all this mayhem and disorder, into tonight's confusion and terror – it will turn out to be solely *our* fault. It always is.

Inside the Olympic Stadium at 9.30 p.m., as we impatiently wait for kick–off whilst reflecting on the madness still unfolding outside, people from Liverpool and from all over the world, many having dreamed of and paid regally for this trip, will have to stand in the aisles or on their seats because others from the city and elsewhere are standing two or three abreast in the spaces in front of them in. All official regulatory systems have now effectively collapsed in some parts of the stadium. God, let's hope there is no panic here, no further tragedy. Would the much touted return of standing areas in this kind of situation have made things safer – or potentially much worse? One large group of Liverpool fans to our left seems to have acquired tickets for a section reserved for Milan supporters. How can this happen? And, in the nature of things, many of these Liverpool supporters who have made it inside illegally – those Reds fans who have shown the Greeks and UEFA that they would not be moved – will now turn to each other and say, 'It isn't our fucking fault. We should have had tickets. Outside was a joke.' And the sirens outside continue to wail as the impossibly rich and beautifully coiffured players of Liverpool and AC Milan take the field having left behind their scented, air-conditioned dressing-rooms.

LIVERPOOL V AC MILAN II

Amidst all this UEFA maladministration and supporter chaos, one of European football's truly extraordinary international contests would now be re-enacted in this most symbolic of European sporting cities. Liverpool Football Club, from the hollowed out Irish–English North West and under their phlegmatic Spanish manager Rafael Benítez, would take on the football aristocrats from AC Milan from northern Italy for the second time in the European Cup (Champions League) final. Just two years before, these two clubs produced a drama so unlikely, one so emotionally and physically draining, that much of Europe seemed to stop, open mouthed, to watch it unfold. In Britain 13.9 million people were glued to their TVs, many returning to the action after hearing about Liverpool's nascent revival. From three goals down at half-time and apparently devastated, Liverpool recovered in just six second half minutes to level the scores and then go on to win the European Cup, on penalties, after extra time. Pretty much everybody knows the story now – and how this fifth European Cup victory after 20 years out of the final meant that Liverpool kept the trophy they won in Istanbul on that unforgettable night. 'We would never see the likes of this again,' most of those who were present that night agreed. 'We must savour this unique moment.' Young boys and girls had their parents write letters to school masters in 2005, explaining that their children's necessary absence for a few days in May was because it was indeed the chance of a lifetime. 'How many other European Cup finals will my son/daughter have the opportunity to see?' It seemed a perfectly rational argument at the time.

But the writing paper had to come out again and the special pleading about the benefits of sport, education and travel began anew. Because here we all were, just two years later, back in southern Europe and facing the same Milan, a proud (if recently soiled) football club clearly bent on revenge. Steven Gerrard had already, in the build up, called the Milan hard man and World Cup-winner Rino Gattuso an overrated 'kitten' and had claimed in his autobiography that Gattuso and his Milanese team mates had been showboating at half-time in Turkey in 2005, laughing and waving to family and friends as they left the pitch as if their job was already done. This disrespect, said Gerrard, had irked the Liverpool players, who vowed that they would show the Italians they still had some pride – that they deserved better. Gattuso was livid at this charge, cursing the Liverpool captain for these accusations of a lack of professionalism and gross dereliction of duty. He said he was bent on righting this wrong in Athens, on reasserting his reputation as a mad dog, a terrier – as a winner.

In the week running up to the final, Liverpool manager Rafa Benítez had also answered hundreds of press questions about what he had actually said at half time in Istanbul in 2005 to turn Liverpool's fortunes around. Benítez was embarrassed, and found it hard to reply, because he had struggled at the time for the right words. The Liverpool dressing-room was actually chaotic and defeated in 2005; the manager had even mistakenly prepared a second-half Liverpool formation made up of 12 players. Bootle's Jamie Carragher admitted later that his only concern at half time in Istanbul was averting a potential five-

or six-goal drubbing by Milan. He wanted only to avoid humiliation, and he had no fancy ideas about getting back into the match, least of all winning it. The Liverpool 'plan', such as it was, was to try to score one goal 'for the fans' and then see what happened. What happened, as we now know, was a comeback inspired mainly by the Liverpool crowd – 'Six mad minutes' Gattuso called it – and then Milanese panic. 'In this [2007] final,' said the Liverpool coach, 'I would like to see the perfect team.' But Benítez would first have to select it.

What was really strange about this European final rematch was that neither of these two great clubs should really have been in the 2007 Champions League final at all. Liverpool's and Rafa Benítez's focus should really have been on winning the Premiership title in 2007. This had been the manager's aim, he claimed later, but he had been thwarted by Liverpool's lack of spending power and by some alleged dithering over key transfer targets. As a result, alleged Benítez, he had ended up with only 'third or fourth choice' players in the 2006 transfer round. He ominously likened the situation at Liverpool after Istanbul to that at Valencia CF after he had won the Spanish title: complacency set in at board level, meaning consistent league success proved impossible. Whatever the reasons, Liverpool's 2007 Premiership dream died in the first few weeks of the new season with a string of by now familiar Liverpool away defeats. As a result, Benítez soon set his sights on Europe once again.

Both Liverpool and Milan were also underdogs in their 2007 Champions League semi-finals, against Chelsea and Manchester United respectively. Both won through against the odds and against British press anticipation of a first all-English final. Moreover, Italian football, for its part, had been mired in corruption and match-fixing charges in 2006, centred on Juventus. Things looked very bad indeed for the 'Old Lady' of the north of Italy, a proud club that was relegated in disgrace to *Serie B* with a nine-point deficit. But police investigations also involved at least three other top Italian clubs and forty-one players and officials. Mighty AC Milan were one of those who suffered a points deduction in 2005–06 and who were forced to start the new season in 2006–07 behind the rest in *Serie A* – an eight-point penalty for allegedly interfering with the appointment of match officials. Milan were also shorn of their star striker Andriy Shevchenko in 2006–07 after he arranged a move to Chelsea in England, perhaps fearing a season in Italy without Champions League football. As football fans in Italy continued to fight with police officers, amongst themselves and with foreign visitors in increasingly outmoded and chaotic stadia, it looked like nothing less than a potential *calcio* meltdown in 2006–07. How little we knew.

In Germany in the summer of 2006, and against all the odds, it was a defiant Italy that emerged triumphant in the World Cup finals, outlasting the South Americans and also the Europeans from England, Germany and Spain before defeating a brave France on penalties in a controversial final in Berlin. Moreover, far from experiencing European club exile, an ageing AC Milan side – the fifth richest football club in Europe in 2006, boasting possibly the world's best player in the Brazilian Kaká – discovered that UEFA had, in fact, no powers at all to exclude them from the 2007 Champions League competition. Milan's retrospective 30 points penalty for their sins in Italy – which had been reduced on appeal – still left the club in third position in Serie A for season 2005–06 and thus eligible for the qualifying round of the Champions League in August 2006.

This situation seemed little short of incredible. UEFA's William Gaillard, rather shamefacedly, reported that the Italian federation (FIGC) had indeed nominated the disgraced AC Milan for the 2007 Champions League, and that UEFA's executive committee had discovered that it had been powerless to object. 'Some of the committee had misgivings about the situation,' he later admitted. 'But when we examined our statutes and regulations, we saw that we could not do anything about it because the national association was sovereign.' UEFA understood immediately the gravity of the situation and felt compelled to change its own statutes at its congress in Dusseldorf in

January 2007. From then on, clubs penalised by their own national associations for attempted match rigging at home could be excluded by UEFA from European competition. But that was for the future. The UEFA executive just had to sit and hope that AC Milan – found guilty of attempted cheating and severely punished by their own national federation – did not somehow manage to win Europe's blue-chip football event, the 2007 Champions League.

Partly because of these serious problems in Italy in 2006, the English Premier League and *La Liga* in Spain were generally argued to be the dominant leagues in Europe. They had the TV cash and the crowds (though Germany had those too), and because of this many of the world's best footballers on show. Liverpool Football Club had also acquired in 2004 Valencia CF's Rafael Benítez, then the most coveted Spanish coach in the game. So, England and Spain were now not only at odds in football but their cultures were also, simultaneously, deeply intertwined, at least in one North West British city.

In the Champions League in 2006, Barcelona eliminated English champions Chelsea following a wild and turbulent first-leg night at Stamford Bridge, while Arsenal accounted for a meek Real Madrid, as well as the Spanish surprises in Europe, Villarreal, in a nervy semi-final. Villarreal had already helped see off Everton and Manchester United earlier in the competition. England and Spain seemed to be the key European football club protagonists in 2006. Before Barcelona and Arsenal met in the final of that year – narrowly won by the Catalans – the two countries were exactly level at the top of the table of European Cup-final wins at ten apiece. In the 2007 Champions League competition, England and Spain were in European football combat once again, with Barcelona falling to both Chelsea and then Liverpool, and the Londoners also getting the better of Valencia CF in the quarter-finals. As Liverpool doused Chelsea once more in the semi-finals, AC Milan's surprise defeat of Manchester United in the other semi-final reminded both England and Spain that the Italians were still a force to be reckoned with in club football in Europe.

So, it was a repeat of Liverpool v. AC Milan. Milan even decided to opt for the all-white kit they wore in 2005 to face their demons head on. Could lightening really strike twice?

'HE'LL PASS THE BALL FORTY YARDS . . .'

Lacking real transfer pulling power, Liverpool at least had some consolation for losing their European Champions cloak in 2006. In the Millennium Stadium in Cardiff on 13 May 2006, with Rafa Benítez pulling the strings, the Reds had contested another epic final – a thrilling, pulsating and error-strewn FA Cup drama. It was one that deserved the promised stage of the new Wembley Stadium, but it would now be treasured, instead, by the good people of Wales – by people we knew we could trust. And what a story they had! And what a background story, too. The thoughtful and rather emotionless Spaniard Benítez and his Liverpool captain, the withdrawn and troubled Scouser Steven Gerrard, had almost parted company in July 2005. They came within a whisker of mutual rejection, as confusion and their cultural and emotional differences seemed to be inexorably driving them apart. Ten months on and it was Gerrard who was, almost single-handedly, saving Liverpool Football Club and its manager from defeat in the Millennium Stadium against an inspired West Ham United.

Rafa Benítez, we knew, had little time for the cult of the individual player. He likes to make a coach's point, an approach which fitted in well with the Liverpool ethos, about having good workers in your team. 'You can have good players who might play fantastic football and entertain the supporters,' he said, 'but if you want to win trophies, then you also need workers who will play and train well every week for nine months of each season, and with quality. But this is the problem: to have enough workers with the quality to win.' Gerrard was exceptional in this last respect: he combined this willingness to work with spirit and a penchant for the spectacular. He was just too good to lose.

This FA Cup final epic was Liverpool's second consecutive major cup final drawn 3–3 and then won on penalties (chalk up the TV viewing figures). It was also the second time that the indefatigable Gerrard had been the key figure in eventually hauling Liverpool back into the battle and then on to an unlikely victory. Losing 0–3 in Istanbul to AC Milan in 2005; 0–2 and 2–3 behind in Cardiff in 2006 and never once looking, at any moment, to be winners in Wales. Until, that is, Gerrard took over. His manager could only look on with a wry smile and wonder, 'How close we came to disaster.' Could his captain really do it again in Athens in 2007? He seemed to be the only Liverpool player of whom AC Milan was truly afraid.

In a recent book about football management in Europe, the ex-Italian striker and former Chelsea manager Luca Vialli has written that one of the things that marks out the professional game in England from that played in, say, Italy or even Spain today is that at 0–2 down the Continentals usually accept defeat graciously. It seems strangely 'unprofessional' abroad, he says, to try to claw back such a clear deficit. So you accept your lot with dignity and move on. And he is on to something here because, contrarily, in England a 0–2 score line can sometimes be seen as a convenient pathway to comeback glory. And it is a positively dangerous score, an invitation to potential disintegration, when the trailing side contains the scowling and perpetually troubled figure of Steven Gerrard. After all, it was Gerrard who showed the heart and the quality necessary to drive his home-town club Liverpool on to victory in both Istanbul and Cardiff. The Huyton man never gave up the fight, not even at the very last. And it was Gerrard who was, unselfconsciously, thanked by his Norwegian team mate John Arne Riise in 2006 after scoring to make it 3–3 in Wales: for 'saving' Liverpool once more; for simply being a 'great' football player. It was the sort of hero-worshipping you see daily among kids nudging each other in a school playground. 'Thanks, Stevie,' Riise seemed to be saying to his captain, 'for being *my friend*.'

In the post mortems that followed Cardiff in 2006, some reporters described the Scouser's second equalising goal at the Millennium Stadium as a 'force of nature'. West Ham's then manager, the impressive Alan Pardew, probably had other words for it, so close was his own team to victory in Cardiff at that moment. There was certainly a visceral quality about the strike, scored as the match drifted into time added on ('four minutes' bellowed the stadium announcer) and, inevitably, towards an increasingly comfortable West Ham win. It was the only Liverpool shot in the last 20 minutes. It was a goal designed to break the heart and spirit of the stoutest of opponents. Just how *did* he score it? The Liverpool man, crippled by cramp, was actually hobbling horribly and trying to catch up with a last desperate Liverpool attack. He was out of the game, apparently beaten (we had already given it up in the stands). Then the ball broke to him from a defensive header from the West Ham man Danny Gabbidon, precisely 32 yards from goal. Suddenly, Gerrard came alive again. Was this luck or fate?

Benítez could see that Gerrard was absolutely exhausted – more tired even than in Istanbul, where his manager had to work to keep him on board. In Wales Gerrard was probably horrified that the ball had even reached him so late and in such an unpromising situation. Nigel Reo-Coker, still brave and resolute in West Ham's midfield, nevertheless could see the danger, and he tried to close the Liverpool man down. So Gerrard struck early for goal, very possibly as a last resort. It was what the new American owners of Liverpool in 2007 might have called a 'Hail Mary' into the Hammers' end zone. But it was actually a more controlled hit-and-hope than that. On another day – on West Ham's day – his raking shot, from an impossible distance, would have dribbled wide or else ballooned into the stands. Blow for time, ref, and we can all go home. But, instead, here it swerved and dived, in a blur, into the bottom right-hand corner of Shaka Hislop's goal – at 68 mph. Some gadget measured the pace: this proved to be the West Ham goalie's new speed limit. And just as it lifted every disbelieving, defeated Red frown in Wales, so this equalising score from nowhere was also the cruellest dagger driven deep into each East End heart. Everyone in the Millennium Stadium knew instantly what it meant, even if the final outcome was delayed by extra time and penalty kicks. Pepe Reina made sure Liverpool triumphed on penalties – he saved three out of four West Ham kicks.

Pardew's handsome face – he is the English Mourinho – was a grisly picture at the moment Liverpool equalised. It was a designer model of distraught and admiring resignation. As a middling, but honest, midfield player Pardew had himself seen off Liverpool with a winning goal for lowly Crystal Palace in a 1990 FA Cup semi-final, an upset of volcanic proportions. That 3–4 reverse in a frenetic, chaotic contest at Villa Park was more than just a defeat for Liverpool Football Club. It was an alarm bell. It announced that the previously dominant Merseyside club had suddenly grown a defensive vulnerability: a canker. Even the master coordinator Alan Hansen was beginning to look human after all. So it was no shock at all that 1990 was also Liverpool Football Club's last league title win in England. Now, 16 years on, the TV Hansen was purring over another Liverpool man, a player whom the Scot argued may well be Liverpool Football Club's greatest-ever player. He meant, of course, the human dynamo Gerrard.

And at the very moment that the Liverpool captain produced the seemingly impossible, so the West Ham boss Pardew was finally repaid for 1990. He offered no touchline scowl. Nor did the London man seek head-in-hands victim status – though he had every right to do so. Instead, he offered a gentle little smile to camera and a rueful 'What can you do?' headshake. He looked calm. But *inside* his head he was silently praising and cursing: 'That brilliant fucker Gerrard'. The ball had ended up at the feet of the only player Pardew feared in the entire Liverpool squad. Just as Gerrard was the only Liverpool player really feared by AC Milan in 2007. 'If he played for West Ham, we would be favourites,' said Pardew. Only Gerrard could possibly summon the strength and the ability to thunder his shot home from this range. He was the only man in South Wales that May afternoon in 2006 with the audacity – with the balls – to even try it. Was it luck – or fate? And could Steven Gerrard keep on producing these dynamic interventions in the season that followed as his manager Benítez insisted on fiddling and moving him around the pitch rather than building a settled Liverpool team around him? We would soon find out.

Commentators, who probably should know better, would later describe this 2006 FA Cup final as one of the greatest – possibly *the* greatest – in the entire history of the FA Cup. Not for forty years, when Trebilcock's Everton overturned Sheffield Wednesday in 1966, had a team come back from *two* goals down to win the FA Cup (only two goals?). Liverpool had scored a remarkable 17 goals in all in winning the 2006 FA Cup. Six goals were conjured up in Cardiff alone, and one of these was an incredible ninety-first-minute equaliser. The journalist James Lawton even compared Gerrard that day to the saintly Bobby Charlton for the quality of his shooting. So, surely, this match was right up there – a classic? The final was exciting, sure – heart-stopping even. Five or six Liverpool players had collapsed with fatigue (who does the fitness training round here, by the way?), so there were even spectres here of the dramas of the 'old' Wembley, before weight training, special diets and multiple substitutions had kicked in and seemed to rule out player suffering as a source of crowd intrigue. All of this public torture of so many young millionaires must have been ghoulishly entertaining for people watching at home.

But was it really the *greatest-ever* FA Cup final? Surely this was hyperbole. Indeed, Liverpool – Steven Gerrard excepted – had been poor, frankly garbage, in Cardiff. Benítez was mystified by the performance. The coach prided himself on preparing his teams for big occasions like that one. But his Liverpool were a shadow of the team that had won 11 straight matches before Wales – the one that had crushed Birmingham City 7–0 in the FA Cup at St Andrews, and had dumped out Manchester United and also Chelsea, later, in the semi-finals. Maybe a Liverpool at the top of their game would have produced a dull spectacle for the neutrals, would have levelled this West Ham – who knows? In any case, Pardew's team would quickly dissolve in 2006–07, and he would soon be sacked. Football is a cruel sport. As it was, this Liverpool side had just four shots on target in the entire match on 13 May 2006, roughly one every half hour.

So, technically, this 2006 final was a rather sorry affair, one full of misplaced passes, terrible defending and unimpressive goalkeeping. The perfectionist Liverpool coach Rafa Benítez must have been bemused by all the talk about this 'great' football match. Typically, he described it later as a 'fantastic' final – but he did so through heavily gritted teeth and from a still limited stock of English adjectives. Jamie Carragher – himself a comic own-goal contributor in Wales – had revealed before Cardiff that even after brilliant defensive performances for Liverpool the obsessive Benítez liked to point out the mistakes made by his defenders, and that the Spaniard moved seamlessly not to celebration but into coaching mode. By this measure the Liverpool back four could expect to be carefully analysed and primed for improvement in the 2006–07 season. Daniel Agger, a young football-playing Danish centre-back, would eventually step into Sami Hyypiä's formidable boots, the major defensive change by Benítez before the European Cup final of 2007.

So, this 2006 FA Cup final had been a piece of great drama, certainly – a game full of reversals and ultimately containing a calamity for a brave West Ham. But it was not a truly great cup final. Maybe Liverpool fans were also poor judges on this score, because their point of comparison for 'greatness' since May 2005 was coming back from the dead against AC Milan in Istanbul. And who, or what, could possibly match that? Indeed, as the 2007 Champions League final approached and Benítez was asked about a possible repeat of Istanbul, he merely smiled gently and touched his chest. 'I hope not,' he said. 'My heart could not stand it.' Not that Benítez was focused too much on the European Cup in 2006 or even in 2007. Having whittled away to just nine in 2006 the embarrassing thirty-seven-point league deficit that had been conceded to Premiership champions Chelsea in 2005, Liverpool were now even being promoted in some quarters as favourites for the Premiership in 2007. It was ultimately an ill-fated favouritism. Of course, Liverpool had managed to win the European Cup in 2005 after finishing, under Gérard Houllier, a preposterous 30 points, and in only fourth place in the Premiership, behind 2004 English champions Arsenal. In 2006 the Reds had finished only third in the Premiership but were in the European Cup final once more in 2007. For some Reds fans these strange new European qualifying rules almost made winning in Istanbul and reaching the final again seem like the most wonderful fraud. *Almost*.

The Frenchman Houllier was eventually sacked in 2004 by the Liverpool board for making too many dodgy (mainly French based) signings and just too little impression on the Premiership race. He had also turned Anfield into a rest home for the paranoid. Rafa Benítez seemed a slightly different personality, and he was rock-solid secure in his job after Istanbul and Cardiff, of course. But he still had some bridges to mend at Anfield. 'I have been delighted with the supporters,' he told *Fifa Magazine* in December 2005. 'You can lose and play badly, but they still support you, which is fantastic.' In 2007 Benítez returned to this theme, saying he had turned down a possible move to Real Madrid because of the special relationship at Liverpool between the players, the staff and the fans. 'It isn't easy to find a club where all the supporters, or at least a majority of them, are behind you.' But this kind of tolerance would soon fade if Liverpool's domestic results did not improve. There were mistakes and many league humiliations to put right in the 2005–06 season. And this improvement would then be expected to be taken on again into 2006–07 – perhaps even to the Premiership title itself. The rejection by Benítez of Real Madrid and the arrival of American finance at Anfield in 2007 suggested that the Spaniard was in for the long haul at Liverpool. But he now demanded the transfer kitty necessary to match his own ambitions.

SPANISH STEPS

Since 2004 there was little doubt that Liverpool Football Club had taken on another entirely different direction under the Spaniard Benítez. If Gérard Houllier had relentlessly mined his Anglo–French connections, ultimately to his own destruction at Liverpool, so Benítez had turned, unapologetically, to Spain and South American countries for many of his own recruits. Not all of these were immediate successes. With Michael Owen, favourite son of Chester and England, long departed from Liverpool – to Real Madrid and then later to Newcastle United – four Liverpool players had been named in the provisional *Spanish* World Cup squad for 2006, one more than in the for England squad for the same tournament. Some of the committed Liverpool–Irish followed Spain, not England, in Germany in the summer of 2006. Liverpool FC was now also the established England club in Spain – even over Chelsea – for many of those who tracked the English Premiership from Madrid, Barcelona and, especially of course, from Valencia, where Benítez had once seemed so unassailable. The new Spanish connections at Anfield – even the history of the Valencia CF club itself and its defining role in shaping the football life of Rafa Benítez – was now another important, interwoven strand of the great story and complex genealogy of Liverpool Football Club. In fact – or were we just dreaming this? – Walton Breck Road and pretty much the whole of the Liverpool 4 area around Anfield, as well as exuding its habitual, communal Scouse vapours, now also had its own distinctive *Spanish* flavour after Istanbul and Cardiff and even in the build up to Athens. What a combustible mixture this was! Close your eyes. Can't you just smell the tanning oil and the whiff of shellfish paella swirling around the arms-spread statue of Bill Shankly? Could Liverpool add to this intoxicating Spanish brew by winning *two* European Cups in just three years under Benítez?

In considering these issues, this book is no simple biography of

Rafa Benítez: it attempts something rather more complicated than that. Instead it is about the specific character of the new 'Spanish' Liverpool under Benítez, his Spanish coaches and Scotland's Alex Millar in seasons 2005–06 and 2006–07. But it is also about Liverpool Football Club's complex origins as well as its various problems in adapting to the new global game. It covers some of the parallel fortunes of the great Liverpool and Valencia clubs from a historic perspective, and the points at which they cross and entangle. It is also about the wider picture of football in England and Spain and the story of Liverpool Football Club and its great Spanish rivals in European club football. And, finally, in the wake of England's failure at the World Cup finals in 2006, it is about club affiliations and the national teams of both England and Spain.

Centrally, however, it is a story about how a Castilian football man Rafa Benítez, a former *Madridista,* and an exceptional 'Celtic' northern British city and football club met head on to create a new 'Spanish fury' in England from 2004. They travelled together in 2005 to the very point where Asia meets Europe, and they flirted with disaster before discovering a kind of football ecstasy. In 2005–06 they pushed on together again towards a new future. And in 2006–07, although failing again in the Premiership, Benítez managed to pilot Liverpool to another European Cup final, an emotional return against AC Milan in Athens. And who knew, just at that moment, where the new Spanish–Liverpool fusion, now under US control, might lead?

POSTSCRIPT

Liverpool lost to AC Milan in the European Cup final in the Olympic Stadium in Athens in 2007 in a largely prosaic contest. Two goals by the arch predator Pippo Inzaghi – the type of pure finisher, we might say, that Rafa Benítez seems to have no place for in his own plans, preferring the hard-working but less incisive Dirk Kuyt – was enough to see off the Liverpool challenge. A fortunate late first-half goal was more than Milan deserved. and as Liverpool pressed on for an unlikely equaliser in the second half Inzaghi showed a striker's instincts in staying onside before rounding Reina to finish the contest. A very late Dirk Kuyt header did little to alter the shape of the evening's proceedings. A rather ordinary AC Milan thus had their revenge.

Benítez may claim to have won the tactical battle with Ancelotti in Athens by suffocating Milan with the excellent Javier Mascherano and even threatening them wide in the first half through Jermaine Pennant, but poor delivery at the crucial moments continued to define the new Liverpool forward signings. Moreover, the Benítez system of playing Steven Gerrard in the Kaká role also arguably robbed Liverpool of its controlling, driving force behind the ball and thus its real identity. Constructing specific formations to face specific opponents – as against Milan – remains Benítez's huge strength, but it is also his greatest weakness. It may offer its occasional rewards, but it also means that Liverpool play few matches on their own terms, assured and settled in their own shape and skin. In the final, Benítez seemed reluctant to try alternative forward options until it was far too late: Peter Crouch played for just 12 minutes in the final, while Craig Bellamy failed to get on the field at all, even though defender Steve Finnan was replaced in the final few minutes. Sadly, this seemed like a glorious opportunity lost for Liverpool rather than an honourable submission to a superior opponent.

Rather overshadowing this disappointing contest were the crowd and ticketing issues in Athens and also some interesting and provocative comments made in Spain before the final by World Cup winner and ex-Real Madrid coach and football intellectual Jorge Valdano. Valdano and Benítez had previously crossed swords when both men were in Madrid. Now, writing in the Spanish daily *Marca*, Valdano claimed that coaches such as Benítez and José Mourinho were destroying the sport because of their focus on producing intensely physical and tactically direct football teams: 'We had better wave goodbye to any expression of cleverness and talent we have enjoyed for a century.'

Valdano was clearly enjoying this attack. He went on, 'Football is made up of subjective feeling, of suggestion – and in that Anfield is unbeatable. Put a shit hanging from a stick in the middle of this passionate, crazy stadium and there are people who will tell you it's a work of art. It's not: it's a shit hanging from a stick.' This was strong stuff, though Reds fans who had closely watched Liverpool labour away from home in the Premiership in 2007 may have had some sympathy with some of these sentiments if not, perhaps, with Valdano's wild and abusive language. Liverpool under Benítez had certainly not always been thrilling or incisive in 2006–07. The manager was a conservative and measured man, not one for always taking matches to inferior opponents with real passion, belief and style.

It was Valdano's second point, however, that was more telling. He argued that Benítez and Mourinho had two things in common: a lack of satisfying playing success and a connected desire to always be in control of the teams they managed. He continued 'Neither Mourinho nor Benítez made it as a player. That has made them channel all their vanity into coaching. Those who did not have the talent to make it as a player do not believe in the talent of players, they do not believe in the ability to improvise to win football matches. In short, Benítez and Mourinho are exactly the kind of coaches that Benítez and Mourinho would have needed to have made it as players.'

There was an obvious flaw to this otherwise interesting proposition: Arsène Wenger was no great player either, but he had produced a creative, imaginative Arsenal team given real freedom to play. Unsurprisingly, Rafael Benítez scoffed at Valdano's suggestions, and he rightly pointed out that the Argentinian had had little success himself as a coach. Benítez commented angrily, 'He is someone I don't think highly of as a professional. He would come out and give press conferences and hang medals on himself while the professionals with talent worked in the shadows.' Benítez was certainly no man for hanging medals on himself. Like Bob Paisley, he preferred to work in the shadows – his very definition of professionalism is planning and restrained hard work. But there was something uncomfortably perceptive in these comments nevertheless. That the Liverpool coach did sometimes perhaps find it difficult to allow very good players to showcase their talent effectively – that the system, the collective, must always win out over individual flair.

Maybe it would require a little less control and just a little bit more license, especially away from Anfield, to eventually take Liverpool Football Club and its Spanish coach to the Premiership title once more. With new American finance in place for 2007–08, the Liverpool coach would at last have the resources available to return the club to where most of its supporters felt it truly belonged: at the very top of English and European football.

1

'In Istanbul, We Won it Five Times'

Liverpool fans 'save' the European Cup; Benítez and Paisley
in Europe, 1981 & 2005; the new traditions of English club
support abroad; Irishness and the roots of Liverpool Football
Club; Dixie Dean on Elisha Scott and Ricardo Zamora,
goalkeepers supreme; the Liverpool FC legacy for Rafael
Benítez.

OR, HOW LIVERPOOL FC 'SAVED' THE EUROPEAN CUP . . .

Any book that claims to deal in even a half-serious manner with the
impact that Rafa Benítez has already had upon Liverpool Football
Club, its fans and the club's recent history must also have at least
some perspective on its deeper traditions and roots. We need this
much in order to understand, precisely, what attracted the cerebral
Spaniard to Anfield in the first place and also how the general
approach and character of Benítez 'fits' exactly with the historical
and contemporary meanings of Liverpool FC. We try to do this, very
briefly, here. To those who view their fortnightly Anfield observance
as much more than a knowledgeable craving, it almost goes without
saying that support for Liverpool FC rather exceeds mere attachment
or even devotion to something as mundane or as profane as 'just' a
professional football club.

But any analysis of the impact that the quiet Spaniard Benítez has
had must also have as part of its foreground, of course, one place and
one date: Istanbul, 25 May 2005. Just saying it makes you smile, right

away, doesn't it? (We are doing it right now – smiling, that is. It is true that we are assuming you have picked this book up because you are essentially a Red – a Liverpool Football Club sympathiser. If you are not smiling now, just return this volume to the shelf and, ahem, walk on.) Try saying this little code of words and numbers in a bar anywhere in Europe – any place, in fact, where they think they know their football. You don't even have to understand the local lingo, or them yours. Give the locals the date and place, and now watch for the appreciative nods, for the growing grins – for the instant *animation*. If you and the locals are divided by language, someone will probably now start aping the flicked Steven Gerrard header which began the second-half Liverpool resurrection from a 0–3 deficit to AC Milan; or Xabi Alonso's personal penalty mini-drama to equalise the scores and complete a six-minute spell in which Liverpool scored three times (three times!); or the sitter that the Ukrainian master Andriy Shevchenko missed for Milan in the last minute, which would still have retrieved the match for the shell-shocked Italians; or even Jerzy Dudek's crazed penalty shoot-out dance that eventually won the cup for Liverpool after an unprecedented second-half comeback. (The American academic and Liverpool fan Grant Farred calls Liverpool 'God's Team' because Pope John Paul II, the first non-Italian pope, was also an amateur goalkeeper in his native Poland – and thus a Jerzy, and Liverpool FC, supporter.)

No football fan from Liverpool – no serious football fan anywhere in Europe, we would say – could possibly forget the crucial sequence of events that night: Liverpool 0–3 down at half-time and apparently finished; then revived to 3–3 at the 90-minute mark; finally winning, dramatically, on penalties. Did this sequence make the new Liverpool coach Rafa Benítez a lucky fool or an inspired genius? It certainly made him an authentic Liverpool hero. Before the Athens rematch with Milan in 2007, he would be asked many more times about this critical half-time in Istanbul. 'As I was going to the changing-room at half-time,' said the Spaniard, 'I heard our supporters still singing, so I said to the players that we must work hard for these people. Then if we get one goal maybe things would change.' Improbably, he was proved right. So tie the name of a previously mysterious and unconsidered football city to a date in the spring of 2005 when Football Europe invaded and captured a corner of Asia, and it will work every time. Nothing in the European game would ever seem quite the same again.

This last bit may seem like a grand claim, we know – a piece of cheap, emotional hyperbole, some might say. But as the *Sky Sports Football Year Book* of 2005–06, the game's bible in Britain, says, 'Any fictional account of a Champions League final would scarcely have dreamed up the events in Istanbul on 25 May.' It is spot-on, of course; the match was an epic encounter, producing Liverpool's fifth European Cup win in just six finals, and the most unlikely victory of all. But Istanbul was also definitely much more than this. It was a potential turning point, both locally in Liverpool and in the European game more widely. We are outrageous enough to argue that it was a night when Liverpool FC and its supporters might actually have *saved* the Champions League and the European Cup.

We can hear your objections right now. What? Saved this unstoppable cash cow? Saved this unmatched televised sporting extravaganza? Saved it from what, exactly? Glad you asked. Saved it, our friends, from its previously numbing predictability, from its increasingly corporate corpulence. Because before this extraordinary day in May (two days, actually – we spilled over into the 26th) the Champions League (or European Cup) final, football's blue-chip club event, was in grave danger of becoming yet more lukewarm TV sporting muzak: a sporting tourist's stopover, shaped mainly for advertisers and sponsors. Because, let's be honest here, this event has been in real peril of morphing into just another fat night for the hangers-on and the moneymen of global sport. Another half-distracting sporting night spent in front of the telly and organised for UEFA's vast ranks of VIPs. But Liverpool FC's crazy second-half revival, and especially the marvellous response of their lunatic, travel-wearied Red supporters to the comeback of all football comebacks – to this back-from-the-dead flatliner recovery, one that took place miles and miles outside the city of Istanbul – well, it somehow helped turn all of this around. Even UEFA's money-obsessed officials marvelled at the heart-stopping romance of it all – at how an inexperienced team at this level, one which had been so thoroughly outclassed and humiliated by efficient and groomed Italian sophisticates but was now driven on by its never-give-up supporters, had just refused, point blank, to surrender.

The usually steely men from AC Milan certainly expected no second-half siege like the one that occurred: what sort of team launches that kind of audacious comeback, unless in some corny Hollywood movie? How can your life be destroyed – or saved – in just six dramatic minutes: three hundred and sixty seconds in which Liverpool Football Club and its bleary followers went from being inept, rank no-hopers to likely winners? After this magical, near mystical night out in the East (it was truly 'The Miracle of Istanbul') all of us – all dreaming football fans everywhere who had ever despaired at their club's failings but had never lost hope – could feel that we, somehow, had our game back.

Admittedly, Manchester United had kicked the European football corpse somewhat in 1999. They did it, dramatically, by stealing the trophy from poor Bayern Munich in front of maybe 60,000 of their own red devotees in Barcelona after scoring two late goals. But gutsy (lucky!) United was still the richest club in Europe at that time. It was already a sporting corporation beginning to bloat on global merchandising. The mystery was not United's return from the dead in the Camp Nou. It was why, given their resources and also the native cunning of their splenetic manager Alex Ferguson, the European Cup was not in near-permanent residence at Trafford Towers, rather than a surprise, (very) occasional guest there. Only two European Cups won in fifty years for the world's richest and allegedly best-supported football club: a miserable return, surely?

FC Porto under José Mourinho had also kicked against the grain in the final of the European football nobodies in 2004. But even then it was a no-thrills, one-sided 3–0 rout of abject Monaco we had to endure. And Porto's gorgeous manager and a bunch of its best players were already contemplating lucrative contracts elsewhere, even as medals were being hung around their deserving, disloyal necks. Where was the real romance in this little tale of winning the final and then evacuating? No, we would claim that it was after the amazing final of 2005 that the game's officials and football fans around the world were reminded that the European Cup actually really *meant* something in sporting terms again. Those massed ranks of the great Scouse unwashed in Istanbul had reminded us all that for all the talk about cash and 'product', and agents and contracts, and all the embarrassingly crappy *OK* and *Hello!* footballers' wives double-spreads – and some Liverpool players are central figures here – football is still a real focus for communities and identity; for a sense of belonging. Football is a timeless tale of triumph and glory, one best hewn, as it was that night, out of near ridiculing despair. Post-industrial Liverpool, whose future seems inextricably based today mainly on packaging and selling its past, was back on the global sporting centre stage with a future once more, shaped by an exciting (and lucky) young Spanish coach. The very best banner in Istanbul that night – one among hundreds – said all you needed to know about Liverpool's astonishing European revival. It was simply a case of: 'Them Scousers Again'.

THE BEGINNING – AND THE END – OF EUROPE

This was not, of course, the first time Liverpool Football Club had starred on this stage. From the early 1960s, the Reds graced European club competition for two decades, initially under the Glenbuck genius Bill Shankly. Shanks lifted his young team to the stars with poetic ardour later emulated by his Kopite disciples: 'Boys, I can't tell you what I would give to play today. This is our life . . . this is what we were born to do; it is the best we do.' His first Liverpool team came tantalisingly close to a European Cup final in 1965 before being cheated in the semi-final at Inter Milan, and, with Roger Hunt crocked, they then narrowly lost a European Cup-Winners' Cup final in 1966 in Glasgow, against Borussia Dortmund. We didn't know it on that filthy and disappointing night in Scotland, but this was the only European trophy Liverpool Football Club would never win in five appearances in the competition – it was scrapped by UEFA in 1999.

In 1973 Shankly won his first and only European trophy, the UEFA Cup, defeating Borussia Mönchengladbach over two wildly contrasting legs. After a first-leg abandonment when the rain cascaded down at Anfield, Liverpool won the rescheduled match comfortably, 3–0 at home, but then had to hang on grimly for dear life in Germany. It was 'wee uncle' Bob Paisley who reclaimed the UEFA Cup for Liverpool in 1976, with the Reds beating Belgium's Club Brugge KV in the final. The County Durham master then took the core of Shankly's by now ageing team – Tommy Smith, Emlyn Hughes, Ian Callaghan and Steve Heighway among them – to Rome for the club's first really 'Big Night Out' on the Continent, the European Cup final of 1977. Deep in gloom after a weekend FA Cup final defeat by Manchester United, 25,000 Red disciples travelled from Liverpool to Rome for the occasion. The Germans from Mönchengladbach figured once again, this time in a 3–1 Liverpool win. The Liverpool team that won the European Cup again in 1978 and 1981 were much more Paisley's own project. It was one built around the inspiration of three brilliant Scots – Alan Hansen, Kenny Dalglish and Graeme Souness – and thus it also signalled a return to the very early Scottish origins of Liverpool Football Club, way back to 1892. Sated, the incredibly shrewd and talented Paisley – will any other British manager ever win *three* European Cups again? – then handed the Liverpool managerial baton to his assistant Joe Fagan in 1983. 'Smoking' Joe famously delivered another European Cup win, in Rome again, in 1984, on penalties, against a devastated Roma.

Liverpool's 2005 victory in Istanbul, under Rafael Benítez, was actually most like that of the 1981 European Cup campaign, under Bob Paisley. In both cases the Liverpool team won unexpectedly in Europe during a huge period of transition at the club. In both campaigns Liverpool had struggled badly domestically, finishing only fifth in the league. In 1981 Paisley was experimenting with a shoal of new, mainly young defensive, signings – Richard Money, Avi Cohen and Colin Irwin – and the Liverpool squad was struck down badly with injuries to experienced, key players. Unlike when the long-time apprentice Paisley became manager of Liverpool in 1974, 30 years later Rafa Benítez was entirely new, not just to the Liverpool club and the city but to English football. But he introduced new faces into the Liverpool team, just as Paisley had done before him. This time the new man's callow recruits were drawn mainly from Spain, with the integration of foreign players into the fast-moving and thrillingly brutal British game a whole new problem for the Liverpool boss. This was a very long way, indeed, from Liverpool's historic reliance, up until the '90s, on mainly Scottish and northern English football talent. But this was the new way in the post-Bosman era; it had to be pursued to satisfy both European and domestic ambitions.

Some of these early new midfield and defensive picks of Benítez – Antonio Núñez, Josemi and Mauricio Pellegrino, especially – like those of Paisley in 1981 – were just not up to the usual Liverpool standards and they struggled desperately. The new Liverpool manager in 2005 also suffered, as Paisley had done in 1981, from injuries to important players: Steven Gerrard, Harry Kewell and Xabi Alonso among them. In both seasons Liverpool lacked solidity in England, especially away from home in the league. In 1981 Liverpool won only four times on their travels (in twenty-one matches); in 2005 it was just five (from nineteen). In Europe, where the physical demands were not quite so intense and the one-off matches were more tactical, Liverpool fared much better. Here both the Durham guru Paisley and the Madrid man Benítez could somehow breathe a little easier.

The truth was that these two contrasting football men – divided by language, education and culture but 'umbilically' linked by their obsession with the game and their commitment to Liverpool football club, although Rafa still had some years to make up on Bob in this latter department – took solace in their respective European adventures and saw them as a welcome antidote to failure and criticism back at home. But let's be honest, too. In the 1980–81 European Cup campaign – which took the Reds to hardly threatening places, such as Aberdeen and Sofia – Liverpool endured only one really serious test in Europe: a crunch meeting with Bayern Munich at the semifinal stage, which was bravely won on away goals. A gutsy 1–1 draw in Bavaria (after a 0–0 at home), improbably inspired by Toxteth's own Howard Gayle and goal scorer, the irascible and talented Ray Kennedy, was enough to see Liverpool through to the final in Paris. A patched-up Liverpool side then faced an anonymous Real Madrid in the final and held them quite comfortably before winning, late on, with a single Alan Kennedy goal.

In 2005 it had been an altogether tougher ride for Benítez, albeit without the constant threat of elimination faced by Bob Paisley and his men some 24 years before. Rafa Benítez in his first season at Liverpool still had to overcome three real modern giants of the European game in the knockout phase to win the trophy: Juventus, Chelsea and AC Milan consecutively. And unlike in Bob Paisley's final European Cup triumph in 1981, this Liverpool generation under their new Spanish coach was actually very inexperienced at this level: the club was some 20 years out of its last European Cup final. It showed, too, as Liverpool struggled in the Champions League group stages in 2004. But as comprehensively lost as the new man Benítez often appeared to be in the early stages in Europe and in domestic Premiership action with Liverpool – especially away from the comforts of Anfield – so he seemed positively inspired by the later, more tactical and cerebral challenges offered by the bigger guns in European knockout competition. This transformation was remarkable – and puzzling.

Although it was the 20th anniversary, no one in Liverpool in 2005 was desperate to recall the *last* occasion that Liverpool football club had contested Europe's blue-chip club-football final. Some of Liverpool's own followers (coupled with mistakes by UEFA officials and the Belgian police) almost destroyed the sport in a quite terrible night at the Heysel Stadium in Brussels. That evening, after all those Liverpool glory years of the 1970s and '80s under Shankly, Paisley and Fagan, football in Europe had looked like an ugly death trap. The carnage that night – 39 lost souls after missiles were thrown, a fan charge and a crumbling stadium wall collapse – had now become the keystone of the Anfield European legacy. It was a cruel and unfair one, given the team's great tradition in Europe, but it was one the club and its fans had to accept, nevertheless. But now, two decades later – after what had been an ineffably stiff sentence – we had the new glories of Istanbul to mark Liverpool's revived and reformed European status. We had the brave, inspiring mass singing of 'You'll Never Walk Alone' to recall, even at a hopeless 0–3 down in the out-of-town hangar that was the Atatürk Olympic Stadium. (How lucky was UEFA that its ridiculous choice of venue and the ineptitude of the organisation for this match was largely lost amidst the joy of the Liverpool revival?) And we had 45,000 travelling fans from Liverpool, all of them slogging a couple of thousand miles across Europe for the occasion – a piffling 10,000 made it from the so-called great Italian sports city of Milan. And they call this northern Italian outpost a *football* town?

Astonishingly, twenty years after those awful scenes in Brussels, there were *no* Liverpool arrests at all in Istanbul, over a three-day visit for many. None. Though one teenage Liverpool fan, Michael Shields, is still held in custody, serving a lengthy sentence after a horrible assault on a local waiter in Bulgaria. It seems almost certain that his case was badly tried: that the offence was committed by another fan from the city. Liverpool supporters and their club are now, rightly, publicly aligned in young Michael's defence. They want him back home, where he belongs. But we should also be aimed at identifying and delivering the perpetrator. Despite this single incident – one in 45,000 wild and woolly stories from this encounter on the border with Asia – the Liverpool club and its fans had largely atoned, at last, for the dark deeds of Brussels. So, after all this, there really was a new feeling that the Liverpool club and its supporters could move on again in Europe, heads held high once more. Not that 39 families from Italy and Belgium – those close relatives of the Heysel dead from 1985 – will probably ever be persuaded that too much has really changed at Liverpool. Nor could we expect them to be. This is why we need to reflect briefly, a little later, on the Reds' disorderly past, which will also enable us to understand more about the promises of this new future.

CELTIC ROOTS – AND GREAT EUROPEAN NIGHTS

In some senses, the great Merseyside Red exodus to Istanbul in 2005 under an ambitious Spanish regime was actually the continuation of a *new* British tradition in European football support abroad, one that seems to have moved on from some of the tired ugliness of the 1980s and before. This new direction also seemed to have infected even England national football fans, so well behaved had these supporters been in both Japan during World Cup 2002, and even in Portugal at a highly charged European Championships of 2004. Germany in 2006 may yet offer another new chapter.

Manchester United fans had first highlighted this new approach among English club supporters in 1999 in their controlled frenzy at the 2–1 European Cup final comeback win against Bayern in Barcelona. These euphoric United followers in Spain in 1999 seemed like new model sporting citizens – founder members of an optimistic new hybrid 'European Community of Football'. Was this just *too* outrageous a suggestion? That these Mancunians seemed to be just the sort of people, in fact, to challenge UEFA's apparently growing certainty that major football events in Europe should, properly, be the preserve of mainly corporate elites and affluent sports tourists?

Ironically, as Arsenal manager Arsène Wenger has recently remarked, it suddenly seemed in England that it might be the previously troublesome child football which was now 'ahead' of politics in making the idea of a pan-European identity imaginable.

Let's not get too far with this. But Liverpool had themselves carried on this new direction, initially, in the UEFA Cup final in Dortmund in 2001, a wonderfully rainy 5–4 switchback ride against little Alavés from Spain: Gary McAllister's final. Some 40,000 Reds made the trip into a wild carnival – with very little frigid English nationalism in sight – and it was as if mass football travel from north-west England was now somehow holding some of the worst football excesses of the 1980s in check. Then, in the spring of 2003, Celtic Football Club under Martin O'Neill also reached the UEFA Cup final, this time after comfortably defeating Gérard Houllier's Liverpool en route. Celtic lost 3–2 in Seville, in a dramatic contest, to José Mourinho's FC Porto. Seville was Celtic's first major European final for 33 years; it had been 23 years since these early Scottish champions of Europe had advanced beyond even the quarter-final stage in any European competition. So this was quite something, this expedition to the south of Europe. An astonishing 75,000 Celtic fans were said to have travelled to Spain for the occasion. (Did *anyone* in green and white stay at home?) Tens of thousands travelled simply to 'be there' for the final. An estimated 35,000 of them pulled every stunt they knew to make it into the Estadio Olímpico, some paying up to £750 to touts waiting outside for their arrival. For a few days this part of southern Spain was awash with green and white, and largely trouble-free Hoops shenanigans ensued. It was quite a party, by all accounts, one not yet forgotten by the locals. Who could *ever* forget it? Many of these local people are said to have now developed their own Glasgow sporting leanings as a consequence. Football, it seems, can still do bloody marvellous things.

Celtic fans, many of them members of the famous Scottish/ Catholic/Irish football diaspora, travelled from all over the globe to be in Spain that evening. Just as 'displaced' Liverpool fans made the much more arduous journey in their tens of thousands to distant Istanbul two years later to follow Benítez's new Liverpool. For three nights in May 2005 it was hordes of Liverpool supporters who partied with the locals on the Europe–Asia border, rather like United and Celtic fans had done before them in Spain. In fact, perhaps it is the pronounced Celtic and independent traditions of the cities of Glasgow, Manchester and Liverpool – and of their famous European football clubs – that now binds them and their supporters strongly together in the reverence they show for their clubs and for football. And this is despite Liverpool FC's own residual and historic *Protestant* roots in the city. Stay with us, here. There is some football history and local culture that is worth exploring briefly because of the deep context it offers for Rafa Benítez's new Liverpool project.

As the historian John Belchem has argued, the city of Liverpool defies easy historical categorisation: it was described in a 1907 publication celebrating 700 years of the granting of the city's charter, for example, as 'a city without ancestors'. In its Victorian heyday, as a would-be 'Florence of the north', the trading city of Liverpool defined itself against industrial Manchester and in rivalry with commercial London. Its striking and distorting lack of diversity of industry, of a manufacturing base and of a skilled workforce, made Liverpool especially susceptible to later economic and trading change. Its strong Celtic (mainly Irish) heritage also meant that Liverpool was always a city that was *in* the north of England but never fully *of* it. Important here was the fact that the huge long-distance in-migration to the city in the mid-nineteenth century – from Wales but especially from Ireland – had 'crowded out' more local migrants and thus helped transform dominant speech patterns in the city from its then native Lancastrian to its now familiar and distinctively binding adenoidal 'Scouse'. Liverpool football fans today still cock an ear to check for the vowels of 'authentic' club fans. In this sense, speaking in Scouse was always a form of linguistic bonding and an assertion of inter-ethnic group identity – of proud 'otherness' – in Liverpool, rather than a product of pollution and local public health problems, as some writers have wrongly assumed.

The sports historian David Kennedy has written recently about how the early boards of directors of the main Merseyside football clubs were dominated not by the rich but by moderately wealthy local businessmen, often with a strong arm in the brewery trade. Liverpool FC's first chairman, Irishman John Houlding, for example, was a local brewer, having also been an errand boy and even a 'cow keeper' in his time. After the famous split within the Everton club in 1892 that helped form Liverpool FC under Houlding, members of the new board at the nearby evolving Goodison Park – a board which was dominated by Liberals, with no Liberals at all on the newly constituted Liverpool FC board – lobbied *against* the involvement of the drinks industry in the club's affairs, effectively blocking all large brewers from direct control of professional football in the city from that point onwards. Not that drink would ever entirely desert football in the city, either culturally or commercially – not by a long chalk.

Despite the very large Irish Catholic population concentrated from the mid-nineteenth century in the north end of the city, where the three main professional football clubs (including initially Bootle FC) were based, the historian Kennedy shows that there were no early Irish Catholic board members at all at any of the Liverpool clubs. This is perhaps no surprise given the communal violence and continued hostility in the city to Catholics in the early part of the twentieth century. Both Houlding and, especially later, club chairman John McKenna, the two most influential figures in the early development of Liverpool Football Club, were staunch Unionists from Ulster and prominent members of the Orange Order. So, Liverpool Football Club, like Everton, in fact, was strongly resistant, right from its very beginning, to the direct involvement of Liverpool Catholics in its affairs. Two-thirds of all football club directors in the city at that time were also members of Masonic Lodges, including, again, the dominant figures of Houlding and McKenna. McKenna, originally from County Monaghan, had worked as an errand boy and then a vaccination-office clerk in Liverpool. His early sporting love in the city was rugby union, before he devoted himself to business, football and 30 years' service as a director of Liverpool Football Club. These powerful men were also members of the Protestant-infused Working Men's Conservative Association in Liverpool. Early roles in running, and even supporting, professional football clubs on Merseyside, then, were certainly a closed shop to nonconformists and to most local Catholics. How different this would all be from 2007 when Liverpool Football Club would ditch its historic local-ownership structure and opt, like a growing number of elite English clubs, for the Yankee dollar.

So why did no one establish a successful professional football club in the northern end of the city of Liverpool, one that directly reflected the aspirations and identities of the oppressed local Irish Catholics who lived there – as Celtic FC had done so powerfully and successfully in the East End of Glasgow, for example? Good question, and there are no easy answers. But perhaps most simply and realistically what divided the Irish traditions in cities like Liverpool and Glasgow was that the prejudice and spatial segregation suffered by Irish Catholics in Liverpool in the nineteenth century – although severe – was not of the same order as in Glasgow, where stronger institutional discrimination meant the formation of a specifically *Catholic* professional football club – at Glasgow Celtic – was more a matter of necessity, rather than one of mere choice. Bootle Hibernian and 5th Irish were Irish Catholic football clubs established, briefly, in the north end of the city of Liverpool in the 1880s, but neither survived. Many Irish Catholics in Liverpool were probably drawn, instead, initially and unsurprisingly to *Everton* football club, the 'original' professional club in the northern Anfield area. Even today, largely working-class Catholic enclaves in the north and around the city still harbour stronger Everton, rather than Liverpool, football sympathies.

Another possible reason why there was no strong Irish Catholic influence in the early years of Liverpool Football Club was the fact that the core of the early Reds teams were predominantly Scottish rather than Irish, even though they were largely recruited by the Ulster Orangeman and club co-founder 'Honest' John McKenna. However, the Liverpool club did its local cause with the Liverpool Irish and other football fans in the city no harm at all by winning early league titles in 1901 and 1906, while also losing narrowly to Everton in a vibrant 1906 FA Cup semi-final. Everton went on to win the FA Cup that year, making it the first league and cup Double for the city of Liverpool, the new centre for national football excellence in England.

Liverpool FC was led in these early championship years by the handsome and stirring Stirlingshire wing-half and Scottish international Alex Raisbeck. The athletic Raisbeck – an ex-collier and one of seven brothers – is almost certainly one of Liverpool Football Club's greatest-ever players. He was like quicksilver. Gibson and Pickwick's *Association Football* (1908) described the Scot's 'swift, rapid movement [and] fierce, electric rushes' as being like watching a man who is 'pulsating to his fingertips with the joy of life'. Liverpool's more vaunted neighbours Everton were certainly placed in the shade by the blonde Raisbeck in his pomp: the Blues' first league title since 1891 would have to wait almost another decade, until 1915.

The complete revamp of the Anfield Road ground in 1906, as recalled by the stadium writer Simon Inglis in *Engineering Archie* (2005), was also probably an important factor in growing Liverpool's local support in the north end of the city. It was overseen by the premier football ground architect of the day, the great Scottish construction engineer Archibald Leitch. This redevelopment constituted 'a new departure from what football grounds are generally supposed to be', according to the *Liverpool Echo* at the time. It produced an impressive new Main Stand at Anfield, the first in Britain to be made of reinforced concrete and described in *The Builder* as 'distinctly worthy of imitation'. It also meant the relocation of the old Liverpool west stand to the east Kemlyn Road side of the ground. All of this was impressively enclosed with modern 'fancy brick setting'. A new, open Spion Kop embankment also mushroomed up in front of Walton Breck Road in 1906, all paid for by funds generated by the two Liverpool league-title successes. Although the Kop remained uncovered until 1928, the once upstart Anfield could now, rightly, claim to be ahead even of the plush Goodison ground across Stanley Park, which was already host to international matches and to the 1894 FA Cup final. Liverpool's home crowds now challenged and frequently exceeded those of Everton's. The two clubs would oscillate from that point on in terms of their relative drawing power, depending upon issues of relegation and league performance. That was until Liverpool FC became more of a 'national' club and began to draw inexorably away from Everton in attendances in the 1970s.

On show in this wonderful new sporting arena at Anfield in the first quarter of the new century - and the major formative *Irish* presence in the early Liverpool sides - was the legendary Reds goalkeeper and Ulsterman Elisha Scott. Scott signed for Liverpool as a seventeen year old in 1912 and played a total of four hundred and sixty-seven times for the club over the next two decades. He was probably the greatest goalkeeper playing in England at the time and was adored at Anfield, as well as being the first Liverpool player to have his very own 'Kopite' chant. Although goal-scoring forward Harry Chambers and the 'prince' of Anfield full-backs Ephraim Longhurst (Liverpool's first England captain) were key figures, it was the 'immortal' Scott who was the unparalleled star of Liverpool's consecutive league championship triumphs in 1922 and 1923, under the little known ex-Oldham Athletic and then Liverpool manager David Ashworth.

Elisha's clashes and exchanges with William 'Dixie' Dean of Everton in the early inter-war years – covered well by the football writer and knowledgeable Liverpool FC observer John Keith - were the stuff headline makers dreamed of, and quite possibly sometimes dreamed up! William Dean was no shrinking violet, of course, and he certainly seemed to enjoy playing at Anfield against the slim and diminutive

(5 ft 9 in.) but brave and athletic keeper Scott. Dean scored nine times against Scott in their eight club meetings, a formidable record. This haul included a nine-minute hat-trick against Liverpool in the Anfield derby of 1931. After the third goal had been rifled in that day, Dean cryptically asked the Irishman, 'How do you like your eggs poached now, sonny?' The furious Scott could only grimace. Dean bowed three times to the Kop, justifiably getting back a reported volley of 'choice language' for his pains. (Today's complaining stars, please take note.) Scott routinely let out his own on-field abuse in his thick Belfast brogue – aimed on that derby occasion at the gallant Liverpool centre-back Jimmy 'Parson' Jackson, a church elder and a man well known for his cordial and generally gentlemanly relations with opponents. He was sometimes rather too cosy with the opposition for Elisha Scott's peace of mind. An alarmed Jackson told Dean, primly, as he trudged back to the halfway line after the latest tirade from Elisha, 'William, I feel like I never want to play in front of *that* man again.' Dean chuckled. Fortunately, few other Liverpool defenders agreed with the Parson's objections.

A newspaper of the day famously described Elisha Scott as having 'the eye of an eagle, the swift movement of a panther'. Dean simply reasoned that Scott was 'the greatest goalkeeper I have ever seen'. He thought the Ulsterman's greatest strength was his 'point blank charge' and that his 'uncanny' secret was early preparation: that the Liverpool goalkeeper was 'never still. As soon as the attack against him crosses the halfway line, watch Scott jump.' Maybe this constant alertness was partly because Scott received a tube of aspirin and a warning note from Dean at his Wallasey home before every derby game. The goalkeeper was not fazed at all by his mail. He often responded in the tunnel before the contest to Dixie with a jovial, 'You'll get none today, you black-headed bastard!' After derby games, the two men invariably retired to the Lisbon pub in Victoria Street where they could discuss, undisturbed, the outcome: Scott over a bottle of Guinness, Dean a pint of bitter. It must have seemed like a simple game then.

Off the pitch, the great Liverpool Irishman Scott could often be brusque but quite self-effacing, rather shy, in fact. The national and local press got little useful copy out of him, save for the many stories revolving around his variously played-up antics with Dean. After saving a penalty – from Dixie again – this time in the England v. Ireland match at Goodison Park in 1928, Scott was required to stand in for the injured Ireland captain Billy Gillespie for the after-match speeches. Typically, he rose uncertainly and said, simply, 'Gentleman, I'm nothing of a speaker in any way. Any speaking I've got to do is on the field of play. Thank you.' He then sat down and happily got back into his Guinness. Scott was, like many Liverpool players who followed him, largely disinterested and suspicious of the fripperies and formalities around the sport. He wanted only to play for the football club he loved.

Elisha Scott cut a very different figure from the goalkeeping star of the Spanish game at this time, the RCD Espanyol and later FC Barcelona and Real Madrid goalkeeper, Ricardo Zamora. Andrew McFarland, a US-based football historian, has shown that Zamora was already a very public figure in Spain in the 1920s, a fêted star whose fame spread way beyond football; he was often mobbed by women because of his good looks and public celebrity. His son, also a goalkeeper, played for Valencia in the 1960s and also shared his father's reputation for being a playboy. No such opportunities came the taciturn Belfast working-class Scott's way, of course. The Liverpool Irishman was still locked into a moderate maximum wage by comparison, and he had few ambitions to be a public figure outside of his role of defending, often with his life, the Liverpool FC goal.

The Merseyside connection with Zamora came when England met Spain at Highbury in 1931. Then, Dixie Dean and his England colleagues thought the famous Spaniard to be something of a Continental dilettante and certainly a much lesser shot-stopper than the teak-hard Scott. Bill Dean and his mates thought that this 'posh' Spaniard, the son of a Cadiz doctor, needed a lesson – a sharp reminder. Now the captain of Spain – another conceit in the eyes of the England players, one seldom afforded a goalkeeper in Britain – and a man who had recently signed for Real Madrid for a world record fee for a goalkeeper, Zamora was clearly viewed by the English as something of a flash 'poseur'. He was a typical Continental theatrical, his extravagant pre-match warm-up routine at Highbury drawing loud guffaws from the English crowd. His exercises did the visitor little good: England duly thrashed Spain 7–1 with Zamora humiliated. This crushing victory also avenged England's historic 3–4 1929 defeat to Spain in Madrid, England's first international loss to a non-home country. The revengeful demolition of Spain in north London assuaged national pride in England while deflating some of the aura – in Britain at least – around the 'great' Spanish custodian Ricardo Zamora. In Merseyside it also caused the stock of Liverpool's own wiry and brave Elisha Scott to rise still further.

But what of the much bigger question? Did Scott attract or repel the local Irish to Liverpool Football Club in the early inter-war years? The truth is we have no strong evidence here either way. But this was a great Irish sporting figure in the city of Liverpool with whom some local people might surely have been expected to identify, almost regardless of his – or their own – religious or political affiliation. Scott had, after all, played for Ireland before partition.

More importantly, both clubs in the city were eventually able to draw on their distinctive and sometimes insular Liverpool Irish heritages, as well as on the sea-trading traditions and cultural imports to the city – music, theatre, song – to produce enormously rich, often sentimental and unusually loyal supporter cultures. But perhaps it was the near mystic influence later of Bill Shankly and also the extensive football experiences and adventures of Liverpool fans in Europe from the early 1960s that especially helped to build on these traditions at Anfield, adding insight, humour and vim to the complex *seriousness* and the deep creativity of the club's support. Its later positioning as a 'national' football club also 'opened up' further local fan cultures, but not without its own tensions and conflicts.

But it was certainly these distinctive aspects of the Liverpool crowd and of Merseyside culture – both its openness and its insularity and perhaps especially its working–class intensity that was signalled historically by the contrasts drawn between the great goalkeepers of their day, the working–class Ulsterman Elisha Scott and the middle–class Spanish sporting celebrity Ricardo Zamora – that Rafa Benítez had been so astonished and touched by so many years later in Istanbul, and also elsewhere during his first season in England. It was a theme he constantly returned to in his interviews with the Spanish press: the imagination, passion and loyalty of the Liverpool fans, for whom football seemed to mean everything; the huge numbers that followed Liverpool everywhere they played; and their patience and understanding of the game. It was clear, right from the outset, that the Spaniard had a deep respect for the Liverpool support and for its general treatment of the club's players and staff. Despite his very real fears about leaving the home comforts of Spain for the dark and dingy English North West (and who could blame him?), Benítez knew right away that he had come to a real football place and that he wanted to win something for these people whose lifestyle, devotion to football and dialect he could still barely comprehend.

THE ROARING TWENTIES: 'SCHOOL OF SCIENCE' MEETS A 'GANG OF BUTCHERS'

But what were the historic *differences* between the Merseyside clubs? The rival Everton and Liverpool Football Clubs, although born of the same seed and even sharing some of the same ethnic influences in the city of Liverpool actually clashed, perhaps predictably, right from the start in terms of both their respective styles and credos. Everton, for example, were historically studiously temperate and 'scientific' in their approach to the game, and were also rich, one of the early moneyed aristocrats of English football. Liverpool had to work rather harder at the commercial side of the new football business and were also much more prosaic – even crude and direct – in their play. Even for the tough Birkenhead tyro William Dean, the post-First World War Liverpool championship team of 1922 and 1923, for example, was little more than a 'gang of butchers'. He was biased, of course, but he also had a point. By all accounts, players such as Jock McNab, Donald McKinley and the Wadsworth brothers were certainly uncompromising in their defensive approach for Liverpool.

A much more strategic approach to defensive play – a counter-attacking philosophy that would certainly have been approved of later by both Gérard Houllier and Rafa Benítez – was to come with the reign of the first modern football coach in England, Herbert Chapman at Arsenal in the early 1930s. Chapman's plan to withdraw the centre-half to a defensive role and his instructions that Arsenal's full-backs – rather than the midfield players – should mark the opposing wingers was to revolutionise defensive play around the world, as well as heap domestic criticism on defensive, 'lucky' Arsenal. Defensive? In 1933 Arsenal won the Football League title scoring 118 goals!

Liverpool Football Club in the early 1920s evidently had little of Chapman's detailed defensive planning. Instead, they were robust and solid, and made up of traditional British stalwarts, but they were dedicated to winning. They were certainly very distinctive in style from the 'school of science' supposedly established by generations of directors over at nearby Goodison Park. Liverpool's more direct and more collective approach relied on recruits who were very different from the 'classical and stylish', more individualist, type of football player then favoured by the famous Everton chairman of the time, W.C. Cuff. According to the football writer and historian Ivan Sharpe, Everton played 'the prettiest football in the League'. But it wasn't the most successful. As the sports historian Percy Young remarked about Liverpool Football Club, the willing versatility of players such as McKinley and Jimmy Jackson in the 1920s 'was the secret of the teamsmenship in which Liverpool excelled'. This credo was later developed and refined, of course, by Bill Shankly, Bob Paisley, Joe Fagan and Roy Evans at Anfield: here, the team was always more important than any single player. Any player who thought differently – no matter his value to the club – was either brought down to earth by the Anfield dressing-room or the famed Liverpool boot room, or else he was quickly on his way. This meant that more than a century after Liverpool's early title successes, Liverpool managers – whether recruited from County Durham, Bootle, France or Spain – were still saying pretty much the same sort of thing about the essence of the club's traditions and playing style. It was still possible to talk meaningfully about a 'typical Liverpool player' in 1966, 1986 and 2006 as it had been way back in 1906.

So these were some of the important 'deep structures' of the Liverpool club and its fan base, the continuities and local cultures, that had helped seduce the thoughtful and emotionally complex Spaniard Rafael Benítez to Anfield; this was, in turn, the valuable prize he had inherited when he joined Liverpool Football Club in the summer of 2004. These features of the club and the wider working-class traditions of the city and the Anfield area had also appealed to his immediate predecessor in the Anfield manager's job, the French autocrat Gérard Houllier. Houllier had also bequeathed the Spaniard a super-modern training facility at Melwood and a new, more scientific approach to player preparation. Benítez had seen many of these wider cultural traits on show even during his first troubled domestic season at the club and certainly on one memorable May evening in Turkey in 2005 when a potent mixture of pride, history and collective desire seemed to pull the club through its most desperate and apparently hopeless plight. He would never forget it; he was a coach who had been on the very brink of public ridicule and was now fêted to the rafters for returning the Liverpool club to the pinnacle of the European game. After that wonderful night in May 2005, who could not now be driven to succeed here?

Even with a more limited transfer budget than at rival clubs in Europe, such as Chelsea, Manchester United and Real Madrid, at least Benítez was free to choose the players he would *like* to sign, a luxury he was never afforded even when winning Spanish and European titles at Valencia. He was also best placed in England to raid the Spanish game for established players and rising young stars. Moreover, Rafa Benítez and Liverpool Football Club, with their sparkly new European trophy in tow, might perhaps even tangle with historic rivals and near neighbours Everton in Europe in 2005–06 for the first time. Everton had achieved the priceless fourth qualifying Premiership spot in England – and over new European Cup holders Liverpool – in 2005.

But all that exciting talk was for later, surely? At least Liverpool fans could now have a few quiet and trouble-free weeks on the beaches of Europe until August, fantasising about a possible Liverpool v. Everton all-Merseyside Champions League final in Paris in 2006. Why not? We could forget, for once, about our football problems, recall instead the penalty-kick glories and drama of Asia, and dream our wonderful dreams about the possible start of a new, cosmopolitan Liverpool dynasty in Europe to match that established by the great Bob Paisley and his mainly British team back in the late-1970s. No, nothing could interrupt the warm glow of 25 May 2005 – not for a few weeks at least. We could relax; even bask a little. What could possibly go wrong now for a bullish Rafa Benítez and his eager Liverpool staff? What, indeed.

2

Pictures of Spain:
Rafa Benítez at Anfield

Two cities, two cultures, one man; always take the weather
with you; holders, but not defenders, of the European Cup;
Benítez versus Gerrard; Rafa shops – and Momo, Pepe, Bolo
and Crouchy arrive at Anfield; Rafa Benítez's winger-less
wonders.

FROM VALENCIA – WITH LOVE?

In what should have been the warm summer afterglow of Istanbul,
Rafa Benítez and his European champions Liverpool Football Club
faced, instead, not one but two new crises as they prepared for the
new season. This must be something of a record, even in the crazy
world of top European football clubs. Each of these crises was wholly
unavoidable, though the first was only partly of Liverpool's own
making. It meant the prospects of no Champions League football for
Liverpool in 2005–06, despite the club holding the European Cup for
the first time in 21 years. The second crisis, the prospective departure
of club captain Steven Gerrard, the very keystone to Liverpool's
future, was laid squarely at the doors of Rick Parry and especially the
manager Rafa Benítez. The conundrum here was how, exactly, could
the club's chief executive, its Spanish manager and the player involved
be so collectively determined that Gerrard should definitely *stay* at
Anfield in 2005 and yet within a matter of weeks let the Liverpool

captain come within a hair's breadth of leaving? This was, without doubt, a painful case of crossed wires, one built out of the personalities and the complex emotions of the two key figures involved, Gerrard and his manager Benítez. It was a culture clash that almost spelled c–a–t–a–s–t–r–o–p–h–e.

By failing miserably to beat Everton even to fourth place in the Premiership in 2005 – Benítez's team lost 14 league matches in his first stumbling domestic campaign – Liverpool now faced the prospect of being excluded from the Champions League altogether for 2005–06. Because his English was still limited, Benítez had not talked much to the British press about the reasons for Liverpool's problems in the Premiership in his first season. But from comments he made in Spain in 2005, it was clear that he thought he had adapted well to his new situation. 'I have a lot of work, every day. Almost every hour is busy,' he had commented to journalists in Spain. 'The club needs a big push forward, and it is necessary to concentrate on numerous areas. Fortunately, I have had the maximum support of Liverpool Football Club, both in terms of my administration as the manager and in the club's facilities. The facilities here are magnificent.' But language, he admitted, had continued to be a problem in England: 'Sometimes, I feel some frustration for not grasping the English language with a little more precision. In the difficult moments, when there is a lot of tension and you need to say something very specific – or you don't have time for very elaborate explanations – you realise that you lack the expressions you need to exploit all your resources as a coach.' Benítez later spoke about this difficulty to *FIFA Magazine*: 'After you start working, you think it will be easy to learn English in six months and to talk with people, but you find you cannot explain things or express yourself properly. That has not been easy.' Maybe language was part of the later mix-up with Steven Gerrard.

Benítez had noted some of the key differences between coaching in England and working in Spain in interviews he had given in the Spanish publications *Abfutbol* and also *El País* during his first two seasons at Anfield. He often spoke at length about the 'unique' character of Liverpool Football Club, for example. 'The first thing is to know the idiosyncrasies of this club,' he told *Abfutbol*. 'It is traditional, more of a family club than other English clubs. The philosophy here has always been aimed at success. That is, playing well, using the correct pass and playing and supporting each other constantly. So you think that if you can manage it, why not carry on in this way.' This seemed like the 'Liverpool Way', all right. So what could the new coach add to it? What were the qualities Benítez himself had brought to Liverpool? 'But on the other hand,' he went on, 'you have to think that if you are here it is because they have signed you for what you have already achieved. Therefore, you cannot change your style too much. In summary, you have to look for your own style: that mixture of what you want to try to make and what they [the fans] would like to see on the pitch.'

El País asked Benítez whether he had noticed any real differences between England and Spain on the football side as well as *outside* the game. Benítez became immediately animated and offered some very interesting insights on the English character, Spanish sensibilities and the role of *climate* in the making of a people. 'I appreciated the difference immediately,' he said. 'It is big. It is as much in the football sense as in the social one – in the ways of life. One lives football here with much more emotion than in Spain. But all that is related to a different way of seeing life. Here, the days become very long. You get up very early, and at seven in the afternoon you are at dinner. But there is not much to do: the winter is very long and it darkens very soon – at four o'clock. Sometimes, these aspects are those that determine the difficulties of adapting to a new situation.'

It is hard to deny that it is the winter weather that partly shapes the outlook of the English, perhaps especially in the grim and rainy North West. Anyone who has ever travelled to Valencia immediately sees a much more 'open' and 'free' approach to family life and public space in this engaging city, one that is strongly shaped by climate as well as by cultural factors. (And by politics: despite the ravages of Franco, Spain, unlike Britain, has not been Thatcherised.) One of these factors is the much more limited role for drinking in the public leisure of men and the young. You can still shop late at night or else comfortably sit out with your kids in shirtsleeves even in November, in well-appointed restaurants and coffee bars around the Mestalla, for example. This whole area around the Valencia CF stadium – a mix of commerce, retail and residential – is affluent, and it exudes a faintly sanitised sense of well-being to British eyes. It is certainly rather different from the homely, but decaying, terraces and the fragile sense of community that spills out of the neighbourhoods surrounding Anfield. Generally speaking, people in Valencia look wealthier, healthier and usually happier than they do in Liverpool. The gap between rich and poor is much narrower – their worlds collide more. Diet is probably much better there, too: much more fresh, local produce rather than industrial quantities of saturated fast foods. Poverty is not so obviously the social ill in Valencia that it clearly still is in this slowly reviving old British seaport in the English North West.

Public spaces in Valencia are also much better resourced and better shaped for family use because of the better climate, more public spending in this area, less social segregation by age than in Britain and less reliance on market policies to solve social problems in Spain. It is also because so many affluent people in the city of Valencia – unlike in Liverpool – live with their children in high-rise city-centre apartments. In these circumstances, there is a detectable, collective interest in having public space in the city that is both safe and properly funded, and that everyone can share.

The city's river has long been diverted outside Valencia, and the surviving old river bed has now been converted to a generous green park that flows through the city as free space and is used by pretty much everyone for play and relaxation. This is in contrast to the heavily class-based and privatised segregation we still tend to get in England that marks off starkly, in terms of both access and provision, the lives of the haves from those of the many more have-nots.

But Benítez denied, in his Spanish interviews, that all these cultural, economic and climatic differences meant that the game of *football* in England was completely alien to that in Spain – that it was all rough and tumble. 'Many English fans also like a lot of "touch football",' he explained to *Abfutbol*. 'In fact, they watch a lot of La Liga on TV in the United Kingdom. Therefore, there are certain similarities between England and Spain that also attracts these viewers.' So what was his problem? Why did Liverpool Football Club struggle so badly to win points in his first season? Here, we were beginning to get to it. 'There are many teams in this league that offer a "traditional" style of play with the high ball,' Benítez continued. 'And I should say that some get good results. Everything is more physical here, there is more contact, and, overall, they base their game a lot in England on the fight for the second ball.'

He told *El País* that you needed to ensure that you do two things to succeed in England: 'The first one is to play good football – well worked out, intelligent, well organised. In second place, we have to adapt better to the situations that still inconvenience us, mainly the direct game of most of the English teams. In many occasions we have not achieved it, and we have had bad results against inferior rivals. If we are able to deal with this problem, the team will leap forward, mainly because of the trust that would be generated in the players.' Liverpool had competed poorly in this crucial area, often being bullied, especially away from home, under Benítez. But there were also other models to follow in England, as Benítez confirmed: 'However, Arsenal introduced a style based on a lot of possession a while ago, and it brought them rewards. Now it is Chelsea that is playing a very direct style of football, and they impose themselves. It is definitely necessary to be pragmatic and to adapt to the type of game that allows you to win. If you can play well, too, then all the better.'

Benítez seemed convinced that his Liverpool project was now moving on, becoming more solid and reliable following the trials of his first season at Anfield. 'This team was a team with some doubts,' he told *Abfutbol*. 'We still have some, although now we have more certainties. Little by little you go sowing the idea that the group and the collective work we do are important. And when you have good footballers that can affect the balance of a match, then the results arrive.' Benítez also identified a key turning point in Europe – the comeback in the final group–stage match in 2004 against Olympiakos – though even this had done little to turn things around in the Premiership. 'When you win some matches like the one against Olympiakos [3–1 in the Champions League] that started 0–1, and you have to score three goals to win, this is important,' he argued. 'When we came back and won in that way, with the whole Liverpool public behind us, that is contagious, and the team became a lot more forceful and confident.' But Liverpool had not been confident enough to overtake Everton in the Premiership, hence the subsequent crisis in the European club game.

LET THE WORLD GO AWAY: TWO SUMMER CRISES

For UEFA, of course, this kind of ruminating on Benítez's processes of adaptation, the differences between Spanish and English culture, and how you could apply Spanish know-how to the unique circumstances and character of football in England was all academic. UEFA had different matters to consider. They just couldn't work out whether the exciting, new European champions – the same club whose supporters had saved UEFA's bacon in Istanbul and effectively recharged the Champions League under its young Spanish manager – would even be allowed to defend the title it had so recently and gloriously reclaimed. How, exactly, did we get here?

Actually, it was quite simple. UEFA rules supposed that the national association of the trophy winners would nominate the holders to defend their title the following season. Implicit here, however, also seemed to be the assumption that the winners of the European crown would always qualify in their own domestic league for the next year's competition. Liverpool's amateurish league bunglings under Benítez in 2004–05 had comprehensively scuppered this theory. UEFA now hoped that the FA would include the European Cup holders Liverpool, rather than Everton, the fourth-placed club in the Premiership, in their list of nominees. The FA's own policy, revealed the previous season and still on its official website at that time, was that the European champions should indeed qualify, with the fourth-placed club in the Premiership to join the UEFA Cup. But two months before the 2005 final the FA, backed by the Premier League, had said the reverse. And to omit Everton now – especially after that club's suffering following the European ban in the wake of Heysel – would be both politically insensitive and grossly unfair. So, having praised the club and its supporters to the rafters, UEFA's bigwigs were now in a right mess over exactly what to do about their own European champions – about Liverpool Football Club.

No one at Liverpool had objected to these daft UEFA rules, which effectively threw their own nomination back into the discretionary court of the national FA. If this arrangement was going to hurt anybody at all, it was likely to be some relative minnow that had lucked into the final and then fluked a win. (Do they mean us?) This rule was hardly likely to be rectified by the European elite in whose favour it was expected usually to operate. Perhaps the most sense spoken on this score came from an unlikely source, Liverpool's usually airheaded striker Djibril Cissé, who now said, 'There are laws, and the rules are there to be respected. If we don't manage to get a change in these rules or a special right to play, then it will be our own fault.' This certainly seemed to be a unique case of 'Out of the mouths of babes . . .'

And it was certainly true, too, that Liverpool were increasingly vulnerable to not qualifying domestically – Chelsea, Manchester United and Arsenal were now all super-powerful rivals in England; Newcastle United were also a potential force (they surely had to be sometimes) – Spurs too. And if David Moyes ever got Everton moving forwards again (as now), then the Blues would also be challenging.

But the other truth here was that the Liverpool hierarchy had considered itself to be reasonably fireproof – or at least very competitive – at home in the league but to have no chance at all of actually *winning* the Champions League in 2005. Jamie Carragher and Steven Gerrard had almost said as much during the campaign. So why bother objecting to or querying a UEFA rule that was never going to apply to your own circumstances? It was a crucial, if excusable, mistake to make.

What did this all mean? Even as Liverpool Football Club began preparations to display the European Cup it could now claim as its own in the club museum, at UEFA HQ much furious head-scratching now ensued. These learned men had a number of important points to consider: with the FA fixed, how can we change our rules now, with European qualification already completed? But how might it look to the outside world if those heroic battlers from Merseyside were now excluded from the competition they had so illuminated? What might Liverpool's omission do to sponsors and to the crucial TV figures? How credible was a major international football tournament that excluded its own holders (although World Cup winners now have to pre-qualify for the event following recent FIFA rule changes)? Who, exactly, would Liverpool FC replace in the competition if the UEFA policy was now changed? The questions kept coming. And much of the time, if the truth be told, the men at UEFA didn't seem to know quite what they were doing.

Eventually, matters became clearer, decisions were reached. Everton would definitely keep their place in the third qualifying round after all, which was exactly how it should have been. Liverpool, unable to qualify through league position, would now play from the very first qualifying round, though they would be seeded instead of Slavia Prague. This seemed the best outcome all round in the circumstances. UEFA also changed the competition rules so that the champions would always qualify in future – but at the expense, if necessary, of the lowest qualifying club in their own domestic league.

For this season only the holders would have to begin their defence of the trophy against Europe's football minnows. Liverpool would also have no national protective status, so they could be drawn against other powerful English clubs at earlier stages of the competition proper. This included Everton, of course, in the third qualifying round. Thanks – for nothing. All of this meant that, probably for the first time in the club's history, Liverpool FC would now be playing competitive European football in high summer – in the first half of July; in fact, just seven short weeks after that exhausting and exhilarating night in Istanbul. Five Champions League qualifying fixtures might already be completed by Liverpool even before the club's first Premiership match, away at Middlesbrough on 13 August.

The fixture programme already looked like an incredible slog for Liverpool: a 12-month, non-stop haul for all the club's World Cup players, for a start. But Liverpool would have been playing competitive friendly matches in the summer months of 2005 anyway. Now these contests would become just that little bit sharper and more meaningful. This might even help Liverpool because it could also make for a more positive start to the Premiership. Even so, this was probably not an ideal itinerary for those elite players who had still been on active duty in late May 2005 and who would now be involved in international action in the summer of 2006. However, Liverpool's main concern was at club level, not sorting out World Cup problems for Sven-Göran Eriksson and his international coaching mates. The Swede couldn't expect Liverpool to protect its England players for the summer's exertions – though this national concern was to become a predictably important and divisive issue in the new season.

More importantly, Rafa Benítez could now have the elite European competition he craved in 2006. He could also grow and develop the Liverpool squad, based on his Champions League success. Who wouldn't want to play for Liverpool, the European champions? He could discard his few Spanish failures and bring more quality players into the club, whilst rotating his squad a little more astutely in the league and cups this time. Liverpool would, certainly, need to get much stronger away from home in the Premiership, perhaps sign a bit more British or northern European beef to help the club front up on its domestic travels. Things would, surely, get even better on the playing side. If only, that is, the club's best footballer could be persuaded that he was still both respected and loved at Liverpool FC.

IF YOU DON'T KNOW ME BY NOW: THE BALLAD OF STEVEN AND RAFA

At the beginning of July 2005, Rafa Benítez and Liverpool Football Club faced a crisis, the outcome of which would help to shape the club's future prospects for the rest of the decade. With European ties only days away, the Liverpool captain – the most important football player in the entire club and in the middle of his career – wanted to leave Anfield. This seemed absurd – we had been through all of this the season before over the captain's proposed move to Chelsea, which he had contemplated because Liverpool Football Club supposedly lacked the players and the necessary clout to win things. But – correct us here – barely a few weeks before all this had seeped out once more from our TV sets, hadn't the Huyton man been seen joyously lifting the game's biggest prize, the European Cup, for Liverpool? His home club was back at football's top table, moving with the elite. Why would he want away now? What kind of cowardly deceit was this anyway? Mind you, Liverpool had finished a monumental 37 points behind Chelsea in the league. And word inside the club was that the major summer signing for the European champions was likely to be the much-travelled lanky striker Peter Crouch from Southampton. Was this beanpole the basis for a serious title challenge?

Liverpool fans were now encouraged to be hostile – to be enraged by this callous Gerrard treachery. One supporter publicly burned his Liverpool shirts for TV consumption and others allegedly scrawled up 'Judas' graffiti at Melwood and elsewhere. There were even dark hints that some of the self-confessed hard men from the city had telephoned in, suggesting it might be 'better' all round if Steven decided to just sign his contract at Liverpool and shut up. His family was being threatened; things were turning ugly. It was another Merseyside passion play with, potentially, a very unhappy ending. Rafa Benítez simply looked perplexed.

But who was really to blame? We all knew that Steven Gerrard was an emotionally fragile and complex young man. You only had to see him edging into corners at public events, or else desperately trying to squeeze out a little smile for TV interviews, to know his sensitivity: that he lacked a little maturity, self-awareness and confidence off the field. He was frequently twisting and squirming inside, torturing himself psychologically. If football clubs are really as smart as they think they are, they would have staff picking up just this sort of thing, working out ways of sorting out the heads of guys who are worth £30 or £40 million to them in sales and even more on the pitch. Gerrard needed some loving. He needed to be cherished and demonstrably wanted by Liverpool. Any fool could see this. He had been at the club since he was a kid, and he was admired and coveted almost everywhere else in the game. He was also a profoundly British product: a committed and passionate battler, rather than the type of Continental professional who saw football more clinically as a job. But his promised contract talks with Liverpool had not materialised. Had Liverpool Football Club begun to take him for granted, lining him up for public ridicule? Like it or not, when you are as famous as these players are and earn as much money as they do, this sort of public symbolism becomes vital – a crucial matter of personal dignity. Had some of his England mates now implied that his manager was taking liberties: that Benítez possibly fancied the cash from selling Gerrard so he could build his new Liverpool around his Spanish blue-eyed boy, Xabi Alonso? Gerrard's emotions were now in turmoil. And still no word came from the club. He was sure he was being messed around: in public.

Rafa Benítez is also emotionally complex – but a rather closed off, cold and analytical man. He says so himself. He is a product of the

Continental game and a culture where both players and especially managers practise their ruthlessness, rather than express their real emotional ties to football clubs or each other. Abroad, players and coaches routinely move on at the whim of sporting directors – moneymen who have little feel for the culture of their club or the feelings of their employees. After all this talk about the importance of 'spirit' to English clubs, for Benítez any 'arm around the shoulders' special bonding with any of his players was beyond the pale – and his own Spanish upbringing – and also potentially counterproductive in his eyes. He saw all of his players as equal to each other, as parts of the jigsaw he was now trying to put together so painstakingly at Anfield. He saw no signs at all of his captain's unrest, his torment, and, frankly, he was not looking for any. There had been heated discussions at training, sure, but that was part of the job. Gerrard was staying: that had been agreed upon after Istanbul. So why all this fuss now, when things had to be built for next season? And why was all this unproductive *emotion* involved in what were, after all, simply professional assessments and decisions?

Benítez certainly *wanted* Steven Gerrard to stay at Liverpool, although the coach was also probably coldly objective about any outcome: if necessary, £40 million could buy him four lesser but nonetheless quality players to shore up the midfielder's leaving. Benítez had told Santiago Segurola from *El País* back in April 2005 about the Huyton man's qualities. 'I see him [Gerrard] very much as a Liverpool player,' said Benítez. 'We don't want him to leave us, in no way. I want him here; we need him here. He is a flagship player, and he knows it. He is very complete. He is the first player to be picked for the crucial midfield area. He has quality; he passes the ball very well; he is brave. His physical commitment is hugely competitive.' This seemed like a eulogy, a real statement of intent. But then Benítez ended with a little caveat about his captain: that, good as he was, Gerrard 'should still mature a little as a footballer'. Benítez had mentioned this fact publicly a few times: that Steven's leadership and running qualities were sometimes ill-used; that he should apply himself on the pitch with a little more focus.

The truth was that parts of both sides of this agonising story were clearly true: that Rafa Benítez *did* want to keep his heroic captain if at all possible; but also, yes, the Liverpool midfield was now to be built around the more mature and organised, although younger, Spaniard Xabi Alonso, not Merseyside's own Steven Gerrard. This hurt the man from Huyton and fed both his insecurities and his burning sense of injustice, no matter how irrational.

As Gerrard now mooched around Melwood avoiding journalists and urchins alike, dressed in a grubby spearmint-coloured polo shirt instantly recognisable on the Sky Sports cameras, Rick Parry began to field complaints from the Gerrard camp about the stall in contract talks. As Liverpool chief executive, Parry definitely looked culpable – Henry Winter, a decent judge, described him as 'dithering' in the *Daily Telegraph* – but he had been on holiday and was simply waiting for a lead from his club manager, singularly unaware that Stevie was about to explode with his uncompromising 'no going back' indignation. Maybe Benítez was weighing up Anfield life with or without Gerrard after all?

SFX, Gerrard's agents, were then told by Liverpool about a proposed offer of a four-year contract extension at £100,000 a week for their client. Chelsea rapidly topped this with £125,000 and a £32 million bid for the player, immediately rejected by Liverpool. But this was not about money – it never had been – it was about honour. Sensing this at last, Benítez now said that he had told Gerrard that, in time, he could do any job he wanted at the club – assistant, coach, manager, chief executive. It was a long list of jobs, no doubt about that. But what about his current one – as the one-man midfield engine and captain of Liverpool Football Club?

Gerrard was mixed up and unimpressed, saying that it was all too late. He issued a statement about how the last six weeks had been 'the toughest of my life, and the decision I've come to has been the hardest I've ever had to make'. Rick Parry looked defeated, admitting that, 'It looks pretty final.' Apparently, no one inside Liverpool Football Club, an organisation that was packed with modern international specialists and technicians who worked on every aspect of player development and preparation, had even picked up a *sign* that the club's most important asset was hurting enough to contemplate leaving the football club he had loved since his childhood. Why should they, given the events of *last* summer? This was exasperating. So these three men – the passionate and emotionally fragile Gerrard, the businessman and committed fan Parry, and the cold professional Benítez – had seemingly been railroaded into a course of action that none of them wanted to take. It looked like an extraordinary outcome.

And then, even as the Liverpool staff were preparing to wave away the captain on the London train, Gerrard, emotional to the last, cracked. There was talk that he had been in tears, overnight, on the telephone to Liverpool teammates. That it was his family that had finally talked him around to staying at Liverpool, especially his heartbroken father. That he simply couldn't face being vilified at Anfield if he returned with another club – with Chelsea. That he had been poring over photographs and the video of the Champions League final with his girlfriend and family, spotting mates in the Liverpool crowd. Whatever the reason, what had seemingly been irretrievably lost in those past six weeks was suddenly found again. Gerrard was staying.

Sky Sports News stopped a bemused and clearly light-headed Rick Parry outside Kemlyn Road as the Liverpool man arrived for work the next morning. Parry looked exhausted but also serenely drunk with pleasure. He had no idea how the club had arrived at this mess, nor how it had escaped from it. He was just delighted that 'Steven' had realised that his ambitions were more than matched by those held by Liverpool Football Club.

Club chairman David Moores – a Scouser – said later that Gerrard's staying at Anfield was the 'big plus' of the summer. 'We did go through a tough spell, and there were some crossed wires,' he admitted. '[But] I never doubted Stevie. He came to my house on the morning after he announced he was staying, and we had a good chat. He had been confused, and there had been a lot of things going on behind the scenes.' Oh, really?

Ultimately, the mess was down to the muddled head of Stevie, but, frankly, it had also been a period of misunderstanding, misinterpretation and (lack of) negotiation drawn from the Keystone Cops school of football management. However, in a strange way, it was also oddly reassuring. The whole soap opera signalled that, even as European Champions, Liverpool Football Club could still act like an unsophisticated local diners' club or a parochial village-hall committee. We were still more of a flawed community than a slick corporation. But at least disaster had been avoided, even if it was more by luck than judgement. Benítez sighed with confusion and relief: Steven Gerrard would start the season with Liverpool Football Club after all.

TRANSFER TIME: ONE TOWER, NO STEPS

It is a good test for a coach, setting up a squad again after a major success. It was one Benítez had also faced at Valencia in 2001, though he was given little cash to spend. He chose then to change relatively little of the team assembled by Héctor Cúper that had played in two consecutive Champions League finals. As a result, Benítez led Valencia – Cúper's team – to the La Liga title in his first season in charge. At Liverpool he had won the European Cup in 2005 with a squad and a team that was basically put together by the Frenchman Gérard Houllier, but with two key changes: the addition of the two men from Spain, Xabi Alonso and Luis García. Fernando Morientes, his other major signing, had been ineligible for European action and had been a major disappointment in the Premiership. Benítez told *El País*: 'Xabi Alonso started up in a phenomenal way. Immediately, he became the reference point of the team. He didn't have any settling-in problems. He received excellent press comment, and people felt charmed by him. His adaptation to the city and to the English Premiership has been magnificent.' This was all true. Alonso had definitely taken the Liverpool team on, offering great passing, organisation, options and flexibility in midfield, while García, though sometimes wasteful, could also produce touches of real class and vital goals. 'Luis García has had highs and lows,' continued Benítez, 'but his contribution has often been decisive. He is a key player for us because he is very clever. He knows how to generate danger among back lines, and he has goals in him.'

Liverpool had earned just under £22 million from match bonuses and their share of UEFA's market pool for winning the European Cup and had probably cleared just under £30 million from the tournament in total. So, even with no outside investor in sight, Benítez could still lay claim to funds to strengthen his squad in an attempt to close the Premiership points gap with Chelsea. It wouldn't be easy: José Mourinho, having failed to lure Steven Gerrard to Stamford Bridge, had instead spent a cool £45 million plus on recruiting midfielders Michael Essien from Lyon and Shaun Wright-Phillips from Manchester City. Benítez spent well under half that amount bringing in three key players for the new campaign: 22-year-old goalkeeper José 'Pepe' Reina for £6 million from Villarreal ('The best goalkeeper in Spain,' according to Benítez), striker Peter Crouch from Southampton for £7 million and the young Mali midfielder Momo Sissoko (just 20) from Valencia – signed from under the noses of Everton – for a reported £5.6 million. Benítez had seen both Patrick Vieira and Sissoko as 18 year olds; he thought the Malian the better player. Benítez also signed, on a free, the experienced 28-year-old left-sided Dutch midfielder Boudewijn 'Bolo' Zenden – 'Middlesbrough's best player', boasted the Liverpool manager – a man who could also play centrally, as he had done brilliantly for Boro in the 2004–05 season while easily undoing Liverpool at the Riverside.

These four new signings annoyed some Reds fans, inspired others. In the annoyed camp were those who thought that the European champions should have been bringing in some bigger fish than these men. None of these guys actually made the heart race. For some Reds, the arrival of the gawky Crouch, especially, suggested that the coach was struggling badly for a convincing aesthetic and for a real feel for the intuitive art of striking. Would Liverpool now look to try to fire the ball in to this beanpole in another version of the sort of 'lighthouse football' frequently seen in the Blue den across Stanley Park? In fact, the word in the game about Crouch was actually counter-intuitive: that he was quite decent with his feet but not great in the air for his 6 ft 7 in. lightning-rod size. But could he add shape to the Liverpool attack and score goals? These were better questions. Also, two Reds heroes from Istanbul were now officially 'annoyed': the Czech Milan Baroš was most likely to be frozen out or sold because of Crouch's arrival, despite the unconvincing form of both the injured Cissé and recent arrival Morientes; and Jerzy Dudek looked set for a long spell on the Liverpool bench behind Reina. The Pole's recent penalty heroics in Istanbul would not save him.

In the 'inspired' camp were those Liverpool supporters who figured that Benítez knew what he was doing. The team had quite enough 'flair players' in it and lacked backbone when the going got tough away from home in the Premiership. These signings would help. Zenden was more reliable and more hard-working than the flaky Kewell; Sissoko could add dynamism, energy and pace to the Liverpool midfield and also help to release Steven Gerrard for more forward duties, a favourite option of Benítez; Reina could be expected to make fewer glaring mistakes than Jerzy; and Crouch? Well, Crouch might just do a better job of holding the ball higher up the field away from Anfield than Milan Baroš had ever managed. The Czech had badly frustrated Benítez, despite the forward's prodigious work rate, his crucial goals (admittedly from plenty of chances) and his unquenchable optimism.

Finally, no fewer than four other potential signings had slipped away from the Spanish coach. Luís Figo, from Real Madrid, decided to join Inter Milan rather than Liverpool, perhaps reasoning (probably correctly after Benítez's similar error with Pellegrino) that the Italian game was less pacy and physical at this stage of his career than the English Premiership. Both Simão Sabrosa from Benfica and the Peruvian Norberto Solano from Aston Villa failed to materialise, even though a £10 million fee had initially been agreed for the Portuguese player. The exciting young Chilean winger Mark González was then signed and mysteriously refused a work permit for the Premiership by the British Home Office. This may have been due to the fact that the Chilean had a serious knee injury when Liverpool lined him up. González would have to be loaned out in Spain for a season while he proved his fitness and ideally qualified for EU citizenship. He would eventually arrive in the summer of 2006 but make very little impact on the 2006–07 season. Add to this the injury that Harry Kewell suffered in Istanbul and it meant that Liverpool now had the towering Crouch in their squad (to remind Benítez of life with John Carew at Valencia CF) but no authentic winger in the set-up to cross the ball to him or to the listless Fernando Morientes – a decidedly strange outcome to the summer's transfer activities at Liverpool 4. When Benítez did eventually sign wingers in 2006–07, they failed to deliver, and the manager also seemed to lose faith in Peter Crouch as the man to lead the Liverpool challenge.

Could Benítez marshal his forces again for another successful assault on Europe? After all, Liverpool Football Club had won all its previous European cups in a cluster – why not another period of European dominance right now? Benítez may not have known too much about the excesses of Liverpool 'scallying' around the back streets of Europe in the 1970s and '80s, but he knew something about the club's fantastic history in European competition – about its great struggles against Spanish opposition and Europe's elite. This was one of the key things that had attracted the ambitious Benítez to Merseyside in the first place. Could the Spanish master now set Liverpool on a mission to retrieve some of its great European traditions – and in the face of his native country Spain's own rather chequered European club football past? We could only wonder, of course – and hope.

3

From Heysel to Istanbul:
the 20-Year Sentence

> Liverpool Football Club and the European Cup; the rise and
> fall – and rise – of the Spanish in Europe; Liverpool's strange
> return to the Champions League.

THE EUROPEAN CHAMPIONS CLUBS' CUP

How little we then knew it, but Rafa Benítez's arrival at Liverpool in
the summer of 2004 would signal an astonishing revival in the team's
fortunes in Europe's premier club competition – the European Cup.
Liverpool FC already had its own proud place in the history of the
European Cup, of course, one which their new and ambitious Spanish
manager was very attracted by. His aim was eventually to return
Liverpool Football Club to the pinnacle of the European game – or
have a damn good try attempting. But he was also well aware of the
weight of the Liverpool legacy and of the undulating fortunes of the
great English and Spanish clubs in 50 years of European competition,
not least the struggles at his beloved Real Madrid to rekindle the
memories of the now distant 1950s when Real had been even more
dominant in European club football than Liverpool had been in the
late 1970s and early 1980s. Madrid's *galácticos* had recently brought
back some welcome memories of these halcyon days to the Spanish
capital, even if they were now in danger of plunging back into the
chaotic state which had made European success for Spain simply

a dream for much of the last four decades. The challenge for Rafa Benítez was to revive similar good memories for older Liverpool fans who had been raised on images of Heighway, Souness, Dalglish, Hansen and the rest routinely lifting the European Cup almost 30 years ago. This story of English and Spanish rivalries in Europe, and the respective periods of dominance and failure for these countries in European football, was central to the rich weave of the European club game, and it had been part of Benítez's heritage as a young player in Spain. But as a coach he now found himself professionally dedicated to both England and Merseyside, even if his thoughts sometimes drifted to European club football history and to the continuing tensions, triumphs and uncertainties in his Spanish homeland.

For more than a decade from the mid-1970s to the mid-'80s, England dominated European football off, as well as on, the field. But the Continent eventually learned to fear our football teams (as well as our fans), especially the one that was honed by Shankly and Paisley and drawn from the Red half of Liverpool. Liverpool under Bob Paisley, and then Joe Fagan, were, arguably, the best team in Europe for much of this time, winning the European Cup four times, in 1977, 1978, 1981 and 1984.

Single clubs or countries have dominated this great competition for periods before and since, of course. The brilliant and fearless young Manchester United team, early pretenders, perished on a European assignment in 1958, well before reaching what would, undoubtedly, have been a formidable maturity. They could have been the first English champions of Europe and could have ruled the game for a generation, thus reshaping the history of European club football in the process. But from Franco's detached and poverty-stricken dictatorship of 1950's Spain, a beautiful white ghost emerged that entranced Europe – and set in train a football-club rivalry between England and Spain that would light up the fields of European football for the next 50 years.

The European Cup was the brainchild in 1954 of the French

football magazine *L'Equipe*, and it chimed well, at a time of great political upheaval, with ambitions for greater European integration and exchange in the lead up to the establishment of the European Economic Community in 1958. But the new competition was really established in order to test the rather desperate claims of English football clubs, following the humiliation of the England national team by Hungary in 1953, that the English club game was still the best in the world. *L'Equipe*'s original plan for a floodlit midweek European league was shelved because of likely fixture congestion. But in 1955 the fledgling European governing body UEFA agreed to organise a home-and-away knockout competition for 16 invited European clubs, though for the 1956–57 season the rules were changed and only national champions and the holders were eligible to enter. The new competition was called the European Champions Clubs' Cup, and the first final was scheduled for Paris in honour of the initiative of the French in setting up the new venture.

French vision was matched only by English introspection. Ironically, Chelsea, the current English champions in 1955, actually refused to take part in the new tournament after taking 'advice' on the matter from the xenophobic Football League. Chelsea officials agonised over the decision but decided not to oppose Alan Hardaker. This was a huge opportunity missed, of course, and it confirmed some of the worst fears about continuing English insularity and hubris in the face of the development of the game in Continental Europe. The Mears family in West London – Chelsea's owners – long regretted their conservatism. The 1955 title was the west London club's only league crown until Roman Abramovich's millions paid off 50 years later. Manchester United sensibly ignored the League advice in 1956: English football's uneasy obsession with Europe had begun.

THE GLORY – AND NOT SO GLORY – YEARS: ENGLAND, SPAIN AND THE EUROPEAN CUP

The great Real Madrid team of Gento and Alfredo Di Stéfano, soon supplemented by the Frenchman Raymond Kopa and the Hungarian Ferenc Puskás, was indefatigable in the early years of club football in Europe and won the first five European Cup finals in succession, from 1956 to 1960. After the first Real Madrid European Cup win in 1956, the club's president Santiago Bernabéu said, as straightforwardly as Bob Paisley himself might have done two decades later at Liverpool, 'I believe we have simply done our duty.'

Spain – like Liverpool later in the 1970s and '80s – certainly needed some uplifting. Franco's rigid regime at home meant isolation and poverty for most of the country's inhabitants, so Madrid's successes offered up a welcome, more benign, international image of his despotic domestic rule – much to the Francoist Bernabéu's satisfaction.

The graceful but deadly Argentinian Alfredo Di Stéfano was Franco's unwitting ambassador-in-chief. But his contribution to Real Madrid's early European dominance was all the more telling because he really *should* have signed for Real's bitter domestic rivals Barcelona. How sweet this irony must have seemed to the Madridistas. Di Stéfano even played a couple of friendly matches for the Catalans in 1954 while still connected to the outlawed Colombian club Millonarios, although his official registration was actually held by the Argentinian outfit River Plate. Real Madrid stepped in to destabilise the proposed Barça deal by talking to the Colombians while Barça continued to doorstep River Plate. It was a stalemate made even more bizarre by the fact that the Spanish government then decided that *no* foreign signings should play in Spanish football. Was this yet another Spanish state conspiracy against the Catalans?

The impasse was eventually broken when the Spanish federation decided that Di Stéfano could play in Spain after all – but only for

Barça and Real in *alternate* seasons for the next four years! How the great man might have managed this unconscionable dual life is unclear. Being both loved and hated at different moments in Spain's two great football kingdoms might have been beyond the psyche of even this balanced genius. Imagine a Rooney or an Alonso playing alternative seasons at Anfield and Old Trafford! It was a ludicrous attempt at a 'fix' to placate the dominant Spanish football powers. But it satisfied neither. The imperious Alfredo was spared the test because, affronted by the alleged duplicity of the Spanish authorities, the Barcelona board soon withdrew their interest in the Argentinian. But the Catalans might better have bitten their tongues, even at the thought of sharing this bounty with their bitter rivals. Costing just £20,000 for his legal release from River Plate, Di Stéfano shaped Real's modern dominance of the Spanish and European game for the next decade. He even scored four goals against Barcelona at the Bernabéu in a 5–0 rout just two weeks after moving to Madrid – and after spurning that club's greatest rival.

Along with Santiago Bernabéu, Di Stéfano was the undisputed colossus of the club game in Europe in the 1950s, and in 1954 he helped his new club win their first Spanish title since 1933. He won eight league titles and five European Cups at Madrid, playing as a forward midfielder – an authentic inside-forward role – of the kind that is still common on the Continent (Zidane, Platini, Baggio) but that remains rather puzzling to British eyes. Di Stéfano scored an astonishing 418 goals for Real Madrid in just 11 seasons. He was unmatched in his influence in Spain and in the European Cup. After their early domination, Real Madrid next won the European Cup in 1966, just as England conquered the international game at Wembley, but the influence of Spain then faded from view in top European club football.

After a brief British ascendance in Europe in 1967 (Celtic) and 1968 (Manchester United), it was the Netherlands' turn to dominate in the early 1970s. Ajax's 'total football', inspired by Johan Cruyff, now transfixed the European game: Ajax won three straight European Cup finals, in 1971, 1972 and 1973, after taking Feyenoord's Dutch lead (the team from Rotterdam beating Celtic 2–0 in the 1970 final). Then the mantle moved south to Germany, where Bayern Munich, under coach Udo Lattek and the on-field leadership of Franz Beckenbauer and goal poacher Gerd Müller, won their own three European titles in a row, from 1974 to 1976. Bayern beat England's Leeds United, cruelly, in the 1975 final in Paris, a match notable for German good fortune and bizarre refereeing but also for the wild hooliganism of some of Leeds' distraught and destructive followers. Here were the early warning signs of later English-inspired tragedy in the European game.

England's own period of *football* dominance in Europe followed, from 1977 to 1984. It was established through the work of Liverpool (four times), Nottingham Forest (twice) and even modest Aston Villa, who were first – and only – time winners of the trophy in 1982. Finally, from Italy, the Dutch-influenced AC Milan side, under Arrigo Sacchi and then Fabio Capello, won three European Cups between 1989 and 1994, including two 4–0 humiliations, first of Steaua Bucharest in 1989 and then of Barcelona in the 1994 final in Athens. The exquisite Milan midfielder Dejan Savićević spent this latter evening completely ruining the Catalans. Milan's high tempo and structured 'pressing' style of play under Sacchi influenced many later successful European football coaches, including, of course, Liverpool's own Spanish import Rafa Benítez.

It seems incredible now that countries, and even single clubs, could ever have established such lengthy periods of European football dominance. But then stronger club contracts, limits on the recruitment of foreign players and a much more limited global market for footballers meant that even the smaller European club winners – in the Netherlands, Germany and England, for example – could more easily build on their experience and success, rather than struggle to keep hold of their stars, as they might do today. Successful coaches also moved around less rapidly and freely in that era, so that in the years that followed Liverpool's triumphs, and with English clubs now in disgrace and banned from Europe, the competition opened up even more. It was Eastern Europe's turn to shine: Steaua Bucharest stumbled through the final to victory on penalties over Barcelona in 1986, and Red Star Belgrade did the same in 1991, this time scrambling past Marseille in the shoot-out. Who knows now whether there will ever be another Eastern Champions Cup triumph in the free-market era? Though why not, when there are Russian billionaires already splashing out fortunes in European football clubs?

Since the new Champions League format replaced the old knockout one in the 1991–92 season, eleven different clubs from seven different countries have won the European Cup in fourteen competitions (up to 2005), a relative spread of the rewards at the same time as the major clubs and the big leagues of Europe have gradually taken a much firmer hold of the competition. FC Porto's victory, in 2004, managed by the hugely talented Mourinho, seems like merely a welcome blip to the dominance of Spain, Italy, England and Germany in Europe today. This new era compares with 18 different club winners in 36 years of the competition in its original format between 1956 and 1991. In the fifty years of the European Cup from 1956 to 2005 Spanish clubs had won the trophy on a total of ten occasions, nine of them by Real Madrid and just one (before 2006) by Barcelona, who were victorious in London in 1992. Before 2006, Spain was tied with England and Italy in respect of the number of European Cups won, though English clubs have played in fewer competitions, because of their early reluctance and the Heysel ban in the 1980s. The three 'other' winners listed in table one include, of course, Scotland after Celtic's famous victory over Inter Milan in Lisbon in 1967.

Real Madrid's early dominance of the European Cup in the 1950s was based on a combination of multi-cultural talent unmatched anywhere in Europe at that time, one that prefigured football's later global age that would be led, once again, by Real. Spain, incredibly, won only one European Cup – Real again, in 1966 in Brussels – in the next thirty-two years. This seems like an extraordinary hiatus. The Spanish drought –called by Real Madrid fans *los años del desierto* (the wilderness years) – was ended, ironically, by Real's bitter rivals Barcelona's sole European Cup win, which briefly revived Spanish fortunes in 1992. Atlético Madrid also lost its only European Cup final during this lengthy period of Spanish failure, to Bayern Munich in 1974 – it was the only final ever to go to a replay.

Table 1: European Cup wins by country, 1956–2005

	No.	*Periods of relative dominance*
England	10	Late 1970s/early 1980s
Spain	10	1950s and late 1990s/early 2000s
Italy	10	1960s and early 1990s
Germany	7	Mid-1970s
Holland	6	Early 1970s
Portugal	4	Early 1960s
Others	3	

So what happened to the early Spanish club – more properly, the Real Madrid – dominance in Europe, often built as it was around expensive foreign imports? Spanish isolationism might, eventually, have taken its toll. The domestic championship – the struggle between Barcelona and Madrid especially – dominated in Spain in a way that was unusual in Europe. But Real Madrid traditionalists suggest that a turning point, of sorts, in the club's troubling post-1950s' direction finally came in 1974 when Miguel Muñoz, the club's Spanish coach for more than a decade, was replaced by an outsider, the Yugoslav Miljan Miljanic. This was a period of generally growing freedom and openness in Spain – signalled by the rise of foreign tourism – as Franco's death approached. The great Di Stéfano once famously remarked that, 'The word runner-up or sub-champion (*subcampeón*) doesn't exist in the Madridista vocabulary.' But if this were really so, the concept would have to be invented, because it took Real another 24 years after the expansive appointment of Miljanic for the Madridistas to finally reclaim the European Cup.

Perhaps the answer to this question about failing Spanish clubs abroad also lies, partially at least, in the Spanish federation's decision in 1965 to allow only players with Spanish roots to play in the Spanish league. As Spanish football expert Phil Ball points out, this soon became known as *El timo de Paraguay* (the Paraguayan fiddle) when it was discovered that a consul in that country was earning hefty sums by falsifying players' documents to help with their passage to Spain. Nevertheless, this new directive would have certainly disrupted Real's European Cup ambitions, compared, at least, to their more cosmopolitan, halcyon days of the 1950s. But then many of the European champion clubs of this period – from Germany and the Netherlands, for example – included very few foreign imports themselves. It was different in England, of course. Liverpool relied on a brilliant trio of Scots – Hansen, Dalglish and Souness – as well as key Welsh and Irish recruits, who were absolutely central to Liverpool's own European and domestic successes in the late 1970s and '80s. Famously, all the members of the Celtic team that beat Inter Milan in Lisbon in 1967 were born within 20 miles of Parkhead, clearly a remarkable piece of Scottish footballing real estate. Finding even *one* above-average elite football player in the whole of Glasgow today might tax any coach of merit, such has been the coruscating decline of the Scottish game since.

Lacking a raft of top-quality foreign imports – two non-Hispanic imports were only allowed from 1973 – there was also no outstanding domestic talent to save the Spanish club game at this time. And they were not alone in their troubles in this respect. The Spanish *national* team – like its English equivalent – was of very uncertain quality during this period. It was run through with the usual Basque/Catalan/ Spanish internecine conflicts, as well as suffering from a paucity of high–class raw material. In 1982 Spain even lost to Northern Ireland at the 'neutral' Mestalla during the World Cup finals. Valencia had to host the Spanish side as a buffer against the political tensions offered from both Barcelona and Madrid.

THE TIME OF THE BASQUES

So what about Real's perpetual historical and political struggles with FC Barcelona as the main potential source for this decline in its European club influence? The rivalry between the so–called 'Franco's club' of Real and Barcelona, a cultural flagship for Catalonian nationalism, has undoubtedly been overhyped, but the Barcelona–Real Madrid rivalry does utterly dominate the history of the Spanish game. Only briefly, in the 1940s, the early '70s and the early '80s, has this duo been under any real threat in Spain – for example, Valencia CF won three Spanish titles in the 1940s. (In England, even as late as the 1960s, eight different clubs could still win the Football League championship.) This domestic rivalry between Barça and Real in Spain seems to have even intensified in the early 1970s as the fortunes of these two great clubs rather slumped, relatively speaking, during a period of social flux and political change. This meant that Spanish football at this time turned increasingly inwards, a process interrupted only by Barcelona's and Valencia's respective minor European victories in the 1979 and 1980 European Cup-Winners' Cup finals, which actually further focused Real on outdoing their domestic rivals – but at *home*.

Barça, for their part, had their own domestic ambitions still to achieve. In fact, when Ajax's Johan Cruyff signed for the Catalan club in 1973, amidst much predictable ballyhoo, Barcelona had already gone 14 seasons without winning the Spanish title. The brilliant Dutchman broke the drought during his initial 'dream season' of 1973–74, but that was that. This was also the time of Bill Shankly's last managerial campaign at a changing, slowly modernising Liverpool. Shankly, of course, had his own rather painful European Cup memories of both

Ajax and Cruyff – a 1–5 defeat in Amsterdam – and had only recently enjoyed what would be his first and only real success in Europe, the winning of the 1973 UEFA Cup.

Real's own relative loss of domestic direction in the early 1970s meant the brief surrendering of their dominance of the Spanish league title. Real Madrid recovered towards the middle of the decade, but not for long: Real Sociedad won their only two Spanish titles for the Basque country in 1981 and 1982 – led by their talismanic, moustachioed striker Jesús Zamora – followed by two titles for their more senior Basque neighbours, Athletic Bilbao, under their rugged English-style coach Javier Clemente in 1983 and 1984. This was certainly the time of the Basques in Spanish football, unprecedented since the 1930s.

Perhaps the best way of crudely comparing Spain and England in football and geographical terms is to view London as Madrid (inevitably) and the English North West as Barcelona. This makes Valencia a faded Yorkshire or Midlands power base, and the underachieving, localistic and passionate Basques as (predictably) the English North East. If you buy into this simple model, then imagine, say, Sunderland and Newcastle United taking the Football League title for two seasons each during Liverpool's era of dominance in the 1980s – and doing so by relying only on players drawn from the North East. Now you have something approaching the world-turning English equivalent of these extraordinary Basque achievements of the early 1980s.

Earlier, Liverpool had dismissed Real Sociedad, quite brutally, in the 1975–76 UEFA Cup, winning by an embarrassingly easy 9–1 aggregate score. Indeed, Spanish football seemed to hold no real fear for Liverpool at this time. Later, at the semi-final stage of the same competition, the Reds also won much more comfortably than the 1–0 score line suggests, beating Cruyff's by now ailing Barcelona in the Camp Nou, before snuffing out the Catalans in a 1–1 return leg at Anfield. In the final the Reds made rather harder work of defeating Club Brugge KV 4–3 over two legs.

A SCOUSE STRIKER, A WELSH POET – AND *LA CANTERA*

In 1989 there was another Liverpool link with the Basques. Real Sociedad sensationally eschewed the region's historic Basque-only player policy, *la cantera*, by signing, of all people, the Reds striker John Aldridge. Aldridge had scored an impressive twenty-one goals in thirty-one league starts in the 1988–89 season for Liverpool, and his record was sixty-three goals in total in just two seasons at Anfield. But this goal return could not salvage his brief Liverpool career.

His transfer occurred well before the time when top football managers in England, such as Houllier and Benítez, would demand three, or even four, quality strikers on their books. In the 1980s two were deemed to be more than sufficient – often one too many. The Scouser Aldridge had recently had a damaging 'fuck off' fall-out with manager Kenny Dalglish's wife Marina, and this was not a great career move. But the striker was almost certainly released by the Liverpool boss in order to accommodate the return of Ian Rush to Anfield after a fairly disastrous season at Juventus. Aldridge was desperately unhappy to be asked to leave Anfield – and to find out that Liverpool had been talking to potential suitors without his knowledge. The club was looking to make a cool £400,000 profit by selling the striker, then 31 years old, to Real Sociedad for £1.15 million. After a full-on slanging match with the Liverpool board about the size of his cut of any deal – the Merseysider was nobody's fool – Aldridge agreed an 'appropriate' pay-off with Peter Robinson before angrily stomping off for the Basque country.

Aldridge was actually the 11th foreigner ever to play for Sociedad, but the first for 30 years. Ironically, Sociedad's history is littered with British coaches, stretching right back to Harry Lowe in the 1930s, and the club and its fans extolled the more physical British style of play, a fact that Liverpool fans would see confirmed under Rafa Benítez in the work rate and commitment of another Sociedad product, Xabi

Alonso. (Alonso's father Periko played in the Sociedad championship teams of the 1980s, and his brother Mikel now plays midfield for the Basque club.) In 2005–06 only one Premiership player delivered more tackles than the rugged Basque midfielder.

Aldridge immediately noticed the more scientific approach to his medical care, diet and training in Spain, and also the open resistance to non-Basques at Sociedad. A slogan on a wall at the club's training ground read 'No outsiders welcome here'. But the ex-Liverpool man conferred with another ex-Red who was now serving his time in Spain. The cod Welsh poet and ex-beanpole Liverpool striker John Toshack was masterminding another assault at the European Cup at still-troubled Real Madrid.

Toshack had moved to Spain to coach Sociedad in 1985. (Sammy Lee and striker Michael Robinson would also make the move to Spain – both at Osasuna – and Robinson later forged a successful career there as a football pundit.) The Basque club that Toshack joined was in sharp decline from its surprise Spanish championship successes in the early 1980s. From the start, Toshack was regarded in Spain as an entertaining and idiosyncratic disciplinarian – his nickname, *El Flemático* (the phlegmatic one), was one often kept for the British – and someone who might add some much needed British steel to the cosseted and ageing stars in Sociedad. And he had some success, his new club winning the Spanish Cup in 1987. Toshack then attracted the attention of Real Madrid in 1989, and in his first spell in Madrid – he returned briefly in 1999 – he lost only eight out of sixty-three matches, but it still wasn't enough. Undermined by failure in Europe and the erratic performances of the talented Romanian midfielder Gheorghe Hagi, he was sacked and rejoined Sociedad in 1991 for four mainly happy years, including a UEFA Cup qualification in 1992.

Later, British coaches working in Spain would be regarded rather less affectionately by the Spanish press: one newspaper described Toshack and the then Barcelona coach Bobby Robson as 'farm hands from the museum of British football'. But back in the late 1980s

Toshack was still widely revered in Spain as a British coach who added discipline and drive to Hispanic flair.

While at Real, Toshack told John Aldridge, the new man at Sociedad, that things would settle down once the striker did what he knew best – score goals. He duly got 22 in his first season, hauling Sociedad to a UEFA Cup place in the process. But even the arrival of the Real Madrid cast-off and familiar replacement Toshack as Sociedad manager for season 1991–92 couldn't persuade Aldridge and his homesick family to stay in Spain for one more year. He returned to the Merseyside area, having piled up 40 goals in just 75 Sociedad matches, to experience more success as both a player and manager with the rather more homely Tranmere Rovers.

PARIS, 1981

Five of the ten Spanish championships won by Basque clubs came before the end of the Second World War. Four others came in the little purple patch between 1981 and 1984. No Basque club from Spain has ever reached the European Cup final. For Real Madrid life has been very different. Once supreme in Europe but about to be usurped, for once, by these hostile northerners at home and regularly falling short abroad, Real finally managed to reach the European Cup final for the ninth time, in 1981. But they came up against seasoned opponents, Bob Paisley's streetwise Liverpool, in what was a pretty poor European summit meeting in Paris. Real coach Vujadin Boškov was unimpressed: he called Liverpool 'programmed, like a machine'. This was Real's first European Cup final for 15 long seasons. It showed. Against a hardened, experienced Liverpool team – but one that had been struggling desperately with injuries – the Spaniards looked listless and functional, relying heavily on England's own ill-fated winger Laurie Cunningham for what little flair and adventure they could muster.

Real Madrid's great European traditions, its evocative name and its emblematic all-white kit, coupled with the wonderful Paris location, all offered the 1981 European final some real allure. It was the famous Spanish *Los blancos* against the mighty Liverpool Reds. And it was much more, because here was a meeting on European club football's biggest stage between the champions of the old European order and the new dominant European force from England. But the Real *team* of 1981 bore little resemblance to the great Madrid sides of the 1950s. It was largely anonymous, built around the defensive strength of the fearsome German Uli Stielike, rather than on any seriously threatening attacking potential of the sort that had marked out Real 25 years before. With Liverpool themselves carrying some injured passengers – Dalglish was barely fit, Alan Kennedy only recently back from injury – the match was disjointed and largely uneventful, and it was fittingly decided by a second-half goal from defender Kennedy after an ugly defensive error by Real centre-back Cortés. A French commentator described the final as 'chloroform football'. The Red celebrations that followed – Phil Thompson took the European Cup to both the Paris Lido *and* to the Falcon pub in Kirkby – and the chaotic deluging of Paris by Liverpool fans, was generally regarded as much more memorable than the final itself. And poor Real Madrid were left without a European trophy once more, still seeking a return to signs of its earlier Continental dominance.

According to the young Manolo Sanchis, later to captain Real in the late 1980s, this 1981 result and particularly the Madrid *performance* against Liverpool in the final especially hurt in the Spanish capital. It focused local attention on what had been lost since the great Real days of the 1950s, as well as the possibilities of getting back to these cherished older Madrid traditions. It convinced the Real Madrid fans, more than anything, of the need for something new. 'We had good players in our team but lacking the glamour of real stars,' he said. 'It was when we lost 0–1 against Liverpool that people began to demand change.' Real Madrid eventually got change, beginning with the brief, but emblematic, return of the great Alfredo Di Stéfano, this time as club coach, in 1982. The much-heralded arrival at the Camp Nou of his fellow Argentinian Diego Maradona, the magnificent urchin, in the same year, upped the domestic ante in Spain but actually did little to revive Barça's flagging Spanish title and European ambitions. Indeed, it would take the presence of Terry Venables, another Englishman, as coach to win the Spanish title for the Catalan city once more (in 1985) and to get Barcelona to a (losing) European Cup final of their own (in 1986). However, these were but small blue-and-red oases in an otherwise whitening Real Madrid Spanish desert. Barcelona fans could still point, of course, to the alleged 'advantages' of nationalist Real Madrid and the supposed 'bias' against the insurgents to account for their own relative underachievement at home – but in Europe? Here there were still many more questions than answers.

THE 1990s – A SPANISH EUROPEAN COMEBACK

Real Madrid slowly recovered its poise under president Ramón Mendoza, with 'the vulture' Emilio Butragueño now rattling in the goals and being ably supported by Michel, Martín Vazquez and the rest of the 'vulture squad'. During the ten years of the Mendoza presidency (1985–95), Real won six Spanish titles – five consecutively – and a UEFA Cup (in 1986). Not bad work, not even by Liverpool standards under Bob Paisley and Joe Fagan. But the Madrid club and its supporters were aching for something else, something more. Mendoza was still forced out of office because of his failure to bring 'home' the 'Big One' – the European Cup – to the Spanish capital. Even with English clubs now banished from Europe, Spain could make little claim to be the new dominant force in European football. Instead, the Dutch, Portuguese, Italians and even Eastern Europeans all now briefly moved centre stage. They tossed the big-eared trophy to each other as if gloating at the long-term European lock-out of the Spanish club giants. Something had to give.

Before Liverpool FC had been forced out of Europe in disgrace in 1985, it was the new Spanish champions Athletic Bilbao that were actually among the most testing of opponents for the prospective European champions, this time in the European Cup in the 1983–84 season. In the second round of the competition the tough Basques forced an impressive goalless first leg at Anfield in October 1983, showing both cynical determination and real resilience in the process. Goalkeeper Andoni Zubizarreta was outstanding in the sort of gutsy defensive show that was now only infrequently seen from European opponents in the crucible that was Liverpool 4. Indeed, such was the Basque defensive strength that Joe Fagan and his staff feared an early elimination in the return in Spain. They were right to be alarmed: Noriega and Gallego might both have scored in the opening exchanges in the second leg at the San Mamés. But then Liverpool showed all their European pedigree with Ian Rush grabbing the decisive goal from an Alan Kennedy cross. Liverpool would now go on to defeat Roma – in Rome – in the final, the club's fourth European Cup win in eight years. Spanish football, 18 years without a European Cup to call its own, could only look on at Merseyside's successes – and dream.

After the failures of the 1980s, it was now all change at Barcelona. As Liverpool FC struggled to adapt after Europe had reopened its doors once more to English clubs, Johan Cruyff, the new talismanic Barcelona coach, was collecting multiple Spanish titles in the early 1990s and, *finally*, via a Ronald Koeman free-kick at Wembley in 1992, the European Cup for the Catalans in the same year as a title success. This was the first such 'Double' in Spain since Real had done it twice way back in 1957 and 1958. This Barcelona feat meant that pressure for another European Cup success at the Bernabéu had now become almost intolerable. Real won only a miserly two Spanish titles in the 1990s, something of a disaster, especially as the new regime at Barcelona, with Josep Guardiola, Michael Laudrup, Hristo Stoichkov and José Mari Bakero all to the fore, dominated the domestic game in Spain and even threatened a new football dynasty in Europe – a mirage, as it turned out. But, crucially, the Madridistas had finally begun building for future European Cup success themselves, a project not without its own various twists and torments. The knee-jerk dismissal of the intellectual Argentinian coach Jorge Valdano midway through the 1995–96 season, for example, meant the disaster of Real missing out entirely on European qualification for the 1996–97 season.

With no European football to act as a distraction for once, the shrewd Italian coach Fabio Capello was recruited for a year, while chastened Real president Lorenzo Sanz went for broke by buying Clarence Seedorf, Roberto Carlos, Christian Panucci, Davor Šuker and Valencia man Predrag Mijatović to aid in the immediate aim of Real winning the Spanish league title once more. It worked. The following season the new Real coach, the German Jupp Heynckes, was left with just one task: to win the 1998 European Cup. To huge celebrations in Madrid, gyrations that caused serious injury to 200 revellers, he actually managed it. Mijatović's goal was enough to defeat a jittery Juventus 1–0 in Amsterdam in a perfunctory final. No matter: it was, at last, *la séptima* – the seventh European Cup for Real – even if it was more than three decades after the sixth had been secured. The European football pendulum was about to swing back to the Bernabéu, and for the first time in over 40 years.

LIVERPOOL FC: FIGHTING IN THE EAST

As Barcelona and Real tried to quell the northern hordes in Spain in the 1980s, and as Valencia attempted, initially unsuccessfully, to build upon their lone Spanish championship success back in 1971, so Liverpool's own period of domestic and European dominance in the 1970s and '80s was briefly interrupted by football successes for some of the game's supposedly lesser lights. But these challengers came from the English Midlands, rather than any independent-minded and separatist 'Geordie nation' that might have had ambitions to ape the regionalist Basque successes in Spain. There were league titles in this period, for example, for previously unconsidered Derby

County (1975), Nottingham Forest (1978) and Aston Villa (1981).

The rise of the Midlands provincials in England seemed to be less about matters of culture, regionalism and politics, as might have been the case in Spain. This local uprising in England was a case of the brief flowering of a managerial genius to rival even the unflappable Bob Paisley. After first leading Derby County to the league title in 1972, for a short time Brian Clough's Nottingham Forest seemed to have a hex on Bob Paisley, first winning the title from under the noses of Liverpool in 1978 and then showing the temerity to knock Paisley's team, the holders, out at the first-round stage of the European Cup in the autumn of the same year. Forest also dumped Liverpool out of the League Cups of 1978 and 1980, so this was no beginner's luck. Paisley definitely seemed to struggle against the chutzpah and the tactical know-how of Clough, who also had the knack of making his collection of stars and misfits play with no fear and considerable collective spirit. It was a formidable combination of attributes, shaped, in an attacking sense, around the shambolic, overweight figure of talented left-winger John Robertson. Forest also had defensive strength assembled in front of the near impassable England goalkeeper Peter Shilton. Clough's men were, in short, a very, very difficult team to beat.

Replicating Liverpool's own back-to-back successes under Paisley in 1977 and 1978, Forest went on to win the European Cup for the first time in 1979 and then retain it in 1980, a quite stupendous feat for Clough and his mixture of expensive stars and baffling rejects and journeymen. Like Forest, Liverpool had benefited from some benign European Cup draws at this time, but they had also had some stinkers: Forest themselves in the first round in 1978, followed by the brilliant Dinamo Tbilisi in the first round the very next year. Both ties were lost. In 1982 (CSKA Sofia) and again in 1983 (Widzew Łódź) Liverpool also lost to Eastern Europeans – this was threatening to become a pattern. But in 1984 Liverpool managed to halt the Eastern rot in the European Cup against Dinamo Bucharest in a brutal semi-final encounter. Liverpool won the final in Rome on penalties, Bruce

Grobbelaar's goal-line antics against Roma being famously copied 21 years later by Jerzy Dudek in Istanbul.

The terrible events involving Liverpool fans at the Heysel Stadium in 1985 felt like the end of football in England – but it was actually probably an early turning point for a sport and for a culture that was long in crisis. Thirty-nine, mainly Italian, fans paid the ultimate price for the lesson. The truth is that when the political Thatcherites of the 1980s effectively dished out a disdainful 'no future' coda for the majority of Liverpool's young inhabitants, many young scallies who were in search of respect, rather than the humiliation they were then offered, simply refused to accept the message. And who could blame them?

Nicky Allt's recent book *The Boys From the Mersey* brilliantly describes the role that football – and especially the technicolor European football adventure following Liverpool FC in the late 1970s and 1980s – played in providing the canvas for the great, sprawling pictures some of the city's movers and groovers were still desperate to paint. The endless bunking of trains, the stealing, the clothes, the determined travel to distant football locations with good mates and, occasionally, the hard lecture of the Stanley knife now increasingly ruled at 'the match'. Questions were even asked in the House as hooliganism started to escalate in English football, with talk of fan membership schemes and the banning of foreign football travel especially when English 'lads' caused unholy havoc on the Continent. But it made no difference at Liverpool. No market-obsessed blue rinse from Grantham was ever going to teach these Merseyside boys how to jive – or dare tell them not to try.

Liverpool 'hooligans' had always favoured stealing and strategic fighting over 'mindless' destruction and vandalism: the game, after all, deserved some respect. And the idea that neighbouring Everton fans were somehow more restrained and better behaved than those over at Anfield – and were therefore blighted by the ban meted out after Heysel – was soon scotched by vivid recollections of football travel at home and abroad published by well-known Blue hooligans.

All this fancy talk about politics, exclusion and a search for 'meaning' is no defence of the old Anny Road boys and their dangerous and sometimes imaginative and entertaining mates. Nor is it meant to be, even if football travel for young men in the '80s – especially in England and occasionally abroad – inevitably meant fronting up to unfriendly forces elsewhere, defending your corner. Because the street attacks and the cute attempts at mass bunking-in at matches without tickets – something of a Liverpool speciality – no matter how easy or attractive, were simply making already dodgy football grounds in England and on the Continent even more dangerous for everyone else.

The routine robbing from motorway services, sports shops and, increasingly, from jewellers' premises abroad, and the attacks on fans and touts for match tickets, also soon meant that *all* Liverpool fans began to be regarded in some places in the 1980s as rather less than lovable rogues. They all became suitable targets for abusive treatment on their travels. We saw a continuation of this Reds tradition, of course, in Athens in 2007. Scally football culture also had some impact elsewhere. According to writer and Spanish football expert Jimmy Burns, some Real Madrid followers trace the origins of their own *Ultra Surs* hooligans, who grew out of the *Peña de las Banderas* supporters club, to those experiences at the 1981 European Cup final in Paris, where some Liverpool fans attacked Spaniards – including married couples – and stole their tickets. Real Madrid Ultra Surs decided to collectively imitate the Liverpudlians – or at least be better prepared for such an assault next time by setting up their own local crews. It just might be that some unfortunate England fans felt the 'benefit' of this harsh lesson at the World Cup finals that followed in Spain in 1982.

But it couldn't go on indefinitely, this sort of theatrical and chaotic football adventure, this violence and plundering; tragically, Heysel, and later the police malpractices at Hillsborough in 1989, told us as much. After 1985 Liverpool Football Club faced a long period of exclusion from the European football elite, by which time our own house would be put back into some kind of acceptable order.

IT'S A BEAUTIFUL DAY? LIVERPOOL'S
RETURN TO THE EUROPEAN CUP

Liverpool FC finally returned to the European Cup – or the Champions League, as it had then become – in the autumn of 2001, a full 16 years after its ignominious departure. It was a very different world the Merseyside club had rejoined. For one thing – quite miraculously, it seemed – Liverpool was playing in the Champions League but had not actually *been* champions of England since 1990. Runners-up and others were now involved in the competition to get the TV revenues up and to try to ensure no more of the bad-for-business first-round Liverpool v. Forest all-or-nothing showdowns we had enjoyed and endured more than 20 years earlier. Back then, the Liverpool boss Bob Paisley was an Anfield graduate, but now the manager was no longer a familiar and tested boot-room product. Instead, it was the inspirational and occasionally high-handed foreign technocrat Gérard Houllier who was in charge and who had already secured the UEFA Cup for Liverpool just a few months earlier.

For another, although the 1990s' Liverpool side had an encouragingly large Scouse core, most of the club's players were now globally recruited – men of a range of languages and idioms. Moreover, the Continental European football superpowers of Spain and Italy had finally reasserted themselves somewhat in the world's greatest football club competition. Real Madrid, especially, had spent serious money on assembling a team of international stars to rival those of the 1950s, when Real had offered a new international face for Franco's austere and forbidding Spain. Valencia CF, an exciting new football force from Spain, even threatened to break the Real–Barça La Liga stranglehold and would reach *two* European Cup finals of their own, in 2000 and 2001 (after taming Liverpool in the group stages) – only to lose both of them, one to an irresistible Real Madrid. A new young Spanish manager would now drive the Valencia club on to a Spanish championship and UEFA Cup success. Liverpool would meet him later.

Football matches in England now kicked off on Sundays, Thursdays and Mondays – as well as all the other usual days – and at weird times. Because of Hillsborough, people in England now sat and watched games rather than stood and participated: no one watched from behind fences any more. Unless, that is, you went to football countries such as Italy, Belgium or Holland, where hooliganism still seemed rife, probably partly as a result. Liverpool FC and the rest of the British game had learned an incredibly harsh lesson at Hillsborough, where the blame lay squarely with the police, but the wider context for that day's events had been established by English fan traditions over the previous two decades.

But by 2001 things had also changed in this latter respect. There were still the equivalents of the Anny Road lads around, of course – increasingly in the Main Stand at Anfield – but travel for football away from home and abroad was now much more sedate, more boring – nicer. Women wanted to go on football trips. Instability, it seemed, was the new stability in global football. Nothing was quite the same – and on the whole, despite the new bullshit and the endless griping about 'authentic' football and 'the good old days', things were generally better in the English game. Thankfully, it was much harder to die in an English football ground, a fact we reminded ourselves of on 15 April each year as people in Liverpool honoured the 96 who had been lost on a once sunny afternoon in Sheffield.

If this was a new football world that Liverpool Football Club was now re-entering – and it clearly was – then the wider world was rapidly changing too. So it was on a rather strange and eerie night – 11 September 2001 – that Liverpool Football Club rejoined the European football elite. Check that date. Boavista from Portugal were the Anfield visitors in 2001 for what was anticipated to be a historic and emotional L4 night. But football was not the main focus of the crowd's attention that evening. Even in a city as football mad as Liverpool, people can still see the bigger picture. Five thousand miles away in New York the authorities were still trying to work out who, exactly, had flown two aircraft full of passengers into the twin towers of the World Trade Center and had crashed other loaded planes elsewhere in the USA. We had seen all this urban horror unfold live on afternoon TV, extraordinary images beamed back direct from Manhattan. The US death toll was still being discussed in terms of tens of thousands as fans settled down rather quietly at Anfield to much-awaited European Cup football action. No one quite knew who might be the next target. The world suddenly seemed under siege.

All of this made Liverpool's historic return to the European Cup and our own daily troubles in football and elsewhere seem rather less important. Suddenly, a name emerged in the press and on TV that was to become chillingly familiar to all of us over the next five years: Osama Bin Laden. He had no known football credentials, but his presence was palpable at Anfield on an evening when Liverpool FC announced its return to the European Cup with a suitably downbeat 1–1 draw. In fact, most people were simply glad to get the match over that night so that we could all return to our homes to try to make sense of where exactly the world and its politicians now seemed to be headed. But despite this new international pall, life eventually went on as, what we began to learn to call, 'normal'. Great football adventures still lay ahead in Europe in the next few years for Liverpool Football Club and its followers: in Monaco, Turin, Moscow and pretty much all points east and west. None of us knew on that September evening, when the world was in such flux and torment, that from this slightly unreal beginning we would all end up – via defeat in Leverkusen in 2002 and poverty in Basle in 2003 – in Istanbul in 2005 facing humiliation. And then end up touching the sky. Or how Liverpool Football Club's future would soon become entwined with that of a modest young Spanish manager who had stiffened unconsidered Valencia CF to title success in Spain. The new man would bring a bunch of Spanish players with him to Anfield, men who would willingly exchange the regional and political rivalries of football in Spain for the intense, entrenched solidarities and localistic feuds of Premiership football in England.

The history of Liverpool Football Club would now be tied, for all time, to a Spanish city and a club that would mirror our own struggles to overcome the football dominance of England's 'national' club, Manchester United, and the new moneymen at Chelsea. Istanbul had been a magnificent opening statement, sure, but was it just a 'one-off', a brief and beautiful interruption in a new European football order that had now left clubs such as Liverpool and Valencia CF miles behind in its wake? Did Liverpool fans even want to try to compete at this level any more? Rafa Benítez had made Valencia CF a real force in Spanish football, even to rival the galácticos of Real Madrid and the 'Star Chamber' at Barcelona. The history of this great Spanish club and its famous Mestalla stadium now suddenly had its own intriguing Liverpool connections and connotations. But first, Rafa Benítez had a European Cup to retain; and it was still the middle of summer.

4

Learning to Fly

Too early even for cricket; Benítez's new youth systems;
Carra's silverware in Monaco; mugged by José Mourinho;
the Liverpool return to Brussels; dishonoured at the Palace;
Benítez says 'No' to goals against.

NO STRIKERS WANTED – OR NEEDED?

Liverpool's first competitive football match of 2005 in Rafa Benítez's
second season as manager was in the Champions League at Anfield
against TNS, the Welsh battlers from the tiny village of Llansantffraid-
ym-Mechain (pop. 1,000). The game kicked off a week before the first
Ashes Test match in England had even begun: that's how weird this
all was. A hat-trick from Steven Gerrard in front of a shirt-sleeved
and very young Liverpool crowd either confirmed his coach's belief in
his captain as a goal scorer or else convinced others that the nominal
Liverpool forwards on the night, Morientes and the young Frenchman
Anthony Le Tallec, were just not up to the job, not even against
European part-timers like these. Le Tallec and young Darren Potter,
who also started here and at the Racecourse Ground in the return,
were getting their Liverpool pitch time in early. Both would spend
most of the season away from Anfield, and their futures now seemed
to lie irredeemably outside Liverpool Football Club. Gerrard scored
two more goals in the gentle return in Wales, Cissé also opening his
account having attempted to score direct from the kick off and spying
the imminent arrival at Melwood of one Peter Crouch.

Giedrius Barevicius provided a shock lead for the Lithuanians
from FBK Kaunus in the first leg of the next round in an ultimately

comfortable 3–1 Liverpool win played out in what looked suspiciously like a local-authority sports complex. Milan Baroš's total absence from the Reds squad confirmed his likely departure, along with a return to Spain for the unimpressive Antonio Núñez. A bemused Jamie Carragher scored from a corner – who needed Milan? – and Crouch and Cissé also seemed to establish a reasonable partnership up front, the Frenchman scoring well. However, Potter looked weak and indecisive on Liverpool's right, and Zenden only workmanlike on the left. Goals from Gerrard and Cissé in a dull return at Anfield confirmed a 5–1 aggregate win as a rejected Baroš watched from the stand contemplating a possible move to neighbours Everton. No Liverpool striker had stepped up to add the goals and leadership that Baroš had failed to provide, but eleven days before the Premiership kicked off for the 2005–06 season Liverpool's previously reluctant, want-away captain and midfield hub Gerrard had already scored seven goals for the European champions. It was some consolation.

Crouch's arrival at Liverpool even seemed to spark the otherwise slumbering Spaniard Fernando Morientes, who now scored two goals away at CSKA Sofia, following Djibril Cissé's opener in the third and final qualifying round. This 3–1 win was also notable for ugly racist chanting directed at the Frenchman Cissé, which brought some typically smug rebukes from England about the way the game here had 'successfully' tackled the problem. Outside the quietening of racist abuse at English football stadia, however, something much, much more horrible was still festering. Just before the trip to Bulgaria, Anthony Walker, a bright 18-year-old black kid from Huyton, was brutally murdered with an ice axe in McGoldrick Park near where he lived. He had been walking his girlfriend to a local bus stop when he was chased into the park. It was an unprovoked racist murder, coldly committed, as it turned out, by a couple of local 'lads', one of whom was 17-year-old Michael Barton, the younger brother of the Manchester City midfielder Joey. A minute's silence was held at Anfield to 'remember' Anthony, who was wrongly described as a

Liverpool fan – he actually liked basketball but followed Arsenal. His parents showed almost unimaginable courage in the aftermath, asking for forgiveness for his assailants. They little deserved it. In Sofia the locals may have been 'stupidly' hooting at Liverpool's black football players, as Cissé described it, but back in Liverpool a young kid could still be coldly murdered simply because of the colour of his skin.

Sofia was also notable for the brief Reds debut of a young Spaniard called Antonio Barragán, an attack-minded right-sided defender who had been tempted by Benítez from Sevilla. Barragán was now part of a new approach to young-player recruitment and reserve-team football at Liverpool. Although Gérard Houllier had instigated some changes in this direction, Liverpool had largely rejected the direction taken by clubs such as Arsenal to recruit globally for the club's youth and young professional teams, relying instead on mainly local and British talent. Now things would change dramatically at Anfield. Teenagers Jack Hobbs (from Lincoln City), Miguel 'Miki' Roque (signed from Lleida in Spain), the Ghanaian Godwin Antwi (Real Sociedad), Paul Anderson (exchanged for John Welsh to Hull City) and Barragán (Sevilla) would all be brought in, and the club's reserve team under Pako Herrera and Hughie McAuley would basically double up as a breeding and preparation ground for globally recruited young players on professional contracts at Melwood, offering vital experience for Liverpool's youth players.

All this meant much more overlap between the two squads (at Melwood and at the Academy at Kirkby) and that young players with real ability at Liverpool would get an earlier chance to test themselves against seasoned professionals. It also meant that the club could now seek out young players with the physique to compete at the professional level in England – Antwi and Hobbs were powerful centre-backs – and youth-team coach John Owens noted how these recruits had helped compensate for the relative lack of beef among the locals who were currently down at the Academy. Merseyside kids were often talented but scrawny, way behind some of the Continentals and others in their football knowledge, physical conditioning and diet.

Dave Richardson, director of youth development at the Premier League, suggested that larger English clubs should set up nurseries at smaller clubs in England so that the latter could 'look after' younger signings for their betters. It seemed like quite a glum picture of the future for the middle-range and smaller clubs: Leicester City, say, raising 14 year olds simply for transfer later to the Liverpool FC Academy. Though Richardson did helpfully point out that some Premier League clubs already operated 'nursery' clubs abroad – so why not here in England?

At least Liverpool Football Club was now fully committed to a global search for young talent. However, this shift in policy under Benítez would provoke the early retirement of respected Liverpool Academy director Steve Heighway, despite considerable recent Liverpool youth-team success. Barragán and Roque were lodging with a vetted Liverpool family, learning English and slowly coming to terms with the Merseyside climate. Barragán's maturity was hideously impressive. 'I think it's very, very important at the age of 18,' he said soon after his arrival, 'to start looking at ways of increasing and widening my experience, both culturally, through the language, and in the football sense as well. It's a different style of football. It's a good age to do that.' How many British players of his age could even contemplate the same? Barragán's supremely confident appearance in Sofia was the first sign in the first-team ranks of the likely long-term success of the new policy – though local kids from the city might now find themselves squeezed out in the process.

BLEAK HOUSE AT THE RIVERSIDE, SILVER IN MONACO

When Premiership action finally arrived for Liverpool, it felt like it was already halfway through the Reds season. There could be no possible excuses about being ring rusty, but Reds fans were prepared for a real dip in performance in a couple of months' time as fatigue inevitably set in. Middlesbrough (away) is not an enticing (or easy) beginning, though Liverpool should really have done better than a comfortable 0–0 draw, having dominated the match. A conservative midfield of Riise (in front of Stephen Warnock), Alonso, Sissoko and Zenden, with Gerrard pushed up behind a single striker, the negligible Morientes, was hardly one designed to produce a flood of Liverpool goals, even after the second-half dismissal of Ugo Ehiogu following a foul on Gerrard. The Liverpool captain did miss a number of passable chances and even Baroš got some pitch time, although we all now knew that he was on his way. Sissoko, however, proved his worth in the match; he was full of driving energy and rangy tackling. It was just the sort of 'difficult' contest that he had been brought in by Benítez to police. But one point should have been three.

A stylish Xabi Alonso free-kick was enough (there was little else) to next see off an enthusiastic ten-man Sunderland in the Premiership at Anfield, before a weakened Liverpool team (Gerrard was injured; Potter, Warnock and Josemi were all involved) lost 0–1 to CSKA in a pretty dire Anfield return. If anything, this toothless display made Benítez's obvious determination to ship Baroš off (to Aston Villa) seem even more mysterious, because Liverpool looked quite clueless in front of goal, both Morientes and Cissé lacking intelligence and drive. Indeed, the more timorous amongst us watched the final ten minutes from behind spread fingers, knowing that any deflection, inspired strike or rush of blood from the inexperienced Scott Carson could add to Valentin Iliev's early goal and end the Champions League ambitions of the 2005 European champions. Liverpool survived the test but not without anxiety.

The next month or so brought seven fixtures covering the Super Cup, the Champions League and the Premiership, all designed to test the legs and mental strength of any team in the world. With no national team protection in the Champions League draw it was preordained that Liverpool would now resume in the group stage against Chelsea, especially after the previous season's semi-final controversy. This meant forthcoming fixtures against the west

Londoners twice, Real Betis (Champions League, away), Manchester United and an improving Spurs in the Premiership. But first up it was another CSKA, this time from Moscow, in the European Super Cup in Monaco. An away Premiership contest against already struggling Birmingham City in the middle of this fixture madness looked like the only reliable Reds banker – or so it seemed at the time.

The European Super Cup turned out to be Djibril Cissé's night, and you would be a hardy soul indeed to say he didn't deserve it, despite what many would perceive as his petulance, occasional lack of application and routine absence of basic football intelligence. Battered by persistent press rumour – not denied by his coach – of his imminent departure as Benítez searched frantically for forward replacements (Michael Owen talk was incessant around Anfield at that time, as the little master sought refuge from his Real Madrid trauma), the gallant Frenchman emerged from the substitutes' bench to equalise Daniel Carvalho's goal in the 81st minute for a generally slack Liverpool. He then scored a rather better goal from Hamann's pass and fashioned a header for a thus far misfiring Luis García in extra time for a 3–1 Reds victory.

Jamie Carragher, captaining in Steven Gerrard's injured absence, did his best to look nonchalant as he hoisted the silverware, but it was all wasted effort. In times past this trophy would have been regarded as a piece of excess baggage in a busy schedule. But now all cups won on Planet Football seemed to be both valuable and hyped in equal measure. According to local wags, Liverpool Football Club now held two titles, though no serious Reds supporter was going to get overexcited about a one-game recovery over tidy but very moderate opposition. But it was important, nevertheless, to bring the cup home in order to maintain a winning mentality at the club.

Next, two solid 0–0 Premiership draws against Spurs (away) and Manchester United (home) sandwiched an impressive 2–1 Champions League win in Seville against a talented but uncertain Real Betis. In the Premier League Liverpool were already struggling to score goals, just one (a free-kick) in four matches up to that point. The draw at

Spurs could have been a win, Riise striking the bar, but Benítez seemed especially conservative at Anfield against an equally hesitant United, starting with only Crouch forward but hoping that Florent Sinama-Pongolle could get up and join him *in extremis*. Benítez argued later that this result showed that Liverpool were now the 'equal' of Sir Alex's side, although most Reds fans demand home wins and attacking verve almost irrespective of the strength and identity of the opposition.

The important symbolic sideshow was won comfortably by Liverpool: the five-star banner hanging over the M62; the USA flags in the Kop; and the full Istanbul repertoire on show. All this Liverpool glee at a bitter rival sold abroad would have to be rapidly revised, of course, in 2007 when the US dollar also arrived on the Anfield doorstep. But as Liverpool began drilling balls forward to the isolated Crouch, the visitors had some sweet revenge in store, gleefully singing 'Wimbledon' at the locals – at us.

'We can't waste time worrying about the gap with Chelsea,' Benítez said later. But it *was* already time to worry. The real story of that match was that neither United nor Liverpool could be content with this sort of result, simply because Chelsea were already steaming away in the Premiership, racking up victories. And it was also cold comfort to learn that Liverpool had never before started a league season with no goals conceded in the first four fixtures – or that Jamie Carragher, of all people, had already accepted that Liverpool's real ambition for the season was a top-three finish.

According to statistical experts, the holders Liverpool had a 3 per cent chance of winning the 2006 European Cup, Betis a 1 per cent chance. At half-time in Istanbul, remember, it was a 0 per cent chance. Nevertheless, the Champions League trip to Seville offered rather more Red promise, with Crouch showing, for the first time, some of the dexterity and link-up play we had been promised by helping, with Zenden, to make a lovely goal for García. This was after he had confused the home defence following a lofted Carragher clearance to allow Sinama-Pongolle to shock most travelling Reds with a terrific lobbed finish in only his third start in what already seemed like a lengthy campaign. These early hammer blows – 2–0 to the visitors after just 14 minutes, which was hardly typical of the team under Benítez – subdued the locals and offered Red solace for the absence, once more, of Steven Gerrard, consigned to the bench until the 73rd minute because of 'tiredness'. By then, Arzu had pulled a goal back for Betis. But Pepe Reina showed his confidence and reliability behind the Liverpool defence (Jerzy Dudek must have been sick), which all meant three vital points won in one of the group's more difficult fixtures.

Reina, our Spanish custodian, was much less reliable at Birmingham City in the Premiership. Here, at least, Liverpool did manage to score a Premiership goal in open play, the first in more than seven hours. But with Warnock and Josemi playing as our full-backs and struggling to contain Pennant and Gray, and Hamann and Alonso toiling in midfield, the Liverpool goalkeeper offered plenty of encouragement to the hosts who were decimated by injuries and low on confidence. Benítez also played into Steve Bruce's hands, the home team ecstatic to see only one Liverpool forward, Crouch, and Steven Gerrard employed in a roving role high up the field that lacked both focus and apparent purpose. This lack of ambition and tactical acumen from the visitors gave City the initiative – and they took it. Later, the Liverpool manager enigmatically said that he had three similar players, Alonso, Hamann and Gerrard, on the field but only one ball. The truth was he had no effective strikers. A second-half goal made by Gerrard for Luis García should still have been enough to deliver the points, but, instead, Reina and his defenders coped poorly with two low crosses and Liverpool were suddenly 1–2 down in the Midlands sunshine. They needed a Cissé penalty in front of the Reds travelling circus, after young Kilkenny pawed Carragher's header off the line, to share the points. But this was the first real sign of the awful mistakes from the previous season being repeated by both the coach and his team: these two points, casually and unnecessarily lost, could prove to be vital at the season's end.

UNDONE BY CHELSEA

How strange this game is: aggressive and inspired right from the off in Seville, quite clueless in the Premiership in the second city. Next Benítez would have a double test to put things right: two Anfield match-ups with champions Chelsea. The first in the Champions League, the second a desperate scrap for Premiership points. Sami Hyypiä was right when he pointed out that the crucial fixture in this pair was the second one. Both sides would settle for a draw in Europe and defeat was actually 'no disaster' at that early stage. But we could pretty much say – only six games into the Premiership season for Liverpool – that the unbeaten Reds would already be out of the title race if they now lost at home to Chelsea in the league. Chelsea would then have a maximum twenty-four points from eight matches, compared to Liverpool's just seven points from six games played. That's how much those points tossed so easily aside at Boro and Birmingham and against United at Anfield had meant: another potential league title already waved goodbye.

Mourinho began the inevitable mind games by saying that he accepted that Liverpool had beaten Chelsea in last year's Champions League competition – but that they had done so without scoring a goal. Benítez would not be drawn, simply saying, 'We can beat Chelsea.' This looked like more than bravado. But the European rerun lacked the white-hot intensity of the earlier meeting, with the Liverpool crowd understandably less frenzied than before. Liverpool dominated again without really making any clear-cut chances. On another night the Reds might have been awarded at least one penalty, but referee Massimo de Santis from Italy reasoned that no single incident demanded the ultimate sanction and both teams now eyed the weekend fixture with growing anticipation.

And then Rafa Benítez, of all people – star coach, tactical wizard – made a schoolboy error: another one. Let's be charitable, maybe it was partly a language problem, because the Liverpool manager told a press conference – where the obvious tack is to say as little as humanly possible – that Chelsea (meaning Mourinho) 'keep talking and talking about us. I think they are worried. *I think they are afraid.*' You really have to rub your eyes to read this in print. Did he really *say* that? No experienced British coach would ever make this sort of claim, would ever fall into this simple trap. Paisley and Fagan would tear a strip off any player or any member of the Liverpool coaching staff – anybody connected to the club, in fact – who ever thought of publicly undermining an opponent in this way. And here was the Liverpool manager *himself* making this mistake, committing this cardinal football sin. Every sensible Reds fan cringed – and feared the worst.

So let's just say that Chelsea were pretty fired up for the lunchtime league meeting. And that Sami Hyypiä was palpably unwell – definitely not himself – and simply unable to deal with the imposing Didier Drogba. And that at left-back Liverpool fielded the hapless Istanbul hero Djimi Traoré, who gifted Chelsea a first-half penalty after *three* opportunities to clear the ball from Drogba, whom he then fouled. Even then, Steven Gerrard was able to equalise, driving in a Carragher flick from a Liverpool corner. But Drogba then tore past a struggling Hyypiä on Liverpool's right side and laid one on a plate for Damien Duff in front of the Kop. At 1–2 there might still have been a way back in the second half, but the indisciplined García then lost the ball cheaply to Asier Del Horno, and it moved through Drogba (who else?) to Joe Cole, who scored – unattended. This was the killer blow.

Rafa Benítez waited until the 81st minute (why?) to reinforce the isolated and ineffective Crouch with Cissé, who was brought on for Traoré. But the Liverpool manager actually made the substitution when Chelsea had an attacking throw-in on Liverpool's right. It was another simple mistake. Drogba received the ball unmarked and crossed simply to Jeremi, who scored – from the spot just vacated by the departed Traoré.

At 1–4 this was Liverpool's worst home league defeat for 36 years, when the now stricken George Best, playing for Manchester United, had dismantled Bill Shankly's transitional side. And do you want to know what really hurt? What really stuck in the home craw? It was the on-pitch huddle that Chelsea formed in front of the drifting Kop to mock the Liverpool manager, the stadium and its fans. 'There was a lot of swear words,' Frank Lampard later revealed. You can imagine. 'We wanted to prove a point,' he continued, 'and we did it with our spirit and our football. A lot of talk comes when you're champions. A lot of things were said that we weren't happy about. The art is to be strong enough to use that to motivate you, and we did that. We showed our character and our strength.' Mourinho also had his point to make: 'I think it's time to respect us a bit more. I think almost nobody gives us the respect we deserve.' Always respect your opponents is another old Liverpool credo. And later in the season, perhaps remembering his mistake with Chelsea, Benítez warned his players: 'Only say you are better than another team after you have beaten them. Never say it before.' He was right, of course. He just needed to remind himself.

BRUSSELS CALLING AND THE LONDON BLUES; PETER CROUCH: GOAL MACHINE

After a bruising and undistinguished home win against Mark Hughes's uncompromising Blackburn Rovers (in which Cissé scored and was also disgracefully reminded by visiting fans about his leg so horribly broken at Ewood Park during the 2004–05 season), Liverpool made their first return to Brussels since Heysel, to play Anderlecht in the Champions League. There was not much talk about marking the occasion. Benítez had already told Spanish journalists, 'We hardly speak of Heysel at all. It is as if we don't want such a painful topic to come out for the club and fans. We know that it is there, in the memory, but we try not to punish ourselves over it.' So we sneaked over, colonised the bars and did some sightseeing.

On the ring road on the outskirts of Brussels a British car screeched to a halt before us and a dishevelled middle-aged man in shorts got out of the driver's side and babbled some Scouse questions at us about hotels and the direction to the centre of the city. We pointed him on his way. It was Jamie Carragher's dad.

At the ground – a fenced off, rather antiquated reminder of the dark days in England – the searching of Liverpool fans and the checking of tickets was a forensic exercise. The match itself was incredibly open, the home team missing gaping chances before Cissé (again!) spectacularly volleyed Liverpool ahead direct from a corner. In the second half Luis García reminded us of last year's crucial European interventions with his running and touch, but there were no more goals. Anderlecht's Serb striker Nenad Jestrović was sent off only five minutes after coming on as a substitute for allegedly racially abusing Momo Sissoko. Referee Kim Milton Neilson was criticised later for his trouble by Anderlecht officials, and Sissoko called for the toughest possible action by UEFA. Do you think he got it?

Later, the Brussels police, idiotic to a man, walked hundreds of Liverpool fans through plush residential neighbourhoods into the early hours as curtains were peeled back by the suburban curious. Reds had to knock on the doors of the local houses to ask to use the bathroom. But spirits were high. A new song was in vogue to celebrate Everton's fall to the foot of the table, a reply to the Goodison 'Ra-ra-rafa Beneath Us' jibe from the previous season. It went 'No one's beneath them, No one's beneath them, No, no, no one's beneath them, not even Fulham or Wigan or Portsmouth.' Even Belgian police officers smiled – and eventually got tired of their aimless chaperoning as we were finally let on the trains and home. Three more points: the reigning European champions moved on.

Fulham (away, 0–2) was a new low. The home fans were emotionally high about the passing of their England legend Johnny Haynes that week, and Liverpool were flat. Harry Kewell's seasonal return was less than earth shattering. Steven Gerrard was absent – but the hopeless Josemi wasn't. Nothing worked – move on. (Later, on Radio

Five Live's 606, a caller recommended replacing Rafa Benítez with George Burley. Call the orderlies, nurse.) Next to Selhurst Park and the League Cup. Benítez decided to do midweek battle with a much changed and youthful Liverpool side (Scott Carson, Stephen Warnock, David Raven, Darren Potter, Zak Whitbread), one only stiffened by the return of Steven Gerrard, who naturally scored. But Palace gradually built their belief and began to realise that these kids and a Morientes–Crouch forward partnership held no fear. Liverpool's defence was porous, and Gerrard didn't really seem to care too much about defeat. Which was, appropriately enough, exactly what he got: 1–2. Liverpool's recent record in London was now quite abject.

Afterwards the Liverpool captain was full of contrition, declaring his team's performance to be 'unacceptable'. 'There's got to be a big reaction to this now,' he went on. 'We've all got to play for the shirt and show how much it means to be playing for this club.' Starting with you, Steven. Alan Hansen said that Liverpool's problem was a fundamental lack of pace up front and at the back. He had a point. Oliver Kay in *The Times* began the Benítez dissection, saying that the Spaniard was a great coach but, at the same time, questioning whether he understood the English game. It was starting to feel like 2004 all over again.

So how did Benítez reply to his critics in 2005? With six wins and one draw from the next seven games through November, that's how – West Ham, Aston Villa, Portsmouth, Manchester City and Sunderland in the league, Anderlecht and Betis (a home draw) in the Champions League. Thirteen goals scored, none conceded. OK, these were mainly ordinary teams, and some Liverpool performances – Manchester City away, for example – were still decidedly average. But it was still much more heartening stuff. Significantly, Steve Finnan returned to play right-back in all these matches, and Riise missed only one on the left flank. Liverpool's back four was made solid at last by the manager. Gerrard was back to full fitness, and Harry Kewell was left on the bench, with Zenden in and scoring goals – until a season-wrecking injury in training sadly wrote him off. Even

Fernando Morientes got a couple of goals in this run, though Peter Crouch played more often and still had none. By this, we mean that he had scored precisely *no* goals *all season*, this £7 million Liverpool and England centre-forward. It was eighteen matches – and counting – and the Reds fans were now getting scratchy and nervous for him. Then it all started to happen for Crouch – for 'Crouchy'. He suddenly sprouted wings and flew, this ugliest of ugly football ducklings.

Little Wigan Athletic had done wonders in the Premiership since being promoted under their no-nonsense Scouse manager Paul Jewell. His motto when winning was, 'Be happy but never satisfied.' Jewell got it from Ronnie Moran when he was a reserve-team player at Anfield in the 1980s. The Wigan boss managed it as he saw it, and his team were nobody's mugs – no one had taken liberties with them. When they came to L4, they were flying in the league, sitting in fifth place to Liverpool's fourth and level on points (25) with the club Jewell still supported. So, it was a very special day for Jewell – he badly wanted to beat Liverpool. But it was not a good day to visit Anfield, where confidence was high again and where the Wigan keeper Mike Pollitt was about to implode and help Liverpool's Peter Crouch out of an embarrassingly deep trough.

The first-half 'shot' in question, when it came, was not even that: it was actually a looping deflection off an outstretched Wigan leg. It arced gently towards Pollitt stationed watchfully under the Wigan bar. He had dealt with these deliveries thousands of times – could do it in his sleep. But his eye seemed to be taken momentarily by an advancing Liverpool body – by Steven Gerrard. Thus distracted, the visiting keeper gently paddled the ball not over the bar as he had hoped but softly into the Wigan net. He fell to his knees as if poleaxed.

It was actually an own goal. A parks keeper could have saved it. Not that Crouch cared as he went careering along the front rows of the Kemlyn Road, high-fiving his supporters, all of them now nodding vigorously to each other that they just *knew* that this guy would eventually come good. The relief was tangible. The more opposing fans had tried to ridicule their man, the more the Kop had offered its unconditional support for him.

Crouch appeared from the Liverpool player scrum tousled and beaming that awkward smile of his: half geeky schoolboy, half Albert Steptoe. And wouldn't you know it, he then went and got himself another one, this time gently lobbing over the stranded Pollitt. What did we tell you? Goal machine, this boy – turn him off before he *hurts* somebody! Poor, bedraggled Wigan now gave up the ghost – who could compete with this deadly striker? It ended up 3–0 to Liverpool (Crouch 2, García).

Which left just two games to see off before Liverpool were to travel to Japan for the FIFA Club World Championship – a week's unwelcome black hole in mid-December in an already impossibly crowded fixture list. With Chelsea surprisingly losing in Seville to Betis, Liverpool found themselves needing only a draw at Stamford Bridge to clinch top spot in the Champions League group – and so avoid other group winners in the knockout stage. Publicly, Mourinho was so disdainful of worrying who the mighty Chelsea might confront next in Europe that he said he would rather beat little Wigan in his next Premiership match than worry about a win against Liverpool in the Champions League. He even pondered fielding a weakened side in the contest. Of course, he did nothing of the sort. But Liverpool, Carragher and Hyypiä imperious, still held a limp Chelsea comfortably: another 0–0 and yet another clean sheet. So Mourhinho got his wish – and he now had to accept his fate with good grace.

Middlesbrough couldn't score either at Anfield in the Premiership, although Liverpool did have Pepe Reina to thank for keeping out a sharp Mark Viduka when clean through on goal. Since Birmingham, the Liverpool keeper had made few spectacular saves but had been sensible and solid, key attributes in a successful keeper. He already had twenty clean sheets to his name that season and, at that point, an astonishing ten in a row. If he could keep out attackers in Japan, it would be Liverpool Football Club record time, in his first season at Anfield.

In the match against Middlesbrough Fernando Morientes (remember him?) snuffed out the opposition with two goals of such staggering quality that one was left wondering why the guy was still suffering so badly in England. After all, he had an astonishing 72 goals in 112 La Liga starts. 'We always had faith in him,' said Benítez, but it still wouldn't wash. The answer to his failure, of course, was that the Spaniard lacked the basic pace and the strength to make it in the Premiership – and a little bit of bravery and desire in the penalty box, too. He wouldn't stay.

At that stage, Chelsea were only (only!) 12 points distant from Liverpool, who were in a threatening third position in the table after a slow start. But who was to claw back these points on the Reds' behalf? Arsenal had won only *one* game away from home all season, and only Manchester United seemed at all competitive with the men from Stamford Bridge.

But, for now at least, Liverpool Football Club, courtesy of the politicians and the moneymen from FIFA, had other fish to fry. For the fans, the lucky travelling few, it would mainly be a case of decent hotels and organised tours in Japan. But plenty of those who grew up and travelled around Europe with Liverpool in the chaotic 1970s and '80s would also be out there in Yokohama. Football in Liverpool (as in Spain) moves on – but it also always somehow stays the same.

And what of the Liverpool boss, the man who was now piloting his Liverpool team into the unknown? He would face his own personal problems in Japan, difficulties and a sense of loss that would draw his thoughts inexorably back to his home in Spain. He had learned his trade in the tough proving grounds of the Spanish professional game – in a very hard and insecure school, and primarily at a famous football club whose own history had often shown clear parallels with that of the club that Benítez was now beginning to manage so cleverly in England. So it was for a very special reason that Rafa's last public words before tearfully leaving Spain for his new challenge on Merseyside had been a defiant '*Amunt Valencia!*' Because, in many ways, this famous Spanish football club was as much in the Benítez veins as Liverpool Football Club had now become.

5

Parallel Lives: Valencia CF and the New 'Spanish Fury'

The origins of Valencia CF; the 'golden' years of the 1940s, and titles in England and Spain; the Inter Cities triumphs of the 1960s; Don Alfredo's La Liga title; 'Don't say Kempes, say goal!'; Valencia's relegation blues; Claudio Ranieri, the Roman general; Champions League agony.

Historians of football seem unanimous: football grew best and quickest in Spain around the end of the nineteenth century where the regional links with British trade and manufacturing were strongest. It is a common tale around Continental Europe. There are records of football being played in Huelva in southern Spain in 1872, and its introduction is attributed to British workers of mining companies. The early British influence in the rest of Spain was also clear, with British water workers forming the Sevilla club in 1905 and Athletic Bilbao being founded in 1898 by traders from the English North East. The Witty brothers, Arnold and Ernest, born in Barcelona but educated at the Merchant Taylors' public school in Crosby in Liverpool, were key figures in the formation of the Catalan club. Barça's maroon–and–blue kit probably derived from the Liverpool school's own official colours.

For Valencia it was the Regional Exhibition of 1909 that was the major trigger for blossoming local interest in the game. The exhibition offered a major opportunity to open external trade links, including, crucially, greater business – and thus more football – contacts with

Britain. Valencia Club de Fútbol (or VCF) was founded by Gonzalo Medina, a local football nut, and seven other enthusiasts in 1919. Young Gonzalo had it bad: he spent the money meant for his wedding on the club's first pitch at Algirós. Medina and Augusto Milego, a local literature teacher, tossed a coin to decide who would be club president – Milego won. Thirty people attended the club's first match, but VCF slowly grew in stature in the local region. The club consolidated its growing status as the premier football club in the Valencian region by joining the new Spanish national league in 1929 and achieving promotion to the First Division of Spanish football in 1931.

As Valencia CF rose to national prominence, Liverpool Football Club, league champions back in 1923, could finish only ninth in the First Division in England under secretary–manager George Patterson. In truth, almost 40 years into its existence, the Merseyside club was now in a period of relative decline, narrowly missing relegation to the Second Division in 1936. Ironically, the Second World War would act as something of a welcome break in what was beginning to look like a terminal descent in football fortunes at Anfield.

Liverpool had already been English champions four times before Valencia had even joined the top flight of the Spanish game. But this comparison is rather skewed. The national Spanish League had only been created in 1929, initially in order to capitalise on the investments that Spanish clubs were now beginning to make when signing and paying players. The influence of the new league quickly grew, and by the mid–1930s it was already as important, in terms of income and attendances, as the previously dominant Spanish Cup, the *Copa del Rey*.

Valencia CF finished its first season in the Spanish First Division in a modest seventh position (out of a total of ten clubs). But the arrival of Luis Colina as technical secretary – the director who selected and signed players – pushed the club on to much greater ambitions and in 1934 the *blanquinegros* (the black and whites) reached the final of the Copa del Rey for the first time, facing Real Madrid. According to newspaper reports, more than 13,000 Valencians travelled to the Catalan stadium at Montjuïc for the final, in which Real Madrid beat VCF 2–1. Many fans were reported to have made the trip to the stadium on bicycles or motorcycles and, in mythologised tales, on foot!

The Spanish Civil War then disrupted the new national Spanish League between 1937 and 1939, but regional football championships in Spain continued to flourish. After the Civil War, sport in Spain became more tied to the state machinery and impregnated with fascist terminology. Sport, for Franco, was a site for the production of obedience, submission and military discipline, and the Royal Spanish Football Federation, which had been founded and managed by the clubs since its creation in 1902, had to get used to being a puppet institution. In this context Spanish football clubs lost their private status and their capacity to self-manage. Club members now became mere ticket-holders at a sports event. It was only in the last period of Franco's dictatorship in the 1960s that Spanish clubs could start to reassert their local influence.

THE GLORIOUS DECADE OF THE BLANQUINEGROS: THE YEARS OF THE 'ELECTRIC' FORWARDS

The 1940s began promisingly for VCF, and by its end the decade would constitute the club's greatest period of success until the arrival more than 50 years later of Rafa Benítez. In 1941, under the Galician coach Ramón Encinas, there were early signs of what was to come, Valencia CF winning the Spanish Cup for the first time, defeating RCD Espanyol 3–1 in the final. This win came with a team known for its famous 'electric' forwards – *La delantera eléctrica*. This striking description came from the widespread shortage of electricity in the post-Civil War period in Spain. Valencia CF, it was said, would have to light up the region and the Spanish game with its football – and it made a pretty good job of it. The team played with an audacious 2–3–5 system, the club's five attackers – Epifanio 'Epi' Fernández, Amadeo Ibáñez, Mundo, Vicente Asensi and Guillermo Gorostiza – making a formidable group made up of two Valencians and three Basque players. The approach involved two skilled and slippery wingers hitting the touchlines and making crosses, two attacking inside-forwards with a strategic vision of game and a centre-forward called Mundo, who was a potent scorer. Just as Liverpool's championship teams of 1922 and 1923 had been mainly noted for their extraordinary defensive strength – only sixty-seven goals conceded in eighty-four league matches over two seasons – it was the forward line of Valencia of the 1940s that dominated, proving to be something of a landmark in the domestic game in Spain. Their line-up became a paradigm of what was considered to be the classic Spanish attacking formation.

It is no coincidence that there were three Basques in this side. Basque footballers had dominated Spanish football before the Civil War, with more than half the Spanish cups being won by Basque clubs during that time. What was described as the 'Basque style' of play was actually very like the dominant approach in England: it was largely based on a fast, direct and aggressive game with lots of crosses from wide positions aimed at the head of an imposing centre-forward. What was also similar to England – and to Liverpool Football Club – was the dominant emphasis in Spain at this time on teamwork and spirit rather than great skill and individualism. The Spanish press and the game's fans in Spain considered this so-called 'Basque style' to be a genuine reincarnation of the English approach, something which suggested that there was more 'authenticity' in the style of football of the Basque clubs, which was widely admired by football fans throughout Spain. This style of play was also one that had been adopted by the Spanish national team that had won the silver medal at the Antwerp Olympic Games in 1920. From all of this arose the myth in the Spanish game of the peculiarities of the *furia Española* (Spanish fury) – an impassioned style of play in the national game. Along with manliness and impetuosity, this passion was also more widely promoted as a national characteristic by the Francoist dictatorship after the Spanish Civil War.

A *'BRONCO Y COPERO'* TEAM

After victory in the Spanish Cup final of 1941, VCF began to be described in Spain as *bronco y copero* (a tough cup team), a description that is still used today to refer to teams that are strong cup fighters. As the war raged over most of Europe, Valencia won the La Liga title for the first time the following season (1941–42). (By this stage Real Madrid and Barcelona had yet to establish the duopoly that was later to dominate the Spanish game and which really began to take hold from the late 1940s.) The attacking Valencia machine scored a remarkable eighty-five goals in just twenty-six matches in the 1941–42 season, enough to stretch out a conclusive seven-point gap over their nearest rivals. Valencia's attacking verve and direct, physical and fast (*eléctrico*) style seemed to be the secrets of this early success. The top scorer in the league that season (the *pichichi*, so-named in honour of the great Basque striker Aranzadi, from the Bilbao side of the 1920s) was Mundo, with 27 goals. Two years later, in 1944, VCF won a second La Liga title, this time leading the table and never being headed from the fourth week of competition. Within five years of the end of the Civil War in Spain, the city of Valencia had become the premier national centre for Spanish football, and VCF was the key club in the Spanish game. It had already won two league titles and one Spanish cup in a rich period covering the five years since the end of hostilities.

1947: LEAGUE TITLES FOR VALENCIA AND LIVERPOOL

Between 1944 and 1946 the blanquinegros reached three consecutive finals of the Copa del Rey in Montjuïc. All were lost: the first two to Athletic Bilbao, the third to Real Madrid. But Valencia recovered from the disappointment of these setbacks to win La Liga again in the 1946–47 season, the same year, in fact, that Liverpool Football Club, under manager George Kay, achieved its fifth title success in England.

It was the first Liverpool championship for twenty-four years and was won in the first season after the Second World War.

Liverpool Football Club – unlike 1939 league champions Everton – seemed to have had a 'good' war. Only moderate performers before the conflict began, and tragically losing their consistent right-back Tom Cooper during it, the new Reds forward trio of record signing Albert Stubbins, Jack Balmer and the incomparable rookie winger Billy Liddell now drove the Merseyside club up the league table. Even surviving the threat of a national players' strike in February 1947 – the maximum wage was raised to £12 in the winter and £10 in the summer in order to quell the revolt – Liverpool were defeated in just one match in their last sixteen fixtures to make good their title challenge. But this was no vintage championship campaign – Liverpool lost almost one quarter (ten) of their league matches, two more than second-placed Manchester United, and had also been thrashed 1–5 at home by title rivals Wolves in December. Liverpool was one of four clubs – Manchester United, Stoke City and Wolves were the others – that could still claim the championship as the season moved towards its climax. The terrible winter in England of 1947 meant that league fixtures dragged on and on, so that Liverpool had no confirmation of its title success until Stoke City failed to win a much delayed match at Sheffield United on 14 June. The news finally came through on the PA during the Liverpool Senior Cup final against Everton at a balmy Anfield. The final minutes were played out against a background of mild hysteria as most of the 40,000 crowd itched to invade the pitch to celebrate the title before the summer had completely drifted away.

In Spain in 1947 Valencia CF would also have to wait to claim their own domestic championship, but the delay was rather shorter. The league campaign became known locally as *Liga del teléfono* (the league of the telephone), because Valencia CF had to wait for the result of the game between Real Madrid and Athletic Aviacion (the name of Atlètico Madrid after the Spanish Civil War) in the last round of matches. As fans waited in the Mestalla stadium for news, VCF officials impatiently manned the telephone for the call that finally announced the result of the Madrid derby – it had ended in a draw. To joyous scenes, the Valencia club's third Spanish championship in just six seasons was confirmed. Just as in Liverpool, where the 1947 Football League title triumph for the Reds signalled the arrival to national prominence of a new star, the great Billy Liddell, so in Spain the 1947 Valencia championship season is forever connected to the emergence of one of the blanquinegros' greatest players, the midfielder Antonio 'Tonico' Puchades. A great passer and an incredible retriever of lost situations, but also a secret smoker, Puchades reached maturity as a player in the mid-1950s. But he had already shown signs as a young man that he was a player who characterised, perhaps more than any other of the era, the fighting spirit and never-say-die attitude of the Valencia club. A French commentator described Puchades as having steely strength, nylon flexibility and silky smoothness. It summed him up well.

Another emblematic figure at VCF at this time was its improbably named club president Luis Casanova, a man who had become interested in football while in England but not at Anfield: Casanova was an Arsenal admirer. Casanova was the VCF president for almost two decades – from 1940 to 1959. He was a master administrator and politician. During the eighteen seasons of his reign, VCF won three of its six league titles and three of its six Spanish cups – it was quite a record. The Mestalla was also considerably enlarged under his presidency, many top players were signed and players from the local 'grass roots' were groomed and incorporated into the evolving Valencia CF success story. Today, Casanova is widely and unsurprisingly perceived to be the architect of the modern Valencia CF. The club concluded the decade – the greatest in its history – still challenging for the top positions in the Spanish game. In the 1947–48 and 1948–49 seasons they finished as runners-up in La Liga to FC Barcelona, and in 1949 Valencia once more won the renamed Spanish Cup, the *Copa del Generalísimo*, beating Athletic Bilbao (1–0) in Chamartín (the stadium of Real Madrid).

In England, meanwhile, Liverpool FC had no such impressive cup record to celebrate, boasting a solitary FA Cup final appearance, which they lost to Burnley, back in 1914. Liverpool were again beaten by Second Division Burnley in the FA Cup semi-finals of 1947, this time after a replay, thus losing a great chance of completing the first English league and cup Double of the twentieth century. (Tottenham would eventually achieve that feat in 1961.) This also meant that the Reds had probably spurned the possibility of building a team to dominate the British game in the 1950s. Liverpool went into steep decline instead, falling in the FA Cup final of 1950 – for which Bob Paisley was controversially dropped – to another north London club, Arsenal. It would take a remarkable 73 years for one of the most powerful and best-supported clubs in the English game to claim the FA Cup for the first time, in 1965 under Bill Shankly. In Spain, by contrast, winning the domestic cup competition had much less national significance and was routinely shared among the nation's elite clubs.

OPENING UP TO THE WORLD – AND FALLING THROUGH THE FLOOR

Almost at the very moment that European club football began to enter the British lexicon in the mid-1950s, Liverpool Football Club slid into ignominy, relegated into the Second Division in rock-bottom place with just 28 points in 1954. Billy Liddell stayed loyal to Anfield, but even he could not drag the Reds out of the mire.

Meanwhile, the World Cup of 1950 in Brazil – England's debut – had signalled the first extended football contacts for Spain with the outside world. The Spanish team included the blanquinegros players Puchades, Vicente Asensi, Ignacio Eizaguirre and Silvestre Igoa and finished fourth in the World Cup, Spain's best-ever performance. As a result many prestigious players and technical staff – especially from South America – soon arrived in Spain, and the Spanish international programme was also expanded, although it was still mainly limited to meetings with other Catholics from Italy, Portugal and occasionally Ireland, as well as the war 'neutrals' Switzerland. All of this contributed to the 'breath of fresh air' that rushed through the Spanish game and initially through Valencia CF. But another new direction in Spanish football was also just around the corner.

The tour of the Iberian peninsula by the Argentinian club San Lorenzo de Almagro in 1947 also had a great impact on the development of Spanish football at this time. This Argentinian team offered a radically different and new way to play football that astonished even these most accomplished southern Europeans. Here was a football philosophy that stressed that the ball, rather than the player, should do the work and that technique and accuracy, rather than spirit and endeavour, were the key to elite-football success. The importance of controlling the centre of the field as a means of building pressure and producing mistakes and goal-scoring opportunities now began to seep into the previously insular, British-influenced, hard-running Spanish football tradition. Coach Jacinto Quincoces, one of the idolised playing members of the 1920 Olympic Games team that gave birth to the myth of the Spanish fury, was now in charge at Valencia CF. He managed one hundred and eighty-eight blanquinegros matches in six seasons – the second-longest-serving coach in the club's history – and took Valencia to two more Spanish Cup finals, in 1952 and 1954, playing against FC Barcelona in both cases. Valencia had now appeared in exactly half the Spanish Cup finals since 1941. Only from the early 1980s in England did a small group of clubs really begin to dominate the FA Cup, with Manchester United and Arsenal then taking something of a stranglehold as the FA Premier League kicked in from 1992. In Spain, from the early 1960s, the cities of Madrid and Barcelona were already ruling in the Spanish Cup. Real Madrid, Atlético Madrid and FC Barcelona account for 67 Spanish Cup final appearances (up to 2005). Valencia lost the 1952 final 4–2 against a fabulous Barça side boasting the brilliant Hungarian Ladislao Kubala as well as Cesar and Basora. The 1954 final was a different story, however, with Valencia CF crushing the Catalans 3–0, including two goals from the star striker Fuertes.

As great foreign players, such as Kubala and the naturalised Argentinian Di Stéfano at an awakening Real Madrid, now began to make their presence felt in the Spanish game – at least 25 years before similar developments began to take hold in even more insular England – the imposing figure of the Dutch forward Faas Wilkes arrived in Valencia, initially to play a friendly match for the Italian club Torino. He was so impressive he was snapped up to play for the Valencia club. Wilkes was a leggy speedster, a star in the dribbling tradition over any distance and at maximum pace. His incredibly long legs seemed to hypnotise defenders and Valencia fans alike: the home crowd adored him. Not only could Wilkes create goals, but he also scored them, seemingly at will. They were greeted by the wild waving of white handkerchiefs in the Valencia crowd. His hold on the Valencian public was such that it was said that the blanquinegros had signed him in order to pay for the impressive new covered tribune that was now planned for construction at the remodelled Mestalla.

However, the Spanish Cup victory of 1954 in fact marked the beginnings of a downturn in the modern history of Valencia CF. The redevelopment of the Mestalla limited the capacity of the club to spend on transfers and players' wages, and the Valencia team continued to decline, performing very modestly in cup and league during the rest of the decade. Although a lack of economic resources prevented the completion of the initial stadium project, the new capacity of the stadium was finally raised to 54,000. When floodlights came to the Mestalla a few years later, the venue was now in the vanguard of the great Spanish stadiums: only Chamartín at Real Madrid was ahead of it for its sophistication and technological advances.

INTO EUROPE: THE 1960s

Football in the 1960s in Spain underwent a spectacular revolution. As television began to be a much more prominent influence in the game and European club tournaments began to intrude into domestic contests – who could rival an already dominant Real Madrid in Europe? – so Spanish society also took a profoundly new direction. The country, thus far crippled by Franco's vice-like grip on its politics and economics, now went down the path of increasing industrialisation and urbanisation: the concentration of inhabitants in the big Spanish cities grew as a result. European football success also helped to 'open' up and modernise Spain and simultaneously loosen the hold of the Francoists. It was another platform for the relaunch of the Spanish game in an era of greater affluence and of increasing celebrity for the world's best footballers.

The performances of Valencia CF in the Spanish league during the second half of the 1950s and early '60s were very uneven, and the decade was mainly the property of Real Madrid – both at home and abroad. So VCF's attentions were turned to other competitions, notably the new, rather strangely titled European Inter-Cities Fairs Cup and an old domestic Valencia favourite, the Copa del Generalísimo – the Spanish Cup. Julio de Miguel, the club president from 1961 to 1974, was a man who knew how to move in the European business environment, thanks to his professional activity as a successful exporter of citrus fruit. It was de Miguel who insisted on introducing the blanquinegros to the Inter-Cities Fairs Cup, a tournament that had been born in 1955 in Vienna with the rather odd intention of providing a football competition to European clubs and cities that might share similar sporting, commercial and industrial interests. The tournament welcomed from around Europe clubs that had little realistic opportunity of ever playing in the European Cup, as it was then constituted. And the city of Valencia was perfectly placed for this new sporting/trading agenda in the new Europe: after all, it hosted the most important trade fair in Spain.

For the 1961–62 season the VCF coach was Domingo Balmanya, but after poor league performances he was replaced by the Argentinian Alejandro Scopelli in the summer of 1962. It was Scopelli who piloted VCF to its first European final. These European exploits helped return the blanquinegros to the elite of Spanish football during a period in which the club did not especially shine domestically, either in La Liga or the old-faithful standby, the Spanish Cup. At the very moment that Liverpool Football Club, under new manager Bill Shankly, was finally clambering out of the Second Division of the Football League, Valencia CF was expanding its European horizons. In the Fairs Cup in 1961–62 VCF eliminated Liverpool's English rivals Nottingham Forest, the Swiss side Lausanne, the formidable Inter Milan (who would be European Cup winners in 1964) and MTK of Hungary to reach their first European final. Valencia CF actually seemed a cut above most of the competition, progressing undefeated to the two-legged final – where a more familiar foe awaited them. However, even FC Barcelona, now coached by Ladislao Kubala, the club's great Hungarian star of the 1950s, had no answer to a famous first-leg Mestalla mauling, the match ending 6–2 to Valencia. The 1–1 return leg in the Camp Nou was a mere formality – though 60,000 still turned up to witness the last rites.

In the 1962–63 season VCF battled against a blizzard of Scottish clubs in Europe, eliminating Celtic, Dunfermline Athletic and Hibernian in succession from the Fairs Cup before despatching Roma in the semi-finals. This time Dinamo Zagreb were dismissed in the final by a comfortable 4–1 aggregate score. Valencia made it a trio of European Fairs Cup finals in 1964, but this time they met their match in Spanish rivals Real Zaragoza, even if the 1–2 score line was described by the press and by VCF fans as *robo* (robbery). This would be Valencia's last European final appearance for some time, one made as Liverpool's own European adventure was only just starting off in the European Cup. VCF would later participate in the Fairs Cup and then the UEFA Cup on a fairly regular basis but without ever reaching the heights they had managed in the early 1960s.

The Valencia team of the 1960s – rather like the very localised Celtic side of the same period – was one mainly built around local products, grass-roots players such as Manolo Mestre, Pepe Claramunt, Roberto Gil, Vicente Piquer, Paco Vidagany, Vicente Guillot and José Manuel Pesudo. Almost all of these men began and finished their careers at the club, something that is much less common in the current global-football merry-go-round. Julio de Miguel added to this solid local core with some astute signings, such as Juan Cruz Sol and the goal poacher Waldo. Valencia CF were able to win the Spanish Cup with these players in 1967 – for the first time in 13 years – beating Athletic Bilbao 2–1 in the final. This win meant that VCF now qualified for the European Cup-Winners' Cup (*Recopa*) the following season, but bad luck in the draw matched them against a powerful Bayern Munich side – including the core of the German national team. Valencia could not survive this challenge. But something remarkable was about to happen to a club that had last tasted La Liga success just after the end of the Second World War. In a domestic league now dominated by the bitter rivalry between Barcelona and Real Madrid, an unlikely figure – a man who had once been fought over by these two great clubs in the 1950s – was about to lead Valencia CF to the Spanish title once more.

DON ALFREDO, COACH OF VALENCIA CF

Although the 1960s had offered some welcome European success for Valencia CF, 1970 was a really special year for the club. During the summer of that year, the legendary Alfredo Di Stéfano returned to Spain from Argentina, where he had won a national championship as the coach of Boca Juniors. Known locally by the Valencians as Don Alfredo, he returned to manage the blanquinegros. Alongside Rafael Benítez, Di Stéfano is probably the most important coach in the history of Valencia CF. He was an inspirational, modernising figure at Valencia, in some ways similar to Bill Shankly, who had successfully revived Liverpool's fortunes just a few years before.

Di Stéfano actually managed Valencia CF in three separate phases: at the beginning of the 1970s; at the end of that decade; and for the final time in the 1980s, when Valencia were relegated. Di Stéfano was already strongly attached to the region, having worked at nearby Elche during the 1967–68 season, and in 1976 he was briefly technical director of the Castellón club.

He had barely arrived at Valencia CF in 1970 when he had important decisions to make. The new manager decided to clear out some of the old guard at the club – Vicente Guillot and the Brazilian Waldo were both discarded – and, ironically, given his own playing success within the superstar system at Real Madrid, he set about building a compact and solid team that was difficult to beat – a trait that was to become a substantial component of the modern identity of Valencia CF.

Di Stéfano's championship side of 1970–71 had few stars, but it had heart, belief and defensive strength – qualities that, if applied well, are good enough to win most domestic leagues. One of the key players already at the club when Di Stéfano arrived was Pepe Claramunt, a man who was as important to the club as Antonio Puchades in the 1950s, Fernando Gómez in the 1990s and David Albelda – Valencia's own version of Steven Gerrard – in more recent seasons. Claramunt is certainly one of the most important midfield players in the history of Valencia CF, mainly because of his unshakeable temperament, his vision across the whole pitch and his immense fighting qualities in the vital central areas. He was the fulcrum of the 1971 Spanish championship team for Valencia – the Emlyn Hughes figure in the club, if you like, and a player every bit as good as the man that Bill Shankly brought to Liverpool in the late 1960s and who would lead the Anfield club to domestic and European success for the next decade.

Di Stéfano's Spanish league-title success for Valencia in 1971 was the club's first for 24 years. It was to prove the sole La Liga title for the club during a span of 55 years, ranging from 1946–47 until 2001–02, when Rafa Benítez won his first league title with the club. Di Stéfano had transformed Valencia into an unspectacular and disciplined team that scored few goals – only 41 in 30 matches, with just 19 conceded. The key to the season was the excellent defensive work of Aníbal and Anton, and the deadly counter-attacks led by the Argentinian left-winger Óscar Rubén Valdez. It may not have thrilled the rest of the Spanish public, but they little cared about that in the Valencia stadium, which had now been implausibly and unpopularly renamed after the old club president Luis Casanova. Di Stéfano, once revered in Madrid, had now become a God-like figure for Valencia fans. Also, of course, this championship win was a passport for Valencia CF, for the first and only time, into the old knockout version of the European Cup, in which the Double-winning Arsenal side was representing England. Neither made much progress, Valencia losing to the Hungarians from Újpesti Dózsa, Arsenal to Johan Cruyff's Ajax. Knockout competitions also offered little solace domestically at this time. It was a case of so near and yet so far as Valencia CF lost three consecutive Spanish Cup finals (as it had done in the 1940s) between 1970 and 1972.

Sadly, Di Stéfano, for all his strengths and his considerable football brain, could not make this little firework of Valencian success in 1971 burn brightly for long. Real Madrid were gaining strength once more – they would win six of the next nine Spanish titles – and he could do little to stem the crumbling confidence of his players. Bill Shankly had been able to pass on the managerial mantle at Liverpool to Bob Paisley in 1974 after winning competitions at home and abroad, but there was no similar line of 'boot room' succession at Valencia. In his third season at the club the VCF team began to show signs of internal conflict and a marked decline of the teamwork and collective spirit that had been so vital in the 1971 title campaign. The club began to plunge down La Liga. In June of 1973, out of desperation, Julio de Miguel abandoned the presidency of the club. In the following season (1973–74) Di

Stéfano agreed to give it one last chance but results remained poor, and the home fans became increasingly restless. Don Alfredo's 'glorious interlude' at Valencia CF was over. So, too, for the time being at least, was Valencia's winning potential in both cup and league in Spain.

The 1970s in Spain produced both a strengthening and a consolidation of La Liga as it became an increasingly important destination for hundreds of South American footballers who could now qualify as 'native' players, or *los oriundos* – that is, as footballers who could demonstrate, by hook and occasionally by crook, some identifiable Hispanic descent. The names of some of these new arrivals clearly suggested Italian rather than Spanish origins, and the Spanish journalist Julian García Candau remarked that it was an ironic and rather suspicious coincidence that pretty much all of these players seemed to have parents born in towns where the relevant files – birth certificates, for example – had been burned during the Spanish Civil War. The Basque clubs were especially virulent in their complaints, of course, denouncing what they considered to be corrupt and illegal practices – and they were almost certainly correct (although it did not prevent a dramatic Basque revival of fortunes in La Liga in the early 1980s). But South American footballers – especially Argentinians and Paraguayans – continued arriving in Spain, and they played unhindered in the Spanish League with pretty much no questions asked.

From 1973, with frustration at the lack of European success beginning to cause strain, Spanish football also started to open its doors to more clearly 'foreign' footballers. Those players who could not enter Spain as 'natives' now entered as 'foreigners'. These changes meant that at the end of the 1960s and the beginning of the 1970s Valencia CF could boast naturalised players such as Aníbal Pérez, Valdez and Adorno, and later 'foreigners' such as Ocampos, Lleida and Catafau. But, in retrospect, these names seem like merely passing ephemera for the club. They were only preparing the way for the signing of *the* great Valencia playing hero of the period – and ultimately for victory for the club in another major European football competition.

'NO DIGA KEMPES, DIGA GOL!'
('DON'T SAY KEMPES, SAY GOAL!')

The 1976–77 season was the first full campaign in Spain after the death of Franco in November 1975. In the years of political transition to democracy that followed, the president of VCF was José Ramos Costa, a man who also plotted something of a revolution in the Valencia team, one that would produce cup riches. With the Paraguayan Heriberto Herrera as coach, a new generation of players arrived at Valencia, including goalkeeper Carlos S. Pereira, defenders Ángel Castellanos, José Carrete, Manuel D. Botubot and Ricardo P. Arias, and forwards Carlos M. Diarte ('Lobo') and Miguel Ángel Adorno. But all of these paled in significance alongside the figure of a leggy and shaggy-haired dynamo who had been bought to score goals and to excite the Valencia crowd. They swooned and fawned over a future Argentinian World Cup-winning hero, one Mario Alberto Kempes, who was signed in 1976 by the technical secretary of VCF Bernardino 'Pasieguito' Pérez. Pasieguito had spent time in Argentina, quietly observing the performances of the then little-known Argentinian striker.

In Argentina they had called Kempes *El matador*, meaning that, like the great bullfighters, he was an artistic killer. Valencia fans used to say *'No diga Kempes, diga gol!'* ('Don't say Kempes, say goal!') when talking about him, or else that he had the 'left leg of God'. (But who had the right?) In the Valencia stadium in the late 1970s it was only Kempes's name that was chanted with real emotion. When Valencia fans screeched for the Argentinian, it was like a battle cry, and visiting teams could be seen to visibly wilt as a result. They seemed intimidated, as if they had been shown a fatal weapon. They had.

In terms of affection from the crowd, real charisma and immediate impact, the obvious Liverpool player to compare Kempes with at this time would be Kenny Dalglish, who arrived at Anfield in 1977. Both men disliked the celebrity side of being a great footballer, even in the 1970s – they each looked lost and inhibited off the field. But they were also very different types of player. Dalglish was essentially a team man, a football thinker and a goal creator for others, as well as a regular scorer. Kempes was much more of an individualist, a pacy and thrilling deep-lying centre-forward and natural striker, and he was a skilled practitioner of the *gambetta* (the fast and incisive dribble). Kenny Dalglish had joined a Liverpool squad that was strong in all areas, with a powerful spine of Ray Clemence, Alan Hansen and Graeme Souness. It was good enough for a further three European Cups to match the one already secured under Bob Paisley in 1977. Things were different for Kempes. He joined a Valencia still lacking confidence and cohesion, and access to a European Cup place for VCF was routinely blocked at home by Barcelona and especially by Real Madrid.

Mario Kempes was an entirely new type of football hero for the Mestalla faithful. His lengthy, uncombed mane of hair and his unshaven features suggested he was some sort of 'alternative' or underground figure – a real loner or transgressive hippy, perhaps? He seemed mysterious, almost mystical. He certainly appealed to younger Valencia fans partly for these reasons. But he also had much more than this, including a powerful, surging stride that took him gliding through defences from deep, and a hammer blow of a shot, especially on the left foot, that made the Valencia stadium positively vibrate with emotion. On the pitch Kempes always looked for open spaces; he was also a prodigious worker, demanding the ball and then making it his own, almost irrespective of the quality of the pass. As he showed with Argentina in the 1978 World Cup finals, given a sight of goal he could finish, either with finesse or with murderous power. He looked like the complete forward – and a man who would prefer to stay out of the limelight offered by both the Camp Nou and the Bernabéu. In short, he was perfect.

Kempes's first period at the blanquinegros spanned the years 1976 to 1981. He made an instant impact and was the leading scorer in the

Spanish league in the 1976–77 (24) and 1977–78 (28) seasons. In the 1979–80 season, although no longer the pichichi, he still scored 22 goals for VCF. In 1981, after a number of serious injuries, Kempes returned briefly to Argentina to the River Plate club. However, River Plate could not pay the agreed transfer fee and so Kempes returned to Valencia CF for two more, largely unproductive, seasons – 1982–83 and 1983–84. It was to prove to be an unhappy ending to a relationship that had promised so much.

DI STÉFANO RETURNS – FOR A EUROPEAN TRIUMPH

In spite of their frustrating and uncertain Spanish League form Valencia CF would now be able to deliver some cup success – a trophy every season for three years. The management board, presided over by José Ramos Costa, had put down the basis of a solid unit made up of mainly Spaniards, including emerging locally raised players, such as Daniel Solsona and Miguel Tendillo. But they had also astutely brought in a number of key foreigners, including a powerful midfielder, the German World Cup man Rainer Bonhoff. With this new Valencia side given extra quality by the recruitment of both Kempes and Bonhoff, VCF was able to defeat Real Madrid 2–0 in the final of the Spanish Cup played in the Vicente Calderón (the stadium of Atlético Madrid) in 1979. The two goals were both 'swingers', coming as they did from the right foot of the profoundly left-sided Kempes, and the victory is still known in the city of Valencia as *'la final de Kempes'* – shades of Cardiff 2006 for Steven Gerrard and Liverpool fans.

It was the fifth Spanish Cup won by the blanquinegros – who also had now stacked up eight losses in the final. But this one had a very special flavour: it had been won over Real Madrid *in* the city of Madrid. Also, Valencia CF had been very inconsistent in the league that season, and few people in Spain had tipped them to overcome Real in the final. In fact, two months before the season's end, coach Marcel Domingo had been sacked by Pasieguito, who became the caretaker coach.

On 30 June, as VCF lifted the Spanish Cup in Madrid, the club had already taken the decision on their next coach: it signalled the return to Valencia of Alfredo Di Stéfano. For the new campaign Di Stéfano hardly changed the team that had enjoyed cup glory in 1979. Diarte had left, but Valencia signed up Orlando Jiménez and welcomed back midfielder Juan Cruz Sol, who was well known to the coach from their Real Madrid days. VCF finished unbeaten at home for sixth place in the Spanish League in 1979–80, but Sporting Gijón embarrassed the Valencia club with a first-round knockout of the holders in the Spanish Cup.

The European Cup-Winners' Cup of 1980 offered a rather different story. After eliminating B 1903 of Copenhagen, Rangers and then FC Barcelona, before defeating the French club Nantes in the semi-finals, Valencia reached another European final some 16 years after their Inter-Cities Fairs Cup final defeat to Real Zaragoza. It was played in the soon-to-be-notorious Heysel Stadium in Brussels, against an uninspired Arsenal side. The meeting was tepid and defensive, played out between two overly cautious teams. It ended, predictably, in a 0–0 draw. Kempes surprisingly missed in the first round of penalties, but Solsona, Pablo Rodríguez, Castellanos and Bonhoff all scored for Valencia, enough to take the contest to sudden death. As the shoot-out progressed, Arias scored for the Spaniards – and when Pereira saved Graham Rix's poorly struck kick, the blanquinegros had won the cup, and over much-vaunted English opponents. It was an occasion, reasoned the club's staff in time-honoured 'football-speak', when the result mattered rather more than the performance. How right they were.

The European Super Cup of 1980–81 now paired Valencia against another English opponent, the European Cup holders and recent nemesis of Liverpool, Brian Clough's Nottingham Forest. The final was played over two legs and, to be frank, had little real status in England. Pasieguito had taken charge of the Valencia team once more, after Di Stéfano was sacked following a poor run in La

Liga. Valencia lost 2–1 in the East Midlands, but on 17 December 1980 won 1–0 in Valencia, a goal scored by the Uruguayan Fernando Morena. The trophy was thus won on away goals, VCF defeating the reigning European champions, another prized English scalp. The victorious 5–3–2 Valencia team that night is still recited in the annals of the club's history. It read: José Manuel Sempere in goal; Tendillo, Arias, Botubot, José Cerveró and Castellanos in defence; Solsona, Javier Subirats and Enrique Saura in midfield; and Morena and the incomparable Kempes up front.

THE WORLD CUP 'HANGOVER' OF THE 1980s

After all this cup glory – and as Liverpool FC were still cleaning up titles in England – the worst decade in the history of Valencia CF began. In fact, it was a very complicated period for the whole of the Spanish game, as an economic crisis struck football. Clubs were paying out more on transfers and wages than they could afford. Promises that the World Cup finals held in Spain in 1982 would somehow 'save' Spanish football from its economic difficulties proved mere hyperbole; Spain crashed out of the tournament in a ferment of national humiliation, held by little Honduras and defeated even by Northern Ireland – and at the Valencia CF stadium!

A more concrete problem for VCF had to do with the remodelling of the Luis Casanova (Mestalla) stadium for the World Cup. Valencia was the headquarters of the Spanish national team, and it was assumed that the cost of the improvements and the modernisation of the stadium would be borne by the national federation. Not so. With World Cup disappointment and financial chaos lingering, the 1982–83 season was almost a disaster for Valencia CF. The club reached the final round of matches – against Real Madrid – tied for bottom place in the league. Alfredo Di Stéfano was now coach at the Bernabéu, and he needed just a draw from his old club to secure the league title from a chasing Athletic Bilbao. Amazingly, VCF got the win they needed, thanks to a solitary goal from Miguel Tendillo, and because of defeats on the same day for Celta Vigo, Osasuna and Racing Santander, they avoided the drop into the Spanish Second Division by the skin of their teeth. This was a real 'West Brom' moment, with five clubs all trying to avoid relegation on the final day and Valencia the least fancied of all to come up with the goods. It was a 'miracle' outcome – but one achieved at the expense of loved former manager Di Stéfano.

But this survival was only a stay of execution. As Valencia's financial situation worsened, so did their results. In season 1985–86 Liverpool Football Club had to recover from the shock and disgrace of Heysel under new player–manager Kenny Dalglish. They did so brilliantly by completing the cup and league Double in England for the first time. VCF had a very different type of sporting shock to contend with: that of being finally relegated to the Second Division of Spanish football for the first time in the club's 55-year history in the top flight. Valencia CF was now a mess, run through with rumour and discontent as players squabbled over wages and argued about who was to blame for the playing crisis. The young players that had arrived at the club, among them Sempere, Arias, Subirats, Castellanos and Roberto Fernández, had quality but lacked the collective experience to fight the drop. Nor was the vaunted Valencia team spirit much in evidence now. But it was the *economic* situation that had been the real killer blow.

Óscar Rubén Valdez, a former Valencia player, had now taken charge of the management of the team, but there was no money to make new signings. Key players such as Saura and Jesús García Pitarch – who later battled Benítez as the club's sport director – had left because of the lack of cash, and in January 1986 Valdez himself abandoned his post, paving the way for the return of the old warhorse Alfredo Di Stéfano (in his third stint as VCF coach). But it was too late to avoid the drop. Di Stéfano then piloted Valencia back into the top flight after only one season, returning to the First Division with a new team of hungry young players. The manager had been a great servant to the club, leading the side as coach for a record 207 times.

Admittedly, this was hardly a figure to match Bob Paisley's 44 years' service at Liverpool as player, trainer, coach, assistant manager and finally manager. Nor could Di Stéfano challenge Paisley's trophy count – who could? But the Argentinian legend had never run from a crisis at Valencia, and he had played a role in many of the club's major achievements in the past two decades. His place in the Valencia CF roll call of great club heroes was secure.

In fact, the generation of players that brought Valencia CF back into the top flight of the Spanish game in 1987 has proved to be a very significant one in the recent history of the club. Many of them became important figures over the longer term; for example, the current coach Quique Sánchez Flores and the club's former sport director Javier Subirats. Fernando Gómez was also a very special figure in this generation of Valencia talent and one of the most outstanding players in the history of the club. He rejected many opportunities to leave Valencia and instead stayed for 15 seasons – the Ian Callaghan of his day – from 1983–84 up to 1997–98. A midfielder, he scored a remarkable one hundred and seventeen goals in the league but played only eight times for the Spanish national team – a criminal waste of talent. His intelligence on the pitch and his technical quality, plus the way he ghosted in for shots on goal, made Fernando Gómez one of the all-time idols of the Valencians. He now commentates on football in Spain.

VCF returned to the First Division of La Liga in 1987–88 with more than 120 million pesetas (720,000 euros) in the bank, and there had been an important rise in its number of *socios* (club members or season-ticket holders) from 16,320 to 20,057 while the club was in the Second Division. In their first season back the blanquinegros ended up in 14th position – OK, but in the ruthless world of Spanish football not enough to save Di Stéfano's job. Before the end of the season, and as the ghost of a possible second relegation began to haunt the club, Roberto Gil replaced the Argentinian. From 1988 to 1991 Víctor Esparrago, a serious Uruguayan football muse, hard worker and man short on words, became coach of Valencia, bringing with him a very clearly defined defensive style. It brought results. A team whose rear guard had been forged in the Second Division of Spanish football now finished in third position of the First Division and runners-up in the 1989–90 season, before falling to seventh position in 1990–91. This was huge progress, taking the Valencia club right back to the highest echelons of the Spanish game. This occurred just as Liverpool Football Club had begun to show the first signs of real vulnerability in England, which would actually turn out to be a signal of its long-term decline.

This new Valencia success was built around the arrival at the club of goalkeeper José Manuel Ochotorena (now Benítez's goalkeeping coach at Liverpool), the forwards Eloy Olaya and the Bulgarian Lubo Penev, the return of Roberto Fernández and the revival in form of Paco Camarasa. The new arrivals merged well with players already at the club, and a sign of the defensive solidity of the new Valencia inspired by Víctor Esparrago was that Ochotorena conceded fewer goals (25 in 38 matches) than any other La Liga keeper during the 1988–89 season. The recruitment of the Bulgarian international Penev was also essential. Penev was a strong forward who worked hard for the team and scored goals as well. Defence for Valencia, as for all good teams, started with the first line of attack – think Ian Rush. It may not always have looked pretty, but the stability and new competitiveness of Valencia CF was the reward for the serenity and relative austerity imposed by the president Arturo Tuzón when it was needed – and the unconditional support shown by the Valencia fans during the years of struggle.

THE NEW SPANISH FOOTBALL, AND THE NEW VCF OF THE 1990s

In the 1990s another new era of Spanish football began. Most of the Spanish clubs became SADs – *Sociedad Anónima Deportivas* (sporting limited companies). Before this, clubs were civil associations whose policies were ostensibly decided by socios. Large debts resulted, and these now required new solutions. Thus began a sporting managerial revolution without precedent in the Spanish game. On 26 September 1991 the general meeting of VCF agreed to transform the club into a SAD and adopt a new form of management, including a board of directors for the first time. On the first board were the next three presidents of the club: Melchor Hoyos, Francisco Roig and Pedro Cortés. The transformation began to take effect in the first few months of 1992, guided by the secretary of the Valencia CF management board Vicente Pons. By October the process was complete with the election of the management board presided over by Arturo Tuzón.

This new management model meant that some cities with smaller clubs began to develop and grow, spreading the wealth in the sport a little. But Spanish football was now almost completely dominated at the top by just two clubs: FC Barcelona and Real Madrid. In the fourteen seasons between 1986 and 2000 the league title in Spain was won only once by a club other than these two giants (Atlético Madrid in 1996); it was a return to the duopoly of the 1950s and '60s. As in England, the technological changes in television in the 1990s seemed to stimulate the growth in public interest for the Spanish game – and to change the game itself. As the two public TV channels began to be supplemented by more and more private TV stations in Spain – some of which covered football – so the sport itself became much more glamorised and entertainment based. This was the age of football as the 'Big TV Show'.

On the sporting side, Valencia CF began the 1991–92 season with an exciting new coach, the brilliant Dutch strategist Guus Hiddink. In England the appointment of foreign coaches was still frowned upon. Liverpool Football Club, for example, still refused to look abroad for coaching inspiration. Instead, it had settled down to a turbulent few years with an ex-player at the helm, the explosive Graeme Souness.

Valencia CF, not unreasonably, now wanted to consolidate the achievements of Víctor Espárrago. But the club also wanted to reach out to bigger targets. Sempere was restored as goalkeeper, and Penev was increasingly the key man up front. The Brazilian Leonardo showed his exceptional skills and magical talent with the ball on the left side of midfield, while Quique Sánchez Flores was a talented right-back, although his career was to be blighted by injuries. The versatile Nando along with Fernando, Roberto, Tomas and Arroyo constituted the tough and adaptable midfield of VCF. Finally, forwards Eloy, Penev, Rommel Fernandez and Toni were key members of the squad that reached fourth place in both 1991–92 and 1992–93, a very decent return.

Back in Europe after many years' absence, Valencia initially found it difficult to adapt and recover their status, suffering UEFA Cup humiliations during the 1992–93 and 1993–94 seasons – they were defeated by Napoli (1–5) and a rampant Karlsruher SC (0–7), respectively. This thrashing by the Germans, followed by a 0–3 home league trouncing by Real Madrid, was the end for Hiddink, and later that same season Arturo Tuzón, the club president, also resigned. Eventually, Francisco Roig would receive the backing of the club's shareholders, and he was elected as the new president of VCF in March 1994 with a campaign that took '*Valencia campeón*' ('Valencia for champions') as its heady title.

In a difficult period for the club – which was suddenly loaded again with on-field problems, resignations, power vacuums, changes of coach and inappropriate media stories – it might have slipped many people's notice that Pasieguito, the visionary who had spotted Mario Kempes for Valencia in 1976, had brought in another major signing for the club from Partisan Belgrade, the brilliant schemer and attacker Predrag Mijatović. Things were looking up again for the blanquinegros.

1995: *LA FINAL DEL AGUA* (THE WATER FINAL)

The 1994–95 season was the first that new club president Francisco Roig could plan for from the beginning. One of his first decisions was an important and symbolic one – to officially reinstate the original name of the club stadium as the Mestalla. His second was to hire the Brazilian coach Carlos Alberto Parreira, who had committed to VCF before winning the World Cup with the Brazilian national team in 1994. The Valencia team was reinforced with the recruitment of Spain's goalkeeper Andoni Zubizarreta, the Spanish international defender Jorge Otero and the World Cup-winning Brazilian Mazinho. Nevertheless, VCF made a slow start in La Liga, depending too much for inspiration on the mercurial Mijatović. Parreira was soon sacked as coach after becoming disillusioned with the city and the club, but the team once again reached the final of the Spanish Cup, beating eternal rivals FC Barcelona and Real Madrid on the way. This was the first such final for Valencia in 16 years, but Deportivo de La Coruña made it an unhappy return, eventually edging out VCF 1–2 in an interrupted climax. The final is remembered in Valencia as *La final del agua* (the water final). The match was suspended 11 minutes from the end, with the score at 1–1, because of a tremendous storm that flooded the stadium. Spanish rules dictate that in the case of abandonment the teams play out only the minutes lost in the return. So three days later the match was resumed – and Deportivo had enough time to score the goal they needed to defeat a deflated VCF.

This setback didn't stop Valencia in their ascent towards the summit of the Spanish game. The infamous elder statesman Luis Aragonés, *El sabio de Hortaleza* (the wise man of Hortaleza), came in as coach. For the English this apparently endless flurry of changes in the club coach position in Spain might seem mystifying and self-defeating. Liverpool Football Club had won no domestic league title since 1990, but by 2006 had still only had four managers since Kenny Dalglish packed in the job in 1991. Football managers in England tend to bring in their own staff, sign long contracts and attempt to change the whole philosophy and approach of the club they join. They control pretty much everything on the playing side – an attraction to Rafa Benítez when he joined Liverpool in 2004. So the top managers in England generally get a few years to try their ideas out. In Spain the coach is seen more as a hired hand – an important one, but still just another employee whose job is simply to manage players selected by someone else. Wider club policy and recruitment is dictated elsewhere. Like players, coaches in Spain are regarded as easily dispensable. And they are routinely dispensed with – meaning continuity at club level is a huge problem in the Spanish game.

Luis Aragonés promised to be more of a stayer than most. Many people in Valencia considered him as the coach who best understood the team and the philosophy of the club. Out went Penev, Roberto, Sempere and Giner, and the team was built around the tandem formed by Mitjatovic and Fernando Gómez. As a result, Valencia finished runners-up in La Liga on 83 points, beaten only by surprise champions Atlético Madrid, who had been revived under Raddy Antic. Barça and Real were out of the top two in the Spanish League – this was almost unthinkable! Aragonés produced a Valencia team that defended well, balanced fighting qualities and creativity in midfield and had in Mijatović a forward player of real potency – he scored 28 goals that season. But his rapid transfer to Real Madrid – who had been stung into action by their own league failure – meant that the Slav went from being idolised at the Mestalla to being loathed by the Valencians.

The following season (1996–97) Aragonés threatened to resign minutes before the first game because of disagreements with the club president Roig regarding new signings. The Russian Valeri Karpin and the Brazilian Romário were then brought in, to much expectation. After all, Romário had been arguably the best player at the World Cup in 1994, but he didn't impress Luis Aragonés, who wanted more committed team players rather than individualists like the Brazilian forward. Romário played just six matches for his new club before returning to Flamengo. Luis Aragonés left Valencia soon after, in November 1996. So much for this 'stayer'.

In stepped the Argentinian intellectual Jorge Valdano, who already had one Spanish title to his name with Real Madrid, where he had clashed with a young Rafa Benítez. But the new man came with a style very different to the one that Luis Aragonés had developed at

VCF. Valdano brought in the Brazilians Leandro and Cáceres, and also Ariel Ortega, an exciting Argentine forward. However, a Valencia team that had been designed to play a brand of football that was rather at odds with the more expansive approach proposed by Valdano could only finish ninth in La Liga.

CLAUDIO RANIERI, THE BEGINNING OF (ANOTHER) NEW CYCLE

Valdano started as coach of VCF the following season (1997–98), when the club re-signed the enigmatic Romário. However, a pre-season injury for the Brazilian and the prompt sacking of the mistake-ridden Valdano meant that there was no chance to see how this intriguing player–coach partnership might have worked out. Next through the managerial swing-door at Valencia was the highly regarded Italian coach Claudio Ranieri, signalling another new direction for the club. Ranieri was the first-ever Italian coach at VCF, and he soon fell out with the precious Romário; the little Brazilian left Valencia in a huff for the second time. The same thing eventually happened to the Argentinian Ariel Ortega: he stayed for the season but barely played. He left the tinkering Ranieri as the worst of enemies.

The Valencia president Francisco Roig had presented Claudio Ranieri to the Valencia public as the *General Romano* (the Roman general). This was one year before Gérard Houllier was to take over from Roy Evans and move Liverpool in a radical new direction as the club's first-ever non-British coach. Ranieri's arrival was also a radical shift. His approach was clearly very different to that of Valdano's, though it did have a certain continuity with the previous, more defensive, reigns of Espárrago, Hiddink and Aragonés. So this was not a total culture shift for Valencia, as it promised to be at Liverpool FC under the new French technocrat Houllier. Like Houllier at Liverpool, Ranieri granted no special favours to the so-called star players at his new club, and he also preferred his players to sacrifice themselves for the team and to play mainly on the counter-attack. Slowly, the blanquinegros began to improve their position in the league under the new regime, but the Valencia fans then began to criticise club president Francisco Roig for his plans for a new share offer. They smelled a rat.

When VCF was constituted as a SAD, 90,000 shares were sold to local people. Soon after the businessman Roig became president of the club he proposed an enlargement of the share capital in order to finance a redevelopment of the Mestalla. But Roig's opponents argued that his real ambition was to place ownership of the club in the hands of a few major shareholders – including himself. Martín Queralt, a law professor at Valencia University, won the vote against the Roig proposal at a shareholders' meeting. But Roig would later return to win his case.

During Roig's time in charge, the Valencia CF president enjoyed great popular support, strong economic resources, good players and coaches, and skilled technical staff. The club also finished runners-up in both the league and cup in his time as president. But the loss of three top coaches in quick succession, and the slump to ninth place in the league in 1997, suggested that both VCF and Roig had rather lost their way once again. The president was increasingly seen as a man who didn't know where to lead the club. In December 1997 the Mestalla crowd screamed *'¡Paco, vete ya!'* ('Paco, get out!') in their anger at the president's proposals, and so Roig resigned. It was the same old Spanish football story. Pedro Cortés, a member of the new board of directors, took over as the Valencia CF president.

On the pitch Ranieri had the speed and precision of the Argentinian wide player Claudio López to call upon, as López now began to shine in his second full season at the club. But the key to Ranieri's approach was defence, with Jocelyn Anglomá, Miroslav Dukić, Fernando Cáceres and Amedeo Carboni covering the veteran Zubizarreta in goal. In midfield the near saintly figure of the blond Gaizka Mendieta began to emerge as the leader of the Valencia team, with Luís Milla and Miguel Angulo honest generals at his side. And up front there was a crucial and lethal contribution from Adrian Ilie, a Romanian who had been signed as a winter reinforcement, but who was now approvingly nicknamed by Ranieri as *La cobra*.

Inconsistency dogged his team – they finished ninth again in the 1997–98 season – but on their day this Valencia could be very dangerous indeed. A 0–3 deficit at the Camp Nou was turned into a thrilling 4–3 win, for example, and Real Madrid were also beaten at the Bernabéu. The following season (1998–99) Valencia claimed their first Spanish Cup for 20 years, thrashing Atlético Madrid 3–0 in the final. There was a feeling in the city that this Italian Ranieri could be turning the team into something interesting after all.

It was here that the paths of the two clubs linked by Rafa Benítez, Valencia and Liverpool, now directly and fatefully crossed in serious competition for the first time. It was in the second round of the UEFA Cup in November 1998. Liverpool FC was, by this stage, jointly managed by Roy Evans and Gérard Houllier, a dog's breakfast of an arrangement and one fated to fail. The two clubs fought out a stalemate 0–0 draw at Anfield that seemed to pave the way for a Valencia win in the return at the Mestalla. But late goals from Patrick Berger and Steve McManaman offered Liverpool a famous result (eventually 2–2), although one that was blighted by three late sendings off: McManaman and Paul Ince for Liverpool and the combustible Carboni for Valencia. After the match, Houllier and Evans fell out over whether the match officials – all Frenchmen – should be offered Liverpool shirts as souvenirs. The incident proved to be the final straw for Evans, who returned to England determined to resign. Liverpool Football Club had won the battle of the Mestalla, but Houllier had been victorious in the Anfield managerial war.

HÉCTOR CÚPER AND TWO CHAMPIONS LEAGUE FINALS

Valencia finished fourth in the Spanish League in 1998–99, thanks to a victory in the last match of the season in the Mestalla, against a Majorca side coached by the Argentinian Héctor Cúper. This secured VCF's entry into the Champions League for the first time – but not under Ranieri. The Italian left Valencia CF – like Benítez later – with tears in his eyes, alleging that he couldn't find a suitable Italian school in the city for his young daughters! He surfaced later at Chelsea – the schooling must be superior in London. It was Héctor Cúper who took over at the Mestalla, and he was offered new signings in the shape of fellow Argentinians Kily González and Mauricio Pellegrino, and a return to VCF of three key players who had been sent out on loan: the inspirational Albelda, and Palop and Gerard López.

Héctor Cúper's was a very pragmatic game plan, with a strong defensive base and an explosive and creative counter-attacking system centred on the creative abilities of Mendieta and the lethal attacking qualities of Claudio López or *El Piojo* ('the louse'), an unfortunate nickname given to him because he was very slippery and persistent. The approach under Cúper was simple but hugely successful, and it helped take VCF to two consecutive Champions League finals, in 2000 and 2001. However, both were lost: the first because of pressure and nerves – and the talent of Real Madrid – the second because of the excessively conservative tactics employed by Cúper.

The 2000 final at the Stade de France in St Denis, Paris, was a catastrophe for Valencia. Having defeated both Lazio and Barcelona in the knockout phase, their final opponents were not the sort of foreign opposition that Cúper might have relished: they faced, instead, the all too familiar figure of Real Madrid. In a one-sided contest VCF seemed absent from the pitch, lacking belief and showing little big-match temperament. It was as if the Real Madrid side – strangely clad in all-black – had cast a spell over them. It ended as a 3–0 stroll for the men from the Bernabéu, Morientes, Raul and Bootle's Steve McManaman all scoring.

In 2001 McManaman's old club Liverpool returned to European glory themselves by agonisingly defeating little Alavés from Spain 5–4 in a remarkable UEFA Cup final in Dortmund to complete a Treble of cup wins for the Reds that year. Things seemed set fair for Gérard Houllier at Anfield – but the Frenchman was soon to lose his way. The senior event in 2001, the European Cup final between Valencia CF and Bayern Munich at the San Siro in Milan, was, in some ways, an even crueller occasion. Valencia CF had lost Claudio López but had undoubtedly strengthened their team since 2000 by recruiting two more Argentinians of unquestionable talent: the uncompromising defender Fabian Ayala had arrived from AC Milan, and the brilliant and elusive Pablo Aimar had joined up during the winter transfer window. The tough and technically excellent Spanish midfielder Rubén 'Pipo' Baraja came in from Atlético Madrid, and the steepling Norwegian forward John Carew joined from Rosenborg. This was now a very formidable Valencia unit and one of the strongest squads in the European game. Surely their time had come?

Valencia steamrollered through their Europe season – eliminating Arsenal and Leeds United in the knockout phases – and in the final they confidently took the lead with a Mendieta penalty. But the Germans responded, and Stefan Effenberg scored an equalising penalty. Pressure can do strange things in football. Fear seemed to take over: the two clubs gripped by anxiety. But of the two, Valencia CF seemed to have the resources and the necessary quality to push on to victory. Instead, Cúper stayed his hand. Extra time could not separate the rivals, and Oliver Khan's save from Pellegrino's penalty in the dreaded shoot-out lottery was enough to win the trophy for the Germans. Perhaps this would prove to be Valencia CF's best-ever chance of getting their hands on the coveted European Cup – it was certainly a wasted opportunity.

Although the club had now restored much of its European

prestige, this was actually an awful moment for the Valencia club and its staff – and some players clearly thought that the Valencia dream of European glory was now over for good. Two key influences, Mendieta and Gerard, departed soon after, and the coach Cúper also left, for Inter Milan. But the core of this impressive side remained. If Valencia could just recruit a talented young coach and try to keep him for a while, then this club and this *team* could definitely still do great things – even win a Spanish title, perhaps – after 30 long years in the domestic wilderness. Valencia could no longer turn to Alfred Di Stéfano for leadership, as the club had so often done in the past. Instead, it put its faith in a largely unknown young coach, an early Madridista, who had shown some talent in the game but who had also suffered setbacks in his coaching career in Spain. This was a major risk, of course. But the 2001–02 league season would finally produce what Valencia CF had been building – sometimes rather chaotically – towards for three decades. A fifth La Liga title now lay ahead for the Valencians. It was a triumph that would be guided by the hand of a semi-stranger to most Spanish football fans, a quietly determined man from Madrid called Rafael Benítez.

6

Merry Christmas, Señor Benítez?

Lost in Japan; Michael's Anfield return; Glorious Goodison;
Big Sam's Bolton play it ugly; Rafa's half-term report.

FULL OF EASTERN PROMISE? CLUB WORLD CHAMPIONSHIP, JAPAN, 11–19 DECEMBER 2005

Roy Collins of the *Sunday Telegraph* called the 2005 Club World Championship a 'ludicrous and meaningless competition, a monument to the ego of FIFA president Sepp Blatter'. You could tell he didn't like it. Liverpool chief executive Rick Parry said Liverpool Football Club's trip to Japan to play in FIFA's puffed-up event was important. OK, we could buy that. Parry also said that the competition was no simple cash cow. Fair enough. He said, finally, that Liverpool wanted to make 'club history' by winning the trophy for the first time to add to the European Cup and Super Cup in 2005 and thus become club champions of the world. This was a little harder to swallow. The 'double whammy of medals and money' is how one newspaper put what was on offer in Liverpool FC's season-slicing trip across the globe. But it was not exactly convincing, was it? Fly halfway across the world to play just two matches, one against some third-rate featherweight, another (almost certainly) against a half-baked Brazilian outfit placed eleventh in their own league – and then argue that this junket was somehow 'more important' than what the club achieved in Istanbul in May? Not really; not likely.

But the key sub-text – Parry's other agenda – was that Liverpool

Football Club could uncover vital investors on the trip to Japan. The sort of high rollers, in fact, they desperately needed to help make the shunted proposed new Stanley Park stadium a reality – or even a possibility. Rick Parry is also bright enough to have known just how potentially important these vast Eastern markets are to the club. But the *real* football club championship of the world surely involves winning the European Cup, the richest and most hotly contested club football competition in the world, a stage dominated by the game's greatest players. By this token, some would say that Liverpool FC were *already* world club champions (though, embarrassingly, with no domestic crown to call their own). If the Brazilian league was so strong – São Paulo were the major threat that week – then why were 800 of their best players abroad, mostly joining better clubs in Europe? ('It's the economy, stupid' was part of the answer.) A possible £3 million in the bank, international exposure, product sales, global networking and extra Brownie points from FIFA and the FA simply for being 'good sports' and taking part must have sounded enough to justify this arduous trip. Otherwise, the junket was potentially a real cost, not a reward, of winning the 2005 European Cup in Istanbul.

The Liverpool manager's father Francisco, 74, died after a long illness in the build up to the Reds' first game in Japan. Remarkably, Rafa did not – no, would not – go back to Spain for his own father's funeral, not given his commitment to this football club and to this event. So he was emotionally beached, instead, in an alien culture. Rafa Benítez is not an overly emotional person – we know that. But we also know how important family is to him and how crucial his father had been to his development and success as a coach in Spain. And we know how important this kind of family loss is to all of us: we who could easily just drop our work and other commitments and be where we were needed most – where we would most *want* to be. The single-minded Benítez gave all of this up for his adopted English football club and for all those who follow it. This was one of those moments when loyal football men like Benítez most deserve our thoughts – and our thanks.

Most Liverpool fans – like Rafa himself – were hoping to get the tournament over with, with no injuries, followed by a trouble-free three Premiership points from Newcastle at home, when 'You-Know-Who' was due to come calling at Anfield. So, the most important thing about travelling to Japan was that it did not obstruct the club's progress back at home. That pretty much summed up how little was really at stake. This was also why Liverpool's history in the forerunner to this event, when South American champions played Europe's in a one-off match, was hardly auspicious: a 0–3 clattering by Brazilians Flamengo in 1981, when Paisley instructed no Liverpool player to get booked and jet lag contributed to a tackle-free afternoon (three down at half-time), and a dull 0–1 reverse to the Argentinians of Independiente in 1984. Both matches were played in Tokyo. Hardly anyone on Merseyside noticed.

But football priorities and finances had changed in the global era. Liverpool Football Club threatened to get serious about winning this fancy tin pot by staying in Japan for more than a week to overcome the debilitating effects of the change in time zones. They might well have beaten their first opponents, Deportivo Saprissa, the chaotic champions of Costa Rica, in their sleep in a game played in the woeful Yokohama Stadium. This sterile bowl – though not quite as desperate as the Atatürk Olympic – had also landed in the middle of nowhere and was host to Didi Hamann's losing 2002 World Cup final. On the day of the match it was a half-full container, with fans scattered miles from the pitch on a too-gentle rake and the winter wind sweeping in, as always. Steve Finnan, still struggling with the change in time zones and thus sleepless in Japan, was fortunate enough to be omitted from the day's 3–0 Reds stroll.

And this comprehensive score line could easily have been doubled. In fact, once Crouch (at last on a roll) and Gerrard expertly put away their first-half chances, the game slowly meandered towards its inevitable finish, Crouch grabbing another goal in the second half after comical Costa Rican defending. Only the 21-year-old left-sided midfielder Christian Bolanos impressed at all for Deportivo. São Paulo looked defensively poor in the other semi-final, scraping through 3–2 against little-known Al-Ittihad. So, it looked like Liverpool would comfortably wrap up the trophy and then get it home to join old 'Big Ears' in the Anfield trophy room.

Back in the real football world, the 2006 European Cup last-16 draw kindly paired holders Liverpool with Benfica from Portugal. From their Japanese garret, Parry and Benítez were properly respectful when talking to the press of their prospective opponents, but behind their cuffs these Anfield men must actually have had the widest of grins. Meanwhile, José Mourinho's reward for asserting that finishing second to Liverpool in the group stage was no hardship at all was to draw the decidedly short straw of FC Barcelona. The Catalans were strolling to the title back in La Liga, and they still had a considerable bone to pick with the Londoners. One of these favourites would now fall, so there were yet more smiles from the Liverpool camp as the team turned to the, surely nominal, matter of securing victory in Yokohama.

But not so fast, hold on. In the final, with Finnan back on the right and Warnock mystifyingly replacing Riise at left-back – and after an idiot local pitch invader held things up for fully five first-half minutes – the Brazilians looked alarmingly lively. With Real Madrid-bound right-back Cicinho prominent, they pinged little one-twos behind the Liverpool midfield and around the flat-footed Hyypiä and Carragher on the edge of the Reds' box. This was very un-Premiership-like attacking – a completely new challenge for the Liverpool defence – and when Mineiro finally found acres of space between Hyypiä and a still-sleeping Warnock on Liverpool's left side after 27 minutes, that long wait for a red mark in the Reds 'goals against' column was finally over. The big question then became: how, exactly, would Liverpool and Benítez react to going behind? But the real response came from the Brazilians, because from then on São Paulo retreated around the expert fouling, feigning and shirt-tugging of their impressively cynical Uruguayan centre-half Diego Lugano. And so the contest became a depressing case of monitoring time-wasting and just how many chances Liverpool missed. 'Goals' – by García and Sinama-Pongolle – were also ruled out by dubious offside calls. The oddball goal-scoring Brazilian keeper Rogerio Ceni also had the match of his lucky life to help keep Liverpool at bay. 'Gerrard thought Liverpool were invincible,' he wryly commented later. But the real truth was something very different: that a dominant side that preferred to play with no assured goal scorer, no serial assassin in their ranks, would eventually be made to pay for their arrogance. This was simply one of those days – and there would be others to come, make no mistake. So, Liverpool actually slaughtered the very moderate new Club World Champions São Paulo 0–1 – and came home from the East empty-handed after all.

EIGHT DAYS, FOUR GAMES: CHRISTMAS FIXTURES, 2005

Endurance and heart are crucial factors in any top-class sporting competition – ask the unimpeachable Muhammad Ali. Ali fought the fearsome George Foreman more than 30 years ago in Zaire in an epic encounter. After taking an awful early pounding from the 'killer' Foreman, Ali could feel his giant foe, 'Big George', beginning to tire. His opponent's breathing became more and more laboured as the two men leaned on each other, mid-round, both gasping for air. Ali grabbed his rival round the back of the neck during one of their more desperate lumbering dances and whispered very gently into the African night, and his opponent's ear, 'Terrible bad time to get tired, George.' Foreman knew at that dreadful moment that he was lost in Africa.

Like Ali in the African jungle, English football managers might have been tempted to play up the tiredness in their rivals' legs over the Christmas holiday period. While footballers in Spain and most of the rest of their Continental colleagues rested their bodies – with Barcelona already halfway triumphant, Valencia CF still hopeful,

Osasuna in dreamland and the bumbling Real Madrid in near despair – in England Premiership clubs would play *four* league matches in just eight days over the gruelling holiday period. And Liverpool's programme followed hard on their losing trip to Japan. The Reds' holiday treat read like this:

26 December:	Newcastle United (H)
28 December:	Everton (A)
31 December:	WBA (H)
2 January:	Bolton Wanderers (A)

This fixture glut was about helping Sven out in the World Cup finals. It was difficult to imagine the resolute club men in La Liga being forced into this sort of arrangement. The fate of Barça and Real counts rather more than that of the men who slope off with the Spanish national team every four years, expecting an exit well before the medals are handed out. Pity the poor *fans* in England, too. At least Liverpool's four Christmas matches were all clutched together in the North West. Some clubs and their supporters were expected to travel up and down the English motorways in search of their festive opponents. Some would have to search pretty hard, too, as the weather kicked in and produced some very late postponements. If you started to lose matches in this phase, it could become a thoroughly miserable and season-defining few days.

MICHAEL ROWS HIS BOAT ASHORE: THE ANFIELD RETURN

Liverpool faced at least three tough, crucial contests over this period, all with delicate little sub-plots. At Anfield on Boxing Day, for example, it was prodigal son time. Michael Owen scored some 158 goals for Liverpool in just 297 games – a proud record. Had we not already been worshipping at the altar of one Robbie Fowler, and had Michael not embraced his national-hero status quite so

Rafa Benítez brings home the 2004 UEFA Cup to the Mestalla. But he was already uneasy at Valencia CF, and he was soon headed for Merseyside. (© Tania Castro, *El País*)

It was European Cup ecstasy for Rafa and Liverpool in Istanbul in 2005 after an astonishing comeback. Two years later, in 2007, it would be a repeat final in Athens – but no repeat glory for Liverpool.

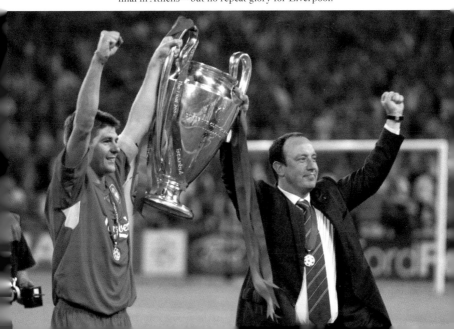

Too early for cricket. Seven weeks after Istanbul, Steven Gerrard gets to grips
with little TNS in the Champions League qualifiers in July 2005.

Early season silverware in 2005–06 as Liverpool players lift the European Super Cup in Monaco.
But frustration would soon follow in Japan in the Club World Championship in December 2005.

Djibril Cissé and Momo Sissoko celebrate the Super Cup win in 2005.
The loan of the erratic Cissé to Olympic Marseille for the whole of the
2006–07 season suggested Benítez was looking for a more resolute Liverpool.
Sissoko's form and fitness would also dip in 2006–07 as Javier Mascherano
gathered strength and admirers at Anfield.

The Miracle of Kenilworth Road. Marlon Beresford saves Djibril Cissé's penalty in the FA Cup third round in 2006, but Liverpool came back from 1–3 down to triumph. Missing penalties in cup competitions was definitely not part of Liverpool's agenda under the meticulous Benítez.

Kop hero Robbie Fowler was brought back to Liverpool by Benítez in 2006, but the striker could not find the necessary pace and form to make a real impact in 2006–07. Nor could Robbie even make the bench in Athens in May 2007.

Fortress Melwood: Rafa Benítez in his natural habitat, watching and preparing on the training ground for Liverpool's next battle.

A bad night in Lisbon as Liverpool concede a crucial goal to Benfica in the 2006 Champions League. Reaching the 2007 Champions League final simply confirmed Rafa Benítez's credentials as a top European strategist – but could he also win the elusive Premiership?

Thrown together again five times in 2005–06 and four more times in 2006–07,
Rafa Benítez and the prickly José Mourinho were fast becoming
managerial giants of the new English game. But Benítez kept on
winning the European contests that mattered.

Pictures of Spain. Xabi Alonso and Luís Garcia celebrate Fernando Morientes's goal at Birmingham City in the 7–0 FA Cup rout in 2006. Morientes would return to Spain after just one season in England and Garcia would be hit hard by injury in 2006–07. But there seemed little doubt that with US finance Benítez would continue his Hispanic transformation of Liverpool.

Steven Gerrard shows what beating Chelsea means in the 2006 FA Cup semi-final at Old Trafford. He would experience the same emotions twice more at Anfield in 2006–07, once in the Premiership and once in the Champions League.

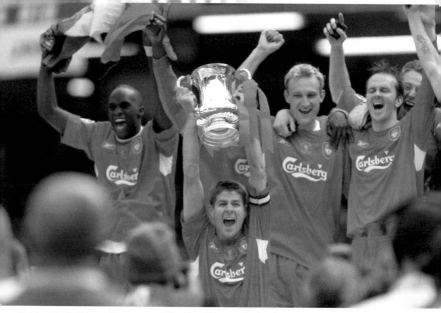

Robbed by builders of a return to Wembley, Liverpool win the 2006 FA Cup in Wales. In one week in January 2007 Arsenal would humble Liverpool at home in both domestic cup competitions. Benítez soon shrugged off the disappointments.

The Liverpool wall can only watch as Filippo Inzaghi appears to handle Andrea Pirlo's free-kick to give AC Milan the lead in Athens in 2007. In 2007–08, and with new American backing, Rafa Benítez would again try to balance Liverpool's success in Europe with necessary home improvements.

enthusiastically, his arrival and achievements at Anfield would have seemed even more extraordinary. Right from the outset, as a tiny 17 year old, he frightened good defenders with his sheer pace and his cheeky schoolboy optimism; he was an energised rubber ball, a man who was nerveless in front of goal. When fame and injury – mainly dodgy hamstrings – eventually depleted him, Owen became much more of a sleeper, a man hiding away in matches before emerging from the arras to commit the dagger wound.

Owen almost always delivered, at least until he, like most of the Liverpool squad, got despondent under a defensive-minded and increasingly paranoid Gérard Houllier. Fewer and fewer opportunities came his way, and Michael increasingly defined himself as a taker of chances rather than as the all-round workaholic goal-scoring pest we had come to expect. Which is partly why our memories of Michael were so unfairly soured. We remembered more the moping, half-committed England man Owen, than the zestful Cheshire school kid who enjoyed embarrassing hulking centre-backs and who loved scoring goals for Liverpool Football Club. Well-respected journalists wrote that the Kop should be thankful for his Liverpool service and welcome him back with open arms to Anfield: wish him well in his new career in the North East.

But nothing in football works quite like that any more. Michael left Anfield under a cloud of his own making, one that will take some shifting. Frankly, Michael and his people (like Macca before him) had been simply duplicitous in dithering over signing a new contract at Anfield when Real Madrid finally sidled in with a predictably nasty – derisory, actually – offer of £8 million in August 2005, plus the unknown reserve winger Antonio Núñez. Rafa may not have even cared about Michael staying at Liverpool, but the club's hands were pretty much tied in any case. It was clear that Owen wanted to try life in Madrid (and their cash, of course), and in less than 12 months he would have been out of contract and worth precisely nothing to Liverpool. So the deal was done – and at least Owen was not moving to an English rival. If you want the honest truth, though, the whole affair still left a very bad taste.

After Michael flew into the Spanish sunset, he never seemed to get a start – at least not with the three galácticos Figo, Ronaldo and Raul all fit and ready to play up front. The English striker scored with embarrassing ease from the Real bench, but when he eventually did get to start, he just couldn't convert and was often substituted. Michael's frustration was evident, and his treatment was greeted with a mixture of mystification, as well as some gloating, back on Merseyside. Real then brought in *two* new expensive attacking Brazilians – Baptista (also fancied by Arsenal) and Robinho – and no forward or midfield player moved the other way. Something had to give. Like Macca – though the Bootle man toughed it out and stayed in Spain – it soon became clear that the England hero was now seen by Real mainly as a means of making a fast buck. And Owen's departure was required to fund the new arrivals from Brazil. You pretty much know the rest. Michael wanted to return to England, and to Anfield, but mainly because he wanted to rev up for his expected international appearances in a World Cup year: 'I had to look after my England place, and I had to look after myself.' Few Reds were exactly happy with this sort of talk, but most nevertheless wanted to see him back in a Red No. 10 shirt. We waited.

With Souness already floundering among the Geordies and Real demanding £12 million for Owen, a desperate Freddy Shepherd then came up with what seemed like a ludicrously bullish (and unnecessary) £17 million Newcastle bid. Unsurprisingly, Real insisted that Michael either go to the Black and Whites or else return to play dugout poker once more at Real. It was no contest, and there were no happy endings, Owen parking himself in football's never-never land in the North East. This was a rather different and more complicated story, of course, than what the *Daily Telegraph*'s usually astute Henry Winter described later as Rafa Benítez's 'bizarre decision not to re-sign Michael Owen'. On the brink of his return to Anfield, Michael's own newspaper column in *The Times* was headlined 'No embarrassment, no guilt . . . and no regrets'. This did Owen no favours. Nor did an assertion in the article itself: 'If I score in my Anfield return, I will celebrate as joyfully as ever.' Why say this? As another newspaper headline put it, 'Owen returns to Anfield with steel in his heart.' All this rather grated. But what really hurt, as we watched the drink-sodden Geordie hordes arrive in the pubs in L4 sporting their gold-lettered 'Owen 10' shirts and singing their stupid little 'Oooooowen' songs, was that back in 2005 Michael – again like Macca before him – had obviously preferred to stash an extra few million quid he didn't really need than do right by the local club that had nurtured and developed his talents, or by the fans who had trekked loyally in his wake. This was not easily forgotten.

All of this intrigue added real vim to the Xmas meeting with Newcastle, and at kick-off time the Kop was positively brimming with malevolent determination. So it was not a complete surprise – but still a tad disappointing – that when Michael made his first pass *against* Liverpool on the green carpet he once graced in red, he actually drew real boos from parts of the Kop. A 'shocked' Steven Gerrard said later that the fans should be more grateful for what his England friend had done for Liverpool. But there was a mix of fear, contempt and frustration expressed here, with some Reds fans convinced that Owen actually chose *both* Real and Newcastle over Liverpool – and, of course, they saw those choices as unacceptable betrayals. There was also a harsh truth contained in some of this censure, because Owen will surely be wasting his gifts at St James' Park. He will score goals there, but he will also be working at a club whose fans positively celebrate their own mediocrity. He will little put up with that for long.

As this amusing little soap opera played out, we quickly saw the definitive Benítez answer to all those who questioned his apparent reluctance to lay out really big money and re-sign the arch goal snatcher. A vibrant Liverpool, stirred by all the Owen talk, thundered forward from the start, and Steven Gerrard soon burst onto a Crouch lay-off and ploughed into that familiar penalty-area inside-right channel that Owen used to call his own, before shooting high and beyond the gallant Shay Given at the Anfield Road end. Crouch himself sealed the bloodless win in the first half with a header that Given fumbled over the goal line. You see, Rafa thought he had an antidote to Owen: he wanted a new type of Valencia-like division of labour at L4, with the whole Liverpool team to take more responsibility for delivering goals. He expected five or six guys to come up with ten goals or more, rather than an injury-haunted Owen-type figure contributing maybe twenty – if he stayed fit. Gerrard and the previously goal-shy Crouch would probably do their scoring share; we could see that already. But would Liverpool also suffer occasionally – as they did in Japan – because they lacked a real poacher like Owen?

And Michael: how did he respond to all this baiting (alongside a weak half-time cheer from the Kop when the points were already assured) and the overwhelming Liverpool dominance? The stark answer was that he didn't really put it in; he didn't try too hard. This may have been, in part, a wily professional's defence: why waste energy and give the locals the extra satisfaction? But maybe it was also a way of showing some 'respect' for what he left behind. 'Look at me,' he might have been saying now. 'I can't bring myself to damage Liverpool.' But the truth of it was probably slightly different. That this was another signal of the late-Michael playing persona, the one that waits for chances to be served up, à la carte, rather than the one that worries endlessly at defenders and chivvies his midfield partners to deliver up something better. This Newcastle side – shorn of Emre, Scott Parker and Kieron Dyer – was quite incapable of offering its forwards anything to chew on. So Michael basically downed tools. At the end he sloped away, seemingly thankful it was all over. But there will be other occasions when Liverpool Football Club may not escape his attentions quite as easily. Injury with England also ruined Owen's 2006–07 Newcastle United campaign, and in the summer of 2007 media talk began to stir once more, encouraged by Scousers and fellow England men Steven Gerrard and Jamie Carragher, that Owen might even return to Anfield as Benítez itched to spend his US dowry.

DISHING UP DIRT AT THE DERBY

The Merseyside derby at Goodison Park was a 28 December 2005 Xmas treat. It explored wildly divergent fortunes on each side of Stanley Park. As reborn Liverpool confidently marched on – eight straight league wins without a single goal conceded – near neighbours Everton were in free fall once more. Already ejected out of *two* European competitions and the Carling Cup, the league offered little solace to these suddenly serial failers under the steely-eyed David Moyes. The Blues were tottering towards the relegation zone: their latest Premiership contests had both ended up 0–4, against Bolton and Villa respectively. They had already lost by the same score at mighty West Brom, so the opponents-who-have-recently-trashed-Everton club was by no means exclusive. And, as if this draining leakage of goals was not bad enough, the Goodison men had also forgotten how to score themselves, with both Tim Cahill and the new man James Beattie parched in front of goal. So when Moyes publicly rallied his troops before this vital clash it rang rather hollow, sounding more like a cry of desperation than a really convincing Blue call to arms.

Apart from the usual derby bile between the fans – with Evertonians even more stoked up than usual following events in Istanbul and their ultimately 'wasted' battle the previous season to beat Liverpool to the fourth Champions League spot – the big pre-match football talking point concerned the contested Mali international Mo Sissoko. Everton had all but signed the spindly 20-year-old Valencia midfielder before Rafa Benítez muscled in – as Houllier had once done with John Arne Riise and Fulham – to lay down a whopping £5.6 million bid for a man he had originally signed as a forward from Auxerre. 'We knew that Everton were talking to him, but it was easy for us to make the signing,' Benítez said, his plain English making him sound dangerously contemptuous for once. Everton certainly fumed at Liverpool's larcenous audacity. Naturally, the spindly Sissoko had few doubts about his latest move – not once his ex-boss in Spain came calling, trailing the European Cup. 'Any player in the world would have done the same as me,' he said. But he now expected a rough ride from the Blue faithful whom he had spurned to join their sworn enemies. Regardless, it was clear that the young Malian would now strengthen Liverpool's, and not Everton's, hand in the battle to come.

Battle? What a thread to follow. Because although most of the players in this most local of football contests are no longer drawn from the city of Liverpool – or even from Britain – this match, populated by Spaniards and French, Africans and Portuguese, was still a bruising whirlwind of an encounter. It boasted more red cards shown than in any other Premiership match-up in recent years. 'The fastest 20 minutes of the season,' said Steven Gerrard, talking about the typical start to the derby. 'You end up with some cuts and bruises on your knees, and then you can start playing as things settle down.' This intensity is not even replicated when Barça meet Real.

Much of the historical rivalry between the clubs still comes from the fans, of course, and even the short trip across the freezing Stanley Park for the match that night felt like a tribal exchange of the kind mirrored everywhere across the globe. It could be a Croatian intrusion into Serbian strongholds; or a Sevilla excursion into the heartlands of Real Betis; or else the coming together of the Italian football tribes of Inter and AC Milan in their uneasily shared stadium space of the San Siro. In the recent turbulent meeting of these Italian dynasties in Milan the Inter fans have predictably revelled in Liverpool's Istanbul victory over their hated housemates, producing huge banners charting the Reds' second-half comeback: '1–3, 2–3, 3–3: Grazie Liverpool!' Internet images of this gloating have been widely circulated among Liverpool loyalists ever since.

Deep cruelty like this, aimed at your closest football rivals, offers sickly satisfaction. Of course, quite horrible things could be heard from the other side and from our own grizzly following that Goodison evening. What can you do but suck in your cheeks, or else chuckle at the sweet black invention of it all? The next day we could return to more 'civilised' values; that evening it was all ugly necessity, a desperate search for the vital upper hand against local rival fans who you might have to face later in work or in the alehouse – and for victory.

Differently from Liverpool in the late-Houllier period, or even under early Benítez, Liverpool captain Steven Gerrard could also now identify the necessary relish for battle in the Liverpool playing ranks. 'I look around the dressing-room, pre-kick-off, now, and I can see a will to win in people's eyes,' he said. 'What we have got is a gang of very hungry players. When you've got that desire in a dressing-room, you've got a winning mixture. It makes you proud to be a Liverpool player.' Gerrard's nod to a 'gang' was no accident: it hinted at the necessary blood trusts, a willingness to lay your body on the line for your mates, of the kind that all successful football teams need. This applies whether you are playing pick-up on a local field or else tottering at 0–3 down in the European Cup final.

None is more willing or more committed than the local man and ex-Evertonian Jamie Carragher. 'I love derbies, absolutely love them,' he said. 'The derby is my favourite game, especially at Goodison. It's like a cauldron, and I love it. To get a result there in that atmosphere is extra special. The stick I get doesn't bother me. It brings out the best in me and makes me want to win even more. It was probably worse a few years ago, when I used to play full-back. I was taking throw-ins then, and trying to get the ball back was a bit of a nightmare.'

Do you like his understatement? 'A bit of a nightmare.' It hides a lot. Remember your own worst school or junior football experience? Maybe it is some scraggy touchline junior psychos reassuring you as you took a throw-in or a corner that you were surely 'dead' if you scored or if you happened, by some dreadful accident, to win the match. Multiply that sort of playground abuse by about 100 – or maybe even 1,000 – and you may get close to what some professionals deal with today. Watch the home crowd begin to boil and ferment as, say, Steven Gerrard runs over to take a corner at the Gwladys Street end. It's not just the stuff thrown at him – the pies, burgers, coins and the rest – but the routine outpourings of hatred you get on these occasions. Footballers have to take some terrible stick from opposing tribes – perhaps even about their family or kids. Why? Maybe simply because you changed clubs, Michael Owen-style. Or else because you just happen to play for the Red side of the city, rather than the Blue. (Or vice versa, because Reds are as bad as Blues.) And the players have to take it all, this kind of assault, and not even smile back at their tormenters lest they 'provoke' another even more brutal crowd response.

In Spain the football fan imagination can run even wilder. Famously, when the winger and Portuguese international Luís Figo first returned to Barcelona, now wearing the hated white of Real Madrid, the locals threw a pig's head at him. A pig's head! In the end the bemused and frightened Figo stopped taking corner kicks – the debris raining down on the field simply became too much either to stomach or to clear.

There were no animal heads on show at Goodison that evening, but there was little obvious respect between these supposedly 'friendly' local rivals, at least not *off* the pitch. But the chaos outside Goodison was soon forgotten (by us) because within seventeen scorching minutes Liverpool were already ahead. Crouch (paired with Cissé) and then Gerrard knifed through the centre of Everton's porous defence to put Liverpool 2–0 up. About 500 angry Blues immediately vacated the Park End to our left, never to return.

These are the best, the real escapist, moments in key matches such as the one that night: the necessarily brief spasms when numbing, twitch-inducing pressure is momentarily replaced by sheer gloating pleasure. Away from home it is like despoiling a hated rival's wedding party, messing up their mansion, tearing down their decorations. All this is laid bare in the barbed singing and heartless finger-pointing at dejected rivals, as well as in the clinching comfort of Red strangers suddenly made friends. The gloom and despair opposite only feeds your own excesses.

Predictably, this moment of ecstasy soon passed, exchanged for torment once more. Apparently undaunted, and with their visitors visibly relaxing, it was Everton who continued to press bravely forward in the first half, especially on Liverpool's left side where the inexperienced Warnock had clearly been targeted for close attention from both Mikel Arteta and the clever Tim Cahill. Crosses rained in from that position and one near half-time from the cultured and spiky Spaniard reached Kevin Kilbane at the far post. He beat Finnan in the air and, via Simon Davies, lobbed the ball to the six-yard-box man James Beattie (described unkindly in the Blues' fanzine *When Skies are Grey* that evening as having a 'club foot'). Astonishingly, Beattie twisted to head the ball gently past both Carragher and a static José Reina – and into the Liverpool net. Hold the front page, for it is a sensation: a league goal for *this* Everton and against *this* Liverpool defence. It put the home club right back in the match.

So, half-time was less a period for calming reflection and cruel Blue-baiting in the Liverpool zones than it was one for barely suppressed anxiety. It was also a time for a rousing battle plan shouted out, no doubt, in the Everton dressing-room. They would surely come out renewed and lifted by the crowd in the second half, buoyed by their late success. But, as it turned out, the fiery Moyes might as well have saved his breath and torn up his little speech. Because within two minutes of the restart, the unpredictable Cissé, freed by Harry Kewell, blundered past David Weir on Everton's right and calmly, for once, threaded a shot home from a tight angle low down to Nigel Martyn's left. As the Frenchman slalomed in celebration towards his delirious Red supplicants at the Bullens Road end, his goal signalled hundreds more early departures from the Park End.

And at a seemingly definitive 3–1 for Liverpool – and with almost a full half left to play – Momo Sissoko, the once near-Blue, started to demonstrate his defensive worth for the Reds. His physical presence suckered in Neville for a deserved sending off before he expertly marshalled the barricades in front of the visitors' back four. There was still time for Arteta to collect his own marching orders and to slouch past his manager earlier than he had planned.

At the final whistle a fist-pumping Jamie Carragher could now confidently look forward to his next visit to his old local, the Blue 'Solly' pub, out in bandit country in the Marsh Lane area of Bootle. Similarly, for departing Liverpudlians the sheer blackness of Stanley Park now felt more like a welcoming velvet cloak than it did a threatening possible post-match battle landscape, even as the Merseyside police helicopter above fired down balls of white light to mark out places around Goodison Road where Blues and Reds were exchanging more than the usual hearty mutual congratulations on a match very well contested. There was no peace any more after the Merseyside derby, as there might have been in the days of Elisha Scott and Dixie Dean. In the end it all meant three more Liverpool points comfortably acquired and more Blue relegation-talk gloom.

BRYAN AND SAM, THE MANAGER MEN

Three days after the derby triumph at Everton, and in the middle of a four-match festive-period slog, Rafa Benítez fielded a surprisingly strong Liverpool team at home to face a much weakened one from West Bromwich Albion on New Year's Eve. Days later Liverpool would face a really tough test at high-flying Bolton, so why risk a strong side here, especially when WBA's manager Bryan Robson saved some of his own best men for an early 2006 home derby with Villa? As it was, we got the 'first-choice' Liverpool defence, plus Alonso, Gerrard and some key forwards all playing again, a mysterious and unnecessary caution against these opponents, especially for a home manager who actually favoured squad rotation. In front of a brain-dead and silent Kop a single second-half goal, from Crouch (again), was enough to seal the contest. The visitors, shorn of all recognisable forwards, offered no discernible threat at all. Three more points gained but would Liverpool now suffer in the Reebok Stadium? We would have to wait and see.

On a darkening Lancashire afternoon in Bolton, Liverpool opted for a decidedly defensive midfield pairing of Sissoko and Hamann – a first in the league – whilst the little-used physical presence of Djimi Traoré returned at left-back. In the absence of the injured Morientes, the also unconvincing Sinama-Pongolle started alongside Crouch. This meant that four of the more creative, regular Liverpool first-teamers – Alonso, Riise, García and Cissé – were on the bench, and Steven Gerrard was plonked wide on the right when we were more likely to need him directing affairs from the middle. Let's just say it was a gamble. To be really critical, it looked like a team that could – perhaps should – have been fielded days earlier at Anfield for a gentle holiday home stroll, rather than for a full-on 'three-falls' contest here. The Liverpool manager was clearly preparing for a bruising aerial battle, so he had involved plenty of his own six-footers. But where, exactly, was the *invention* going to come from in this formation – the key that would be needed to unlock a hulking Bolton defence? The 'mix-and-match' Sinama-Pongolle and Crouch combination looked half-baked and was untried.

On a grey sponge pudding of a pitch, with a dead bounce, we got exactly what we expected from Bolton. Forget the 'new science' at the Reebok – yoga, dance, psychologists, computers and a vast medical back-up – the Wanderers were no modern 'Fancy Dans' at all. Despite all the media talk about Big Sam as an England prospect, a man who was making bricks out of straw, Wanderers were a team mainly made up of physically uncompromising guys who would fish for free-kicks, throw-ins and any other dead-ball opportunities they could use to break your resistance. Sam Allardyce – with Liverpool's Sammy Lee now on his staff, a man breaking away from a career's worth of more sophisticated work – aimed at producing a non-stop, wearing pressure that had often done for Liverpool before and had already comfortably seen off Wenger's timid Arsenal at the Reebok during the 2005–06 season.

Bolton's main forward weapons were the unlamented ex-Red El Hadji Diouf, a man for whom no swan dive seemed too outrageous, and the square-shouldered Kevin Davies, who convincingly seemed to reason that his uncompromising 'style' would gain as many promising free-kicks as he conceded thoroughly useless ones. Needless to say, it was quite horrible to watch, a calculated and frustrating procession of fouls and stoppages, the ball humped forward by Liverpool (to Crouch) and by Bolton (to Davies), with the canny Diouf in an apparently ceaseless search for preferred locations upon which he could deposit his gravity-fixated frame. Carra was soon abusing the familiar Senegal man after a few of these belly flops had conned the usually reliable referee Mark Clattenberg. But it was actually another dubious touchline foul, by Finnan on Stelios Giannakopoulos, which produced the free-kick that led to Bolton's first goal. An unchallenged Pepe Reina dropped an easy high ball in the box, and Hyypiä also failed to clear. In short it was a defensive mess – and in an awful first half.

As the early evening mist hovered threateningly over the Reebok, and with Liverpool now a goal behind, even Benítez could see that more than sheer grunt was probably required to break down the hosts. Alonso replaced Hamann in the second half, and maybe it was this that inspired Harry Kewell to thread his own Xabi-style pass inside the green Bolton full-back O'Brien for Steven Gerrard to chase. The Liverpool man was just too quick and strong for the youngster, who was panicked into fouling him – inside the penalty area. His victim scored easily from the spot, in front of the now roused Liverpool faithful. But Diouf was determined to have his day, and he quickly restored Bolton's lead by bundling in Davies's left-wing low cross, with Finnan mysteriously missing from his right-back berth. Back came Liverpool once more, García (on for the anonymous Sinama-Pongolle) now chesting a delicately chipped Alonso pass beyond Gardner before thrashing a low left-footed shot inside Jussi Jääskeläinen's near post for the equaliser. Phew.

Two-all, honours even, but Liverpool were still searching for a winning goal and cast in the unlikely role of the double equalisers, a situation that was almost unimaginable under the past regime or even during the previous season. The Reds under Benítez in 2004–05 would have, indisputably, fallen under the same circumstances that they faced in Bolton. When the Liverpool 'creatives' had finally been unleashed, the visitors took charge, but it was too late for victory. Later Sam Allardyce was visibly upset by Benítez's post-match complaints about Bolton's playing style and about all those (unnamed) home players who embraced 'diving'. This meant that the big Lancastrian had to dream up some of his own stuff about Liverpool's 'dirty play' – which was soon dismissed as phooey by the referee and even by his own players. Sam actually looked quite sad under this sort of attack. He seemed worried that he might be perceived as a football dinosaur when he obviously thought of himself – no matter how misguided this might be – as a serious student and real strategist of the beautiful game. Tellingly, both Hidetoshi Nakata and Jay-Jay Okocha, Bolton's talented playmakers, had been reduced to the bench in recent matches, as their manager sought results. Notwithstanding Big Sam's troubles, most Liverpool fans would have settled for ten points out of the Xmas twelve, even if taking the last one from Bolton's Horwich HQ had proved as frustrating and difficult as nailing jelly to a wall. It also confirmed that Rafa Benítez had learned plenty from his first troubling season in England.

RAFA'S HALF-TERM REPORT

So what had so improved Liverpool's Premiership showing in the first half of 2005–06, with only one game lost away from home? The list of reasons was a long one.

1. The increased knowledge and experience of Benítez and his staff was definitely one positive development. Gone was the Spanish assumption that some away trips in the Premiership were simply 'gimmes' for a club of Liverpool's size. They now knew exactly what

was required on all trips away from Anfield; there were no more hidden trap doors.

2. The early Liverpool Carling Cup defeat at Palace in 2005 finally proved that most of the club's youngsters still didn't make the grade at that level, so they soon disappeared from the first-team frame. This group was distinctive from the 21-strong nominated Liverpool first-team squad. The latter now included only Warnock and Sinama-Pongolle from the younger Liverpool crop, and, as in Spain, first-team players would only play reserve football when returning from serious injury. Rafa was also judging his young players much more severely that season – and more accurately.

3. A Valencia-like defensive solidarity had become the new key for Liverpool, especially after the poor early performances and results at both Birmingham and Fulham. The new Spanish goalkeeper Pepe Reina had been generally sound – and much more communicative – and there had been much less player rotation generally, but especially at the back, where Traoré and Josemi had been used only sparingly. Admittedly, the manager had also been hugely fortunate with match fitness in his central defence, where cover was thinnest. Carragher had been brilliantly consistent and only once, against Chelsea at home, did Sami Hyypiä's fitness dip: Liverpool were duly thrashed.

4. Benítez had also had four talented and combative midfield players simultaneously at his disposal for the first time. Again, this was a lesson from Valencia. These players had offered vital strength and consistency at all times in the middle of the park, as compared to the 2004–05 season – Momo Sissoko for the erratic Igor Bišćan, for example. This was an absolute key requisite for domestic play in England, where you often have to grind out away victories.

5. Rafa had already pointed to another of the key issues: signing players who had more obviously 'English' characteristics in their make-up – work rate, strength, stamina, physique and commitment – such as Sissoko, Zenden, Reina and Crouch. This had proved to be a major cultural shift. All these recruits had some quality and were

good trainers – honest professionals. This had been crucial to the Liverpool cause and had added a real 'British' solidity to the squad, which now had few obvious weaknesses.

6. The imported Spanish players had also had more time to adapt culturally to England and to the sheer pace and physicality of the English game: they, mostly, looked much more at home, and their concentration and fitness levels had become much more attuned to the high tempo of top football in the Premiership. Benítez was asked by the Spanish press in 2005 if the English game was too 'traditional' for Spanish players, whether there was a danger that they might be rejected in England. 'No,' he replied, 'for several reasons.' Benítez argued that the English league had changed from the time of the Bosman ruling in 1995. 'Fans have not only gotten used to the presence of foreigners, but they have also seen that their influence has been crucial in the successes of Arsenal, the Manchester United of Cantona or van Nistelrooy, or at Chelsea. The important thing is having good players. If they are English, it is better still.' This was all true. But what did the new Spaniards bring to the English game? 'My interest is that the Spaniards contribute what is necessary for the progression of the team,' said Benítez, 'but with the maximum care taken to maintain the very best of English football. For me, this is the perfect balance. I want our game to be focused and also direct, even more so in a team like Liverpool that, for many years, was not really like an English one. I refer to their style of play, to their search for possession of the ball as a fundamental aspect of the game – to the inheritance of Bill Shankly.' Ah, Shankly – this young coach knew his Liverpool history. He went on, 'Intelligent players such as Xabi Alonso, Morientes or Luis García, they can add the necessary subtlety without contradicting the essence of English football.' He was stretching it there – Morientes was hardly a success and García had his critics – but basically this made sense: Spanish vision with English heart.

7. Playing forward players who could battle for and hold the ball higher up the field, especially away from home – such as Crouch,

occasionally Morientes and even Gerrard – had allowed the whole Liverpool unit to play further up the pitch. This had reduced pressure on the Liverpool midfield and defence. Much more of the general play away from home now took place in the opponents' half, and Liverpool kept the ball much better than they did in the first Benítez season, increasing confidence and improving decision making.

8. Benítez had also used his growing personal confidence and his much improved language skills and knowledge of English clubs and their players to make more and better tactical adjustments, a point made strongly by Luis García. He said, 'I think the manager has had to change some of his methods to suit the game here. He has maintained the main things, such as work rate in training and out on the pitch, but I think he is more adaptable now, depending on the opposition. He didn't use to do it as much, but now he might go from 4–2–3–1 to 4–4–2 or 5–2–3.' For García, Benítez was now a better manager than when he had arrived in England: 'He learns from his experiences all the time. He knows more about the other teams and players in England this season, and so he can manage our team much better.' García was right. Benítez was certainly managing his resources more efficiently, and he was making changes on the pitch more out of choice and less out of panic or necessity.

9. Benítez and the squad had gained the full confidence in 2005 of key players, especially the club captain Steven Gerrard. Largely gone now were the Huyton man's drooping shoulders and often negative body language of 2004–05. His personal chemistry with Benítez seemed to have improved since the summer confusion. He also seemed much more convinced since Istanbul and the summer signings that Benítez was a rather different foreign coach from the failed Houllier. Gone, too, was Gerrard's overambition; he no longer tried to do other people's jobs while his own was poorly performed as a result. He looked more relaxed and happier on the field, a major change. This new Gerrard also signified the spread of a wider mutual trust among the Liverpool players in 2005: they believed in each other,

and in the club and its manager. They seemed convinced that the club could win trophies once more, the kind of mental strength that was central to future success.

10. Finally, keeping a large squad of experienced players largely fit in 2005–06 had been a critical boost to Liverpool. In Spain injury problems were less of a problem to Benítez because of the relative lack of physical intensity. He had had to learn quickly in England. It was sometimes easy to forget in the wake of Istanbul just how much Benítez and his staff had suffered from injuries in the previous campaign. In the 2005–06 season up to that point – and with a much stronger squad – only Kewell, Morientes and Bolo Zenden (a bad knee problem) had suffered serious injury. Apart from the last named, all his players were now fit as Liverpool faced the increased rigours of Europe and the second half of the domestic season. Benítez would need all his best players fully charged and ready to face what lay ahead.

As it turned out, this general improvement in Liverpool form was sustained after Christmas 2005, but building upon it for the following campaign was to prove beyond the Liverpool manager in the 2006–07 season when the fixture computer belched up a horrible early run of Liverpool away fixtures against the Premiership's elite clubs. Moreover, Benítez's new signings in the summer of 2006 – which were shaped, the manager argued later, by the club's inability to act decisively in the transfer market – failed to produce the form he had hoped for.

THE LONG HAUL HOME

With 35 fixtures already completed by Liverpool in 2005–06 – more than any other Premiership club – and with a possible 32 matches left to play (excluding any FA Cup replays), the coming months could prove to be a very busy period if the club was really successful. Some wild thoughts occurred at this point. Could Liverpool – as had been outrageously predicted by the prime rationalist Alan Hansen – actually win the European Cup *again* in 2006? The squad was better than the year before, after all. But could it possibly repeat the intensity and desire of the last European campaign in the face of quality opposition? And could Liverpool survive in Europe without a proven goal scorer? Even given the uncertainty at Real Madrid, the Spanish threat in Europe that year seemed more formidable – Barcelona, especially, looked daunting. Could Liverpool also reach the FA Cup final again, due to be held at Wembley in 2006? It would be ironic if they could win it after their Spanish manager seemed to rubbish the whole domestic cup concept back in 2004–05. Finally – the most unlikely prospect of all – could Liverpool make any inroads at all into Chelsea's league dominance, whilst still chasing their own Champions League place? Why not? To do so would mean Benítez drawing on the experiences that had hardened him in the game and led him to come to England in the first place. 'A manager can contribute many things to add to the role of the coach,' he told *El País*. 'But it is necessary that he is responsible. He is a very respected figure in England. That gives him enormous power. The problem is that the power tends to corrupt. It is necessary to keep clear from that temptation, to maintain firmly the right approaches. It is important to stay well clear of the idea that the manager is above the club. That is what I seek to do here.'

It was clear that Rafael Benítez had come to England for an entirely new challenge, a new direction. But the hard lessons he had learned in Spain between 2001 and 2004 would now be vital to his development as a successful Liverpool boss, one perhaps to rival even the great office-holders of Anfield's still-recent past. He knew football managers in England were vulnerable, of course – his immediate predecessor Gérard Houllier had once seemed as bombproof as Benítez would later appear to be at Liverpool. But Benítez also thought that the role of top football manager in England offered rather more stability and freedom to act than he had been used to at home.

It was back in 2001, the Red Treble year in which the Frenchman Houllier stamped his name indelibly on the list of great Liverpool managers, that the largely untried Rafa Benítez had taken on the coaching reins at a crestfallen Valencia CF. He followed in the footsteps of the gloomy Argentine Héctor Cúper, who could not convince either the Valencia board or its fans that he was worth saving, despite having taken the Spanish club to two consecutive Champions League finals. For the three extraordinary years that followed, Benítez, the most exciting young coach in the European game, would take his new club on a wonderful football adventure. It was one to better even the Houllier revolution that had been going on at distant Anfield. Valencia CF under Benítez would directly challenge the Barcelona–Real Madrid dominance of Spanish football and would even threaten to become Spain's modern powerhouse in the European game. Frankly, the future looked limitless for this new Valencia and their strong-minded and idealistic football leader. But even as he was collecting European honours and La Liga titles with his players, the ambitious young Spaniard understood something that would change his life and that of his family for ever. When he was at the height of his powers in Spain, the simple fact dawned on Benítez that he had never wanted to be *just* a hireling football coach. It was an epiphany, a realisation that would eventually bring him and his loved ones to a decimated old seaport in the North West of England, a place that would finally match in its intensity the Spaniard's own life-long obsession with football.

7

Call the Fire Brigade?
Rafa Benítez Joins Valencia CF

Searching for the perfect coach; Héctor Cúper's war with the
Mestalla; Rafa Benítez –who *is* that man? At odds with Valdano;
winning ways in the Canary Islands; Rafa Benítez, scientist
of football; Rafa and his backroom boys; Paco Ayestaran's
'Integral Coaching Method'.

HOPELESSLY LOOKING FOR A COACH (THE FOUR NEGATIVES)

May 2001 was a time for uninhibited celebration and a real sense of
renewal on the Red side of the city of Liverpool. It wasn't difficult
to see why. After all, *three* major trophies had been won by Liverpool
Football Club for the first time since 1984, one of them in Europe. In
three years Liverpool manager Gérard Houllier had seemingly swept
the Anfield stables clean and now looked ahead to future Premiership
and European Cup challenges as the undisputed master of all he
surveyed in L4.

And why not be hugely ambitious, even in this era of marketing
millions and global super-clubs, an elite group to which the 'new'
Liverpool could still only aspire? After all, Liverpool Football Club
also had its great heritage to draw upon to add strength and substance
to the Continental technocratic revolution already under way at
Anfield. Houllier was certainly aware of Liverpool FC's cultural
power, and he valued the club's history – if he later felt haunted by

it. And had not a previously unconsidered club in Spain actually reached the final of Europe's premier football tournament for the past *two* successive seasons? So why not, the argument went in 2001, Liverpool Football Club?

Strangely perhaps, and in total contrast to the sense of unity and purpose that seemed to be bursting out of every pore at a rejuvenated Anfield, May 2001 was actually a period of unsettling uncertainty and considerable disturbance at just that Spanish club, Valencia CF. Here was a club that could now boast two consecutive European Cup finals to its name, despite having little of the financial power of its main domestic rivals; but, ultimately, all Valencia had to show for the experience was two confidence-draining defeats. Some top players at the club had also begun to listen to those who argued that the Valencianistas had had their chance – that if these almost-stars wanted to be truly successful, then they needed to understand that their own futures now lay elsewhere. In a psychodrama for Valencia fans, midfielder Gaizka Mendieta – the team's 'leader' – followed the example of Claudio López and the Spaniard Gerard, who had both departed in 2000, by leaving the club after the 2001 final, bound for Lazio. The move hardly paid off. In fact, none of these players matched their Valencia achievements at their new clubs. The Valencia coach Héctor Cúper, frustrated by these near misses in Europe and also by his treatment from the stands by some at the Mestalla who frothed that he had brought too much defensive caution to their club, was already waving goodbye to Spain himself. He was soon to disappear into the black hole that has swallowed up a raft of coaches at the failing stronghold of Inter Milan over the past 30 years.

Although we little knew it then, Gérard Houllier, far from being immovable and on the brink of greatness, had actually already reached the height of his powers at Liverpool Football Club. There would be neither league titles nor further major European glory at Anfield during his reign. Illness would intervene. And despite his great achievements at Liverpool in 2001, the complex Frenchman would soon alienate many of the Liverpool faithful and local media commentators, and be revealed as a manager who ultimately had feet of clay.

Meanwhile, far from being the end of an interlude of near-greatness at Valencia CF, it was actually the beginning of a brief era of fantastic success at the Mestalla. Even before the Champions League final of 2001 Héctor Cúper had already made his new deal in Italy. So, the Valencia club would play their second final under a coach already committed to pastures new. Rumours thus began to circulate in Spain about his successor. It was widely claimed that the Basque coach Javier 'Jabo' Irureta would be the next incumbent. Jabo Irureta had already broached the matter with Augusto César Lendoiro, his president at Deportivo de La Coruña. Irureta, a rather downbeat but shrewd tactician, had led Deportivo to the Spanish title as recently as 2000, but now he seemed to want a new challenge. Publicly, he never denied that other clubs in Spain 'interested' him – including Valencia CF. In fact, this was the second time that the Valencianistas had made an offer to Irureta. The first had been a decade earlier, when he was considered as a candidate to replace the Uruguayan coach Víctor Espárrago.

The new Irureta lobby at VCF actually grew stronger when José Manuel 'Mané' Esnal, coach of the gallant Alavés side that Liverpool had just beaten (5–4) in the 2001 UEFA Cup final, was also approached by Valencia about their vacancy in a sounding-out process. But Mané soon confirmed that he had no interest at all in moving to the Mestalla. Why should he? Mané confessed that he enjoyed the relative tranquillity and low-pressure environment of the north, where he also felt – unusually for Spain – in control, secure and well supported by his board. He had noted Valencia's recent achievements, sure, but he had also looked closely at the through traffic in coaching jobs at the Mestalla over the past decade, and he had no plans, thanks very much, to be its latest victim.

This negativity on the part of Mané, coupled with the reticence of Cúper and the relative diffidence of Irureta, now sparked suspicions in Spain that the Valencia job was fraught with unseen difficulties: *un hueso duro de roer* (a hard bone to gnaw). Officially, Mané rejected Valencia's offer because he was enjoying the sweetest time of his career with Alavés. But four years earlier, he had abandoned Valencia's local rivals Levante UD because he had felt unsettled by what he called 'too much interference' from people inside the club. He suspected the position was the same now at the Mestalla, where Juan Carlos Rodriguez was the technical secretary. But above him was the sport director at the club, the real fixer at Valencia CF, Jesús García Pitarch – *un hombre de la casa* – a longstanding Valencianistas servant.

The surprise refusal of Mané to even consider the Mestalla job caused consternation at VCF, who now tried to get Héctor Cúper to reconsider his decision to leave. Cúper had built Valencia CF into a defensively resilient *contragolpe* (counter-attacking) team with very quick forward players, especially the destructive Claudio López, VCF's equivalent of Michael Owen. When López left in 2000, his work was taken up by the brilliant Pablo Aimar, the in-form forward Juan Sánchez and Vicente Rodríguez, a talented left-winger who had risen through the Valencia junior ranks. Before the 2001 Champions League final Cúper had said that he trusted in this combination of solid defence and the capacity of his key attacking players to improvise and score goals. But the Argentinian clearly had trouble getting the balance exactly right, between being secure at the back and being threatening up front, a conundrum that arguably sealed Valencia's fate in the 2001 Champions League final.

Strangely, this penalty shoot-out defeat to Bayern Munich might have been expected to *aid* a little in the increasingly difficult task of filling the managerial vacancy at the Mestalla. After all, being European champions would mean that the only way was down for a new coach – and who would possibly be able to improve on Cúper's achievements and also manage expectations among Valencia's fans? An honourable defeat suggested, instead, a highly talented core of key players at the Mestalla that could go on to do even better things under the right coach.

Boosted by Champions League cash, Valencia president Pedro Cortés now formally offered the still-reluctant Irureta an annual salary of 300 million pesetas (1.8 million euros), way above what he was earning at Deportivo. Irureta refused again a few days after the San Siro defeat for Valencia CF, declaring that he was definitely staying in Coruña, having piloted Deportivo to Champions League qualification once more. Valencia themselves had no Champions League slot secured for 2001–02. Irureta privately thought that the Mestalla club could now be on the slide. Many people seemed to agree with him.

By this stage the beaten European Cup finalists Valencia CF had not one but *four* managerial negatives to contend with. The first was that Héctor Cúper was leaving the club after two pretty successful years at the Mestalla, mainly because he had failed to connect well with the demanding Valencia fans. The second was that Mané, the great alternative, had backed out of a proposed move to the club, choosing to stay instead at little Alavés and thus stirring rumours about the dangers of the coaching job at Valencia. The third was that Irureta had been offered buckets more money than he was earning at Deportivo but was staying in Coruña nevertheless. And there was a fourth negative. It was that old Valencia favourite Luis Aragonés, 'the Sage of Hortaleza', had also turned the club down.

Aragonés had coached modest Mallorca to third place in La Liga in 2001, the best finish in the club's history, and also to a Champions League spot. This was an extraordinary success story. But neither Valencia nor Mallorca could lay claim to Aragonés's skills and leadership for the *following* season: he had already pledged himself to his *club de toda la vida* (club for life) Atlético Madrid, who were then fighting for promotion from the Spanish Second Division. Perhaps this was the hardest blow of all for the blanquinegros to take – being rejected for a team that would eventually fail even to win promotion to the top flight of the Spanish game in 2001. What was so unattractive, exactly, about the coach's job at the Mestalla?

The rejections by Irureta and Mané probably gave the biggest clue.

Valencia CF, to these coaches at least, seemed to offer a climate of near-permanent internal conflict, in contrast to the relative security they enjoyed in the rather less pretentious clubs that currently employed them. This situation could only get worse at the Mestalla, they reasoned, because expectations were now so high at Valencia after the club's recent adventures in the Champions League. Also, why were the Valencian fans so critical of Héctor Cúper when the Argentinian had taken the club to *two* Champions League finals? Who could satisfy these dilettante supporters, especially given the loss of the emblematic Gaizka Mendieta to Italy? Lastly – and a little more obscurely – the absence of Paco Roig, the club's major shareholder, from the Valencia board caused uncertainty among prospective coaches. The best working atmosphere for the notoriously insecure coaching positions at Spanish football clubs tended to be that where a strong personal bond existed between the president–owner and the coach, of a type that offered the latter at least some protection from excessive external pressures. But how could this arrangement operate at Valencia CF when some of the real power brokers involved actually remained outside the club?

These four managerial negatives, coupled with the second Champions League final loss, now sank the Valencia club into a veritable swamp of despondency. A faction on the club's board even talked about trying to bring back Claudio Ranieri, but the Italian still had three years to run on his contract with Chelsea, and he showed few signs of wanting to leave Stamford Bridge. More Valencia players now became restive, with speculation that forward Kily González was leaving for Juventus, Inter, Lazio or even FC Barcelona, depending upon which paper you read. Daniel Pasarella, former coach of Argentina and Uruguay, was now offered to the blanquinegros, and the Spanish press came up with the name of the Brazilian Wanderley Luxemburgo, then at Corinthians, as well as the Dutchman Ronald Koeman, the Italian Marcelo Lippi and the little known Argentinian coach Carlos Bianchi. Bianchi had worked successfully at Boca Juniors, and he had his supporters among the Valencia players. But he had never worked in Europe, and the Valencia board was still determined to try to appoint a *Spanish* coach if they could, reasoning that the new man might settle down more quickly and also get on better with the Mestalla fans than did the sometimes morose Argentinian Cúper. But surely this poor chemistry between Cúper and the fans was not the only reason why the Argentinian had departed his post? Maybe there *was* a real problem at the heart of the Valencia club.

WHY DID HÉCTOR CÚPER LEAVE VCF?

Although his relationship with the Valencian fans was far from sweet, the real reasons why Héctor Cúper left Valencia CF were actually professional ones. Cúper had two problems: the first was that he wanted to have more of an active say in the policy of selecting and signing players at VCF. At Valencia, this business was done at the executive level and little involved the coach. And the other was that Cúper didn't want to be constantly second-guessed by the Valencia board about his decisions. He couldn't understand why the club's directors endlessly discussed, over their lunch and dinner tables, the players that the club should or should not sign. He thought – like most coaches working in Britain might – that these sorts of debates were for club professionals and the technical staff only. Cúper was angered when the club's directors questioned his methods after what seemed like every Valencia defeat. Who was in charge of this team, anyway? In his departing comments Cúper revealingly said, 'When somebody works in a club, he has to have total support. To continue to work here was to take a risk, not because the ambitions were high . . . but because there are people here that have no patience.'

Cúper was also frustrated by local accusations that he was an overly conservative coach – that he was showing little respect for Valencia's traditions and history. So he responded by calling for radical changes within the club to show he really could move Valencia forward. His ideas were not welcomed. Cúper wanted to get rid of the sporting commission on the club board, and he wanted all football policy decisions to be made not by club directors but by the coach and his professional staff. He wanted a football *manager's* right to sign, select and direct his own players. In Spain, he was actually asking for the world.

In the end Cúper left for Italy after just two years and after taking Valencia CF to the very brink of European football greatness – he was not unhappy to leave. And now Valencia CF could find no suitable replacement for the man many of the club's fans loved to hate. They would have to gamble. On 31 May 2001 – not even a week after the club's second consecutive Champions League final defeat – a new name began to appear in the Spanish press in association with the Valencia job. No one took much notice, to be honest. For the first time a young Spanish coach called Rafa Benítez was suggested as a surprise candidate to coach the great – if now troubled – Valencia CF. And the question slowly began to circulate amongst fans, journalists and directors in the sport in Spain: who, exactly, is this man Benítez?

RAFA BENÍTEZ? WHO *IS* THAT MAN?

In 2001 Rafael Benítez was not very well known in Spain, and he was pretty much a complete unknown outside the Spanish game. He certainly lacked both the glamour and experience of many of the coaches who had worked at Valencia CF in the previous three decades and more. Back in 1997 he had summed up the Valencia CF situation well: 'It is a club with great possibilities; it has almost everything. But it lacks calm.' Not much had changed since.

When he joined the club as their new manager, he was just 41 years old – some of the senior Valencia first-team squad were only just his junior by a few years. Benítez had no real playing record in the Spanish game to speak of: he was no Di Stéfano, nor a Valdano, a coach who had also been a great player. Benítez had signed for Real Madrid in 1972 as a 12-year-old midfielder and had come through the club's junior teams as an unspectacular but well organised young player. By his mid-teens he was already known as an obsessive thinker and strategist, often giving marks to his fellow players for their performance. In 1979 he travelled with the Spanish university squad to Mexico for the World University Games and suffered a serious ligament injury to his right knee. He never fully recovered, and although he played for Spanish lower-league clubs Parla and Linares up to the age of 26, he already knew that his main contribution to the game – if he had one to make at all – would be as a coach or a manager rather than as a player. Presciently, Benítez finished as a professional footballer in 1986 – just as Valencia CF were reaching their lowest ebb with relegation to the Second Division of the Spanish League. Both were in turmoil; neither knew that their paths were destined to cross 15 short years later.

For the next eight years, Benítez served his time at Real Madrid as a junior coach, even briefly acting as assistant to the temporary first-team coach Vicente del Bosque in 1993–94. When Real recruited the charismatic and intelligent Argentinian Jorge Valdano from Tenerife to take over as first-team coach, Benítez returned to reserve-team coaching duties with Real Madrid Castilla CF, Real's second-string side, in the Spanish Second Division. But he was soon in conflict with his first-team boss, a dispute that tells us a lot about the man. The free-thinking Valdano wanted Benítez to play some expansive and talented players in roles that were free from the shackles of any tactical plan. Benítez resisted strongly, wanting all of his players to work hard, fit the system and always fight for the team. Something had to give, and Valdano had the upper hand on this occasion because, although there was no success in Europe to speak of, his Real Madrid team won the Spanish title in 1995, thrashing Barcelona 5–0 in the process. Valdano was the toast of Madrid.

With the first-team manager's star in the ascendancy, Rafa Benítez left Madrid in the summer of 1995 to coach at Real Valladolid – a club he thought had been relegated to the Spanish Second Division. It had, but a very late decision to expand the Spanish League to 22 clubs – thus ruling out Valladolid's demotion – meant a rather different challenge was in store. The season's opener – his first as a coach outside Real Madrid – was against FC Barcelona rather than some obscure junior club. It was an unexpectedly tough baptism, and his new team unsurprisingly struggled throughout the season. Benítez held on and lasted until a midweek thumping in January 1996, when he was finally sacked. The club that inflicted the final wound, a 2–5 hammering, was Valencia CF.

Benítez next moved to ambitious Osasuna in the Spanish Second Division, in 1996, where he met fitness coach Paco Ayestaran: the two were inseparable in the sport from then on. A serious cash injection in Pamplona meant that his new club expected – demanded, even – immediate promotion. When this already looked in doubt after just seven games, Benítez was summarily sacked. It was a crazy decision – and it showed. Another three coaches were needed that season to save Osasuna, and its hapless president, from relegation.

Then, in 1997, Rafa moved to CF Extremadura in the Second Division, and he really started to show his mettle. Based in Almendralejo, a town of just 25,000 people, the bright young manager amazingly drove his new club to promotion at the first attempt. The obsessive focus he placed on preparation, fitness and attention to detail at his new club had really begun to kick in and show results. The co-tormentors Rafa and Paco flogged their players, demanding from them the highest possible levels of fitness, tactical awareness and knowledge of the opposition. The club's stars found themselves waking up in the middle of the night dreaming about a coordinated team response to losing the ball in the final third and about hours of video footage of their immediate opponents. And it very nearly did the trick. But little Extremadura were eventually relegated, following a gallant season-long fight and defeat in a winner-takes-all, two-legged play-off against Madrid's Rayo Vallecano.

Out of a job once more, Benítez used his enforced sabbatical to travel around Europe studying coaching methods in countries such as England, Germany and Italy. He was a good learner, committed and studious – but always practical. However, book knowledge alone was of no use to a coach still to make his way at the highest levels of the sport. When he returned to Spain, Benítez looked for work. He got lucky. Early in 2000 Javier Pérez, president at Second Division club CD Tenerife, took a chance on offering the refreshed Benítez and his willing assistant Ayestaran jobs. The duo were keen, but they preferred to study the Tenerife club from the outside first and then start with a clean slate in the 2000–01 season rather than take over in the middle of a campaign already under way. It was a typically astute piece of negotiation by Benítez, one that allowed him to consult and carefully weigh up his new challenge before starting to remould his Tenerife side.

This was the first real opportunity that Benítez had had with a reasonable-sized club. Tenerife were down on their luck but still had good-quality players and staff, and their size meant they had great potential. The club was in its second season in the Spanish Second Division but had previously spent ten uninterrupted seasons in the Spanish First Division (1989–90 to 1998–99) and had also had a very good UEFA Cup run in the late 1990s. Real Madrid, Valencia and Barcelona were among the many larger Spanish clubs that positively hated visiting Tenerife's Heliodoro Rodríguez López stadium, which was a real stronghold for the home side. The best clubs in Spain had often suffered defeats there. So, although training facilities were basic, there was a powerful base for the new boss to launch his promotion campaign: a home stadium that few clubs, including the giants of the Spanish game, were confident about visiting. Winning home games by turning the home stadium into a fortress became part of the Benítez credo at every football club he managed.

At his new club Benítez quickly doused the complaints of the soured veterans and hangers-on and sorted out those who wanted to be part of his new project. He concentrated on developing his team around the team's promising younger players – José Luis Marti, Mista, Curro Torres and the early Luis García. His strategy worked brilliantly. CD Tenerife worked harder than any other team in the division, barely gave anything up at home and were duly promoted, proving that Benítez could coach at a medium-sized club that had some stature at the higher levels of the Spanish game. But he would get no chance to test his theories with Tenerife at the apex of Spanish football. His was not yet a totally conclusive case, far from it, but it was enough to convince key figures inside Valencia CF – if not all of the Valencia supporters – of his value.

When mention of Benítez's name in the Spanish press revealed him as a potential candidate for the Mestalla job, an enormous debate arose among the local fans about his suitability. Many were dubious: after all, here was a club with two Champions League finals to its name. How could a relative unknown, a man without even a winning season to boast of in the Spanish First Division, take on the mantle of the great Valencia managers of the past? Benítez also had no experience of any kind in European competition and would now have to pilot Valencia in the UEFA Cup, a competition the Spaniards were warm favourites to win. This was a huge leap of faith, especially for Benítez's main backer Javier Subirats, the sport director at Valencia. But Benítez also had five big pluses to his name that probably swung the decision to appoint him: first, he was Spanish; second, he was young, so he carried few hang ups and brought no hampering football baggage with him to his new club; third, he embraced all the new techniques of football coaching and management – he was a modern, 'scientific' coach with computer back-up; fourth, as a relatively inexperienced coach at this level and at a club this size, Benítez was unlikely to challenge unduly the authority of the Valencia board; and finally, although he had had his disappointments, Benítez was also a proven winner.

One man had a special role to play in bringing Rafa Benítez to Valencia CF: Javier Subirats. Subirats had played for VCF for twelve seasons, from 1977–78 to 1988–89, and had won one European Cup-

Winners' Cup and a Super Cup at the club. He knew the game, and he could see in Benítez some of the necessary qualities for success at the highest level. More established coaches might be less willing to take the risks necessary to move the club on, might be too defensive of their own reputations to make the necessary changes. Valencia CF was faced with some key choices: either it could continue to be an 'almost' club of the modern era, or it could try to drive on to the very summit of the modern European game. Benítez was ambitious, young and fearless, and so Subirats thought that the ex-Madridista was a perfect recruit to ensure the club did not stagnate – that he was capable of piloting Valencia CF into the next phase of their development. Subirats had the backing and support of two key people at the club: the president Pedro Cortés, who would be forced to resign weeks later after a row over Mendieta leaving Valencia CF; and Manuel Llorente, the general manager. The players were also sounded out before Benítez was hired. There was no massive enthusiasm from them but no loudly dissenting voices either. He was in.

One of the (many) doubts that board members and fans at Valencia CF had about their new man was whether Benítez would be able to assert his authority inside the Valencianistas dressing-room. Admittedly, Benítez was known to be a tough coach, a man with a firm character who was happy to have a dialogue with players as long as they didn't expect to have things their own way, but this club had some seasoned internationals and a few 'difficult' customers. Benítez was so young, with no playing pedigree to fall back on, and just keeping their own players on board might be a task in itself. This made the appointment of Benítez a more than risky bet – much more so than had been the case when Héctor Cúper was appointed two years before. But the VCF board could also see that the young man was well prepared to dive in at the deep end. He was willing to work till he dropped, and he had a real desire and hunger for success. They also saw some fire in the belly of the dapper Benítez that contrasted with the slow-burning, deliberate Cúper. The Mestalla could expect to enjoy this guy a little more than their previous anti-hero coach.

Other coaches praised Benítez's positive outlook, his training methods and his modern willingness to be open and honest with his players. This was not an overwhelmingly obvious trait among coaches in the Spanish game at the time. Crucially, too, his agent Manuel García Quilón was perfectly happy for his man to sign a relatively modest one-year contract. He was convinced that the achievements of Valencia CF under Rafa Benítez would allow the coach to come back to the table in 12 months' time to negotiate a much better deal; his man just needed a chance to prove himself. The Valencia board eventually got the message: Benítez signed on a two-year contract. His big break had just arrived.

WHAT WAS BENÍTEZ'S PLAYING PHILOSOPHY AT VALENCIA?

Another of the concerns of the Valencianistas board was, of course, the *style* of play that would be preferred by Benítez. The club had no desire to hire another overly defensive coach, one who risked the sort of ugly divorce between the players and the fans that had been witnessed under Cúper. The press and the Valencia fans began to debate the matter. Curro Torres, a player who followed Benítez from Tenerife, declared that Benítez was no defensive coach. Sure, he liked his sides to defend well, but the most important thing for Benítez was that his team always looked to score goals. Maybe he was different from Cúper in this respect? Curro Torres considered Benítez to be a well-balanced coach in his general outlook – the Madrid man wanted both organisation *and* innovation on the pitch. But the new man was also especially focused on preparation and tactics: every aspect of the opponents had to be weighed and understood, every move rehearsed and worked through on the training ground. Nothing could be left to chance.

Some said that Benítez was yet to find a defined style of his own, that his football philosophy was in constant evolution and that this was something that would allow him to adapt to the game of Valencia CF over the next few years. All said that his approach was painstakingly methodical, that he had the style of a 'school instructor'. He was a perfectionist who liked to rehearse each play a thousand times – a strategist who simulated every possible outcome on the pitch in training. In sum, Benítez was a 'scientist' of football. In this respect it was fitting that in 2002 his name appeared in the committee of professional advisers for a journal of scientific investigation entitled *Ciencias Aplicadas al Deporte* (*Sciences Applied to Sport*), a journal that was produced by the National University of Distance Education (UNED) in Spain.

His methodical and scientific approach was one of the reasons why Benítez preferred and mainly used – some thought in an inflexible way – a 4–4–2 formation: four solid ranks of midfielders and defenders when the opposition had the ball. He could vary the system, occasionally, in the course of a match, but he wanted his players to be absolutely conversant with 4–4–2: to know exactly where they should be on the pitch whenever the opposition picked up the ball. Innovate in possession; organise in defence. This emphasis on formation and structure was a crucial part of his enthusiasm for the 'zonal game' when opponents had possession. He wanted his players to mark space rather than pick up specific individuals. He thought this approach offered both flexibility and comprehensive cover of the key danger areas, and it also meant that his players knew *exactly* how their own responsibilities intersected with those of their teammates. It made his teams like a powerful single organism, one that was constantly mutating to repel dangerous viruses, otherwise known as opposition attacks.

But at Liverpool – where players had traditionally man-marked, especially at corners and free-kicks – it took time for Benítez's defenders to completely understand the system. No one was now 'picking up'. As a result, Liverpool's defence leaked goals from set-pieces at the beginning of Benítez's tenure at Anfield. It was perhaps easier to apply the zonal system in Spain, where corners and free-kicks offered less of a threat from headers from beefy forwards or centre-backs. In England strikers or centre-backs seemed better able to pick the holes in zonal marking – at least at the start of Benítez's reign.

Generally speaking, it was thought that Benítez's methods wouldn't actually mean big changes in the way the team was coached at VCF, so there would be some welcome continuity with both the Ranieri and the Cúper eras. In many ways Benítez seemed to combine the strengths of each of these former Valencia men: the solidity and discipline of Cúper and the greater imagination and vision of the Italian Ranieri. But Benítez was most compared in Spain to the great Italian coach of AC Milan in the 1990s, Arrigo Sacchi. It was a comparison he liked. When Sacchi had first taken over from Fabio Capello at Milan – in a situation similar to the one that Benítez found himself in when he took over at Valenica – few people in Italy thought him to be a credible replacement. But the 'pressing' zonal game high up the field that Sacchi developed at Milan produced enormous success, and it also had a huge impact on coaching globally and on Benítez's own thinking. Milan was a key destination during the young Spaniard's coaching sabbatical in 1999–2000. And when Sacchi had coached in Spain at Atlético Madrid in 1998–99, he had been faced with regular visits on the training field from one of his most diligent international students: an eager young Spanish coach called Rafael Benítez.

RAFA AND THE BACKROOM BOYS

Benítez arrived at VCF accompanied by his friend and collaborator Paco Ayestaran, along with the fitness coach Juan José Rivero and the goalkeeping coach Helder Catalao. Ayestaran had had other offers, of course, after the Extremadura failure, but he had decided to take time out with his mentor Benítez in order to continue enlarging his own football knowledge. The two men possessed national coaching qualifications, and they were both university graduates in physical education and sports. (This meant five years of university studies, so it was equivalent to an undergraduate and then a Masters qualification in England.) Ayestaran was also a qualified national coach of athletics and had a Masters in high-performance sport from the Autonomous University of Madrid. These boys had the theory as well as the practice. It perhaps says something about the Spanish game that this deep background in study and learning about sport did not disadvantage the couple in their football ambitions as it might still do here in England. Here, and despite the successes of the learned Continental figures of Wenger and Houllier, 'doing' is still much more highly valued by the players and press than any knowledge about sport that might be generated in an academic context.

Benítez also brought his assistant Antonio López with him, a close friend and a man who had obtained his coaching qualifications at the same time as Benítez. López had coached at Las Rozas, the Atlético Madrid Under-19s, the Atlético Madrid B team and at Aranjuez. Later, he was the coach at Club Bolivar and was the Bolivian national team coach before returning to Spain to coach Lleida and Sporting Gijón. The third man in the Benítez camp was José Manuel Ochotorena, who would eventually take over as the head coach of the club's goalkeepers. Ochotorena was a personal friend of Benítez and had been a goalkeeper at VCF for four years, after arriving from Real Madrid in the 1988–89 season. He was a hard taskmaster and a man who only gave up goals himself with great reluctance: he had won the annual Zamora trophy for the fewest goals conceded in Spain in 1988–89.

Ayestaran immediately changed training patterns at Valencia, introducing his 'Integral Coaching Method', an approach to match preparation devised with Benítez that surprised the Mestalla players because of its unusual and singular focus. The fundamentals of this method were no great secret: they had long been published in a collection of three videos made by the coach that were easily available in Spanish sports bookstores. Put simply, his approach argued that training must replicate, as far as possible, real match situations, and, by the same token, the team must also play as it trained. Ayestaran described it as 'consisting of using simplified game situations and, starting from them, developing all the variables that impact on performance in order to ensure that it improves'. Simple, huh? It was a method that always combined the physical, technical and tactical aspects of the game in an integrated way. This was its central insight. For Ayestaran, attempting to break down in training the component parts of being a professional footballer made no sense. All components had to be on show simultaneously in a real match – so why not coach this way, too? For example, he argued that, 'Running only works on the physical dimension of sport, on the speed or stamina aspect. But a possession exercise improves the physical condition of the player and the concrete technical and tactical aspects of the game. It can also teach players about the importance of losing your marker and support play.' He was, therefore, in favour of a system of coaching that pretty much demanded the presence of the ball almost all of the time.

Ayestaran's coaching techniques, in fact, suggested working 80 per cent of the time with a ball and only 20 per cent without it. No wonder the players enjoyed his sessions so much. But his emphasis on regularly working with the ball was also designed to ensure ample physical preparation of players, because these sessions were also often intensive workouts, aimed at developing stamina and physical conditioning. This method of coaching broke with some of the prevailing ideas of the time – that developing physique was decisive in football-player preparation. Ayestaran commented on this issue, rather enigmatically, in July 2001 soon after joining the blanquinegros. He said, 'The physical thing is not especially important for the type of game favoured by Benítez. At the end of it, this is not the fundamental thing. It will help, but you can have a well-organised team on the field that gives the impression of being at a great physical level. It is worse to have the opposite – being physically strong but badly organised.'

HOULLIER AND BENÍTEZ – AND NEW CHALLENGES AHEAD

While Benítez settled in at Valencia, over at Liverpool Football Club Gérard Houllier was positively bursting with ambition and hope that 2001–02 would bring the club its first league title in 12 years. OK, Manchester United and Arsenal looked formidable opponents again, but the Frenchman's standing with Reds supporters could barely be higher. The confidence drawn from Liverpool's 2001 cup Treble, coupled with a few positive summer signings – Riise and Baroš among them – and the continuing progress of local boys Carragher, Owen and Gerrard, made the future seem bright. The league title seemed to be in reach once again. By contrast, Rafael Benítez and his coaching staff at Valencia CF were now facing possibly their greatest challenge. In the past Benítez, like all young coaches, had been pressed to make bricks from straw. His previous jobs in Spain came with relatively low expectations, so success was usually a bonus, a way of marking out the measure of the coach and his backroom men. If they failed, well, it was a small earthquake; there was usually little harm done, and they could reasonably hope that another job might come along. Now they were in an entirely different world. Valencia CF was probably one of the top six or seven clubs in Europe in the early years of the new century. Expectations were sky high, and they would be played out in the full glare of the world's media. Fail and you were likely to be damned. You may never get another serious chance.

Valencia and their fans also had to be dragged out of the disappointment of successive Champions League final defeats, and their simmering disquiet over the approach to playing the game established under previous coaches had to be overcome. These supporters not only wanted success, they wanted it with bells on. Benítez and his staff had established international players to work with, sure, but could they convince these stars that their futures lay with this rookie coach and with a club that some critics argued had already overachieved? Looking at their main domestic rivals, Barcelona and Real Madrid, just made things seem worse. Real Madrid spent money like water, and they were reigning Spanish champions with a team full of great stars – Fernando Hierro, Raúl, Zinedine Zidane, Luís Figo, Roberto Carlos among them – while Barça would be busting a gut (and the bank) to match them, you could bet on that.

So Gérard Houllier at Liverpool and Rafa Benítez in Valencia each set out for the 2001–02 season as hugely excited men. Could the Frenchman win the league title with his rapidly recovering Liverpool to build on the cup Treble of 2001? Could the young Spaniard deliver something tangible to the Mestalla after so much promise and Champions League disappointment? Benítez looked to have the tougher job. After all, Liverpool looked reasonably harmonious, the fans were behind the manager and Houllier already seemed to have got the Reds back on track. In Spain the Valencia club was full of political intrigue, as always, the Valencia fans waited to be impressed and the players at the Mestalla were still gloomy about their failure in Champions League finals. The Spanish club was now 30 years without a La Liga title and 20 without a major European trophy. Was Benítez up to the challenge? Although the two men met in friendly contests, they would not cross swords in serious battle yet – Liverpool were in the Champions League, Valencia in the UEFA Cup – but they might have recognised the size of their respective tasks as they gazed across Europe at the football opposition. As it turned out, only one of these football men was to succeed in their present project – the man from Madrid.

8

This Land is Your Land

The Miracle of Kenilworth Road; going down to Rio – at Old
Trafford; Rafa and Robbie – when worlds collide; February
is the cruellest month; cheated by Robben; pure hatred
at Liverpool 4; Benítez falls to Benfica; seven high at St
Andrews.

THE MIRACLE OF KENILWORTH ROAD

Initially Rafa Benítez had seemed mystified by the deep attraction
the FA Cup still clearly held over the English, including Liverpool
fans. The manager saw himself as being recruited primarily to deliver
in the Premier League and, ideally, in Europe. What else was there?
After all, cup football in Spain – as in most of the rest of Europe
– was often played in front of tiny crowds and offered too little in the
way of status, excitement or financial reward. Benítez – like Paisley
and others in the Liverpool tradition – was a football rationalist,
reasoning that knockout domestic-cup success measured only fortune
and performance on any given day rather than the sustained excellence
demanded in the league or even in Europe. He saw the FA and League
Cups mainly as a chance to blood some of his younger squad players
in a relatively low-risk environment. When else were these guys
supposed to get their time? He may not even have realised that the
2005 third-round meeting with Burnley at freezing Turf Moor had
its own distinctive Lancastrian history – including an FA Cup final
in 1914 – and that the locals would certainly fight tooth and nail to

unseat their vaunted neighbours. Moreover, a Liverpool team sheet that night containing an unfamiliar mix of domestic youngsters and foreign squad players was simply provocative: it invited the hosts to further fancy their chances and bare their professional claws. The Reds were duly bundled out 0–1, and a penitent Benítez felt the flack: plenty of Liverpool fans wanted him out there and then.

In 2006 the Liverpool squad was stronger, and the Spanish manager was unlikely to make the same mistake in the FA Cup. The third-round opposition this time was broadly similar – a moderate Championship side, Luton Town – but now Benítez had the FA Cup fully on his radar. He even discussed it as one of the trophies that he had ambitions to win for the club. All of this showed in his selection for the visit to a grim Bedfordshire: only Scott Carson in goal hinted that something different was expected from the more cerebral tests demanded in the Premiership.

Luton Town had their own history of cup heartaches – injury and defeat in the 1959 final – but were now managed by Mike Newell, a Scouser, ex-Anfield trainee and shrewdly laid-back Bob Paisley devotee. In any other circumstances Newell was a passionate Reds fan, but Luton's excellent home record showed that he would test his home-town club, thus demanding an ultra-professional approach from Liverpool to survive the afternoon. Luton's ugly and tight Kenilworth Road ground, glued right back into the 1970s and holding fewer than 10,000 fans even when full – as it was that day – probably shocked Rafa and his staff. But the pitch was reasonable, and the general view was that Luton, under the thinker Newell, would get it down and try to play – which should have suited the visitors. At least, that was our thinking.

When Steven Gerrard scored early on, using his right foot to sweep in a pass from Cissé – the latter's only meaningful contribution on what would prove to be a difficult afternoon, by the way – it looked like a Liverpool stroll. But Luton steamed back, pouring through on Liverpool's left side vacated by the roaming Gerrard. Utilising the empty space, the fast and skilful forward Rowan Vine was getting behind Finnan and running directly at Carragher. It was a cute little plan – simple but effective. For once the Bootle man, boasting recent European defensive lockouts to die for, looked exposed and all at sea. Steve Robinson and Kevin Nicholls were also outplaying and outfighting Sissoko and Alonso in Liverpool's midfield. Luton Town suddenly looked formidable. Before long the muscular Steve Howard was through the centre of the Liverpool defence and in alone on Carson. With a jink to the goalkeeper's left the Luton man lifted a clever shot over the retreating Finnan for a deserved equaliser in front of Liverpool's growling 1,800 visiting fans.

What was going wrong? Maybe Liverpool were being complacent, assuming victory would simply follow? One sure thing was that Crouch, Cissé and Kewell were all anonymous in the first half: none of them was getting usefully on the ball or holding it up. Crouch was out-muscled, whilst Cissé was just listless and irrelevant. As a result, little of the contest was now being played out in Luton's half; instead, the ball was returning to the Liverpool back four with alarming regularity. When Robinson then turned Carragher cleverly to score the second goal for Luton just before half-time, no one present was really that surprised – except by the ease with which the Liverpool man had been deceived once more. It stayed 1–2 until the break but more by luck than judgement. Liverpool had been unrecognisable, quite wretched. But Rafa would now sort it out. At least that was what we told ourselves.

To his credit, referee Mark Clattenburg then tried to get the European champions right back in the game. Early in the second half he gift-wrapped a dubious penalty for Gerrard's fall in front of the chasing Paul Underwood, after Kewell had ineptly overhit what should have been an easy low cross. Mystifyingly, Cissé and not Gerrard took the kick – and predictably missed, Marlon Beresford stretching easily to his left to save. Was this why Rafa Benítez was now visibly throwing a lively wobbler on the left-hand touchline? Or did he want the home protagonist dismissed – surely he wasn't that desperate? But within minutes there was more 'wobbler' work to be done in the Liverpool dugout, because the usually reliable Sami Hyypiä was caught haplessly messing about in midfield and was robbed by Vine. The Luton man sped off before collapsing over the advancing Carson – penalty for Luton. There seemed little doubt – but TV replays suggested later that it was *Vine* who was actually doing the fouling – and *outside* the area. None of this mattered to Nicholls, who scored easily, and at 1–3 it threatened to be another third-round cup exit under Spanish supervision for a terrible, uncommitted Liverpool. Sinama-Pongolle's immediate introduction – Liverpool's only forward on the bench – for the ineffective Sissoko hardly filled the Liverpool fans with optimism. How wrong we all were; we should have had more faith in the braided one.

It was actually finally applying Steven Gerrard's talents and energy to central midfield that was the crucial change made by Benítez to turn the match around, one that ate away at Luton's tired nervousness. Soon Cissé on the right and Sinama-Pongolle down the middle were chasing precise Gerrard passes through the home defence, the little French substitute scoring from one of these with a low shot that beat Beresford for pace. Little 'Pongy', hair-beads flying, scooped the ball back to halfway, and Luton were suddenly visibly wilting, the home crowd silenced and anxious. Even Xabi Alonso had woken up (finally) and next looped a near-40-yard shot over the stranded Beresford and in – 3–3!

The Istanbul comparisons were obvious – and a mock European Cup appeared in the Liverpool end to make the point. But, unlike in Istanbul, Liverpool now pushed on for victory. Finnan crossed for Sinama-Pongolle, who thrillingly headed in his second goal on 69 minutes. The little tassled one had saved us after all. Which meant that in just 16 minutes this football match – this searing FA Cup contest – had seemingly swayed definitively to Luton and then astonishingly back to Liverpool.

There was still an opportunity – in injury time – for goalkeeper Beresford to come up for a last Luton corner and then to get hilariously stranded in Liverpool's half as the ball broke to Xabi Alonso. Typically, Gerrard still had the necessary gas to career down Liverpool's left, screaming for the simple pass that would surely offer him a clear run in on Luton's unattended goal. Instead, the Spaniard calmly curled the ball towards the Luton net from fully 60 yards.

The Miracle of Kenilworth Road (2006) was thus complete. The lesson? That even the European champions could be outplayed and outbattled for a time by supposed inferiors – by a committed team that had been properly prepared and had tactics astute enough to focus on isolating with pace the Reds' central defenders, Carragher and Hyypiä. This match also reminded us that muscle and application could still be enough to discourage lightweights such as Kewell and Cissé, both of whom were shown to have desperately faint hearts. Frankly, Crouch had been little better, and Sissoko had also been exposed as lacking real defensive intelligence and creativity when faced by determined and resourceful opponents such as these. He would improve for the experience – he would have to.

WHEN ROBBIE MET HARRY

After the cup thrills at Luton it was back to the grind of the league, when third played fourth, as Liverpool hosted Martin Jol's Tottenham. But the day's loudest cheer was reserved for L4 pubs just before 2.30 p.m. A tumultuous Manchester derby was drawing to a TV close with City leading 2–1 and attacking an increasingly chaotic United. Their end was nigh. As bodies flailed around him, the stocky City No. 7 – in the eye of the storm – now stood limp and relaxed just inside the penalty area demanding the ball on his left foot. When the pass finally arrived – as we knew it would – the ball was immediately flashed past the left hand of the helpless Edwin van der Sar with the unique and deadly combination of power and grace that took all these Liverpool fans right back to the near-glory years at Anfield in the mid-1990s. Only one man alive could strike on his left-hand side quite like that.

As the scorer wheeled away to be enveloped in sky blue, he flashed five European Cup fingers to United's gloomy disciples. Robbie Fowler, Toxteth's finest, had downed Manchester United once again. The TV cameras now switched to show Sir Alex purpling on the touchline, to more Liverpool cheers. Because of Robbie, cruelly discarded in 2001 by Gérard Houllier, Reds could now walk to the Kop in the winter sunshine with an optimistic spring in their step.

Ledley King, Edgar Davids and the Egyptian striker Mido all returned for Spurs. Rafa Benítez seemed to have discarded, almost entirely, the rotation principle at Anfield. He didn't get many opposers. Morientes for Cissé was the only Liverpool change, with Gerrard once more asked to play wide right. 'With Steve on the right side,' Benítez said, 'he has a lot of freedom. We then have more options there, and we can also play Sissoko and Alonso in the middle, and it means we are able to regain a lot of possession and attack well.' This was the new Liverpool plan. But the Reds would need to be patient. With powerful formations on both sides, the first half was just the sort of high-quality, tight contest you should expect at this level – but seldom get. Travelling London fans derided the Kop's long first-half silences, but on that occasion this home drowsiness was actually a sign of serious football study and appreciation rather than one of ennui. With Finnan more influential than Gerrard on Liverpool's right, Crouch and Morientes tested Paul Robinson with headers, but the visitors were confident and they kept the ball well. England hopeful Michael Carrick and Edgar Davids were prominent; the aggressive Teemu Tainio forced back Alonso. At half-time it was a credible, heavyweight stalemate.

Pepe Reina performed a little superstitious ritual for the start of the second half. As we watched him at the Anfield Road end, he back-heeled the right post, walked across the goal line – pausing at halfway – and did the same to the left one. He then returned to the middle of the goal before pacing to the edge of the penalty area, pausing this time on the penalty spot on his return. When he reached the goal line, he crossed himself. Now he was ready; his benevolent God was in his six-yard box. Pepe soon needed His help when Riise missed a simple ball on Liverpool's left just after half-time and let in Jermaine Jenas. The England man sensibly whipped a low cross to Robbie Keane, who had his eye taken by Reina's expansive dive and so missed what some people wrongly described later as an 'open goal'. The Kop now roused itself, realising it had to help raise the tempo and increase the pressure on a jaunty-looking Spurs. It worked. Unsurprisingly, Finnan was the source, crossing long to the far post, where a dozing Young-Pyo Lee had left a Liverpool man fatally unattended in front of the Kop.

It is safe to say that Harry Kewell had not been the most fêted player at Anfield over the previous two years. He had arrived in 2003 with cash thrown at both him and his agent to secure the deal. He was Rick Parry's 'get you out of your seats' gift for a still-too-defensive Gérard Houllier. But a combination of injury and apparent lack of commitment had reduced his effectiveness and his appeal to football fans raised in the British tradition that hard running and a willingness to spill blood can help mask bad luck or a lack of technique. Kewell still had his Anfield believers – Benítez among them – who argued that he had the necessary quality but needed an injury-free spell to show it. Harry's 23-minute performance in Istanbul had lowered his stock still further with his many L4 detractors, but as Jamie Carragher had argued – and what better judge? – who actually *wants* to go off in the European Cup final? Harry was now well and pain-free for the first time in two years. He could start earning some of his reported £60,000-a-week wage and justify his European Cup winner's medal.

It was Kewell who now watched Finnan's delivery onto his left foot, striking it high on the volley. We had seen these flayed up to section 207 on the Kop before, but not today. Like the master Robbie Fowler before him – don't get ahead of yourself, now – this time it was a clean and controlled contact, one that arrowed inside Paul Robinson's near post. It was enough to see off Spurs.

Harry will never *be* a Robbie, of course – who could be? He will never garner even one tenth of the local affection, nor the local respect, afforded Robbie or even, say, a Hyypiä or a Hamann. The respect that comes from being able to convey to fans the key message: that playing for Liverpool Football Club really *matters* to you – that you really care. It is partly the way Kewell dips his head like a schoolboy when carelessly surrendering possession. And the way in which he sometimes pulls out of the sort of shuddering tackles that a Didi or a Sissoko sees as a duty and honour to commit to for Liverpool. Unfair as this might be, it is for such reasons that Harry Kewell will always have his braying Liverpool critics.

But at least he had given Liverpool *something* against Tottenham – that potentially vital 'bit of quality' that even the utter pragmatist Jamie Carragher had conceded the team needed to unlock a convincing Spurs side and to steal the points when the team had been largely outplayed and under the cosh. Kewell had shown it here.

The current Liverpool under Benítez needed little more than this single goal at home it seemed. Out of eleven league home matches played that season, *ten* had now been rendered scoreless for the opposition. It was also the tenth consecutive game in all competitions that Liverpool had successfully defended their goal at home. The new Liverpool back five was even threatening to look just a little like the famous sixteen-goals-conceded, best-ever 1978–79 Liverpool defence. The current manager's only real defensive worries were the lack of suitable cover and the possibility of injury. Add to these two other irritations: the sheer number of matches some of these guys already had under their belts that season – 37 played so far, with Spurs, for example, aiming for a maximum and paltry 40 matches *in total* – and also the uncertainties of the left-back slot. Riise sometimes lacked consistency and defensive resolve on the left side, and both Warnock and Traoré failed to convince as his replacement. Liverpool now had to take this putative defensive solidity into the heart of darkness 20-odd miles east along the M62. It was a potentially season–defining moment.

JUST LIKE TEAM SPIRIT

Jan Kromkamp, 25, a leggy attacking Dutch international right-back, had joined Liverpool from Villarreal in a deal which had seen Josemi go in the other direction. Frankly, if the new man had his own boots, it was a decent piece of business. But he would have to do brilliantly to oust Steve Finnan, the most consistent right-back in the Premiership. Not that the new boy lacked for confidence, saying right away that he had already marked Wayne Rooney out of two games in the past twelve months. (We did say he was Dutch.) A young Danish international centre-back named Daniel Agger, 21, had also arrived, signed from Brøndby for £5.8 million. This was the end of a long Liverpool search for youthful cover for Sami Hyypiä, and Benítez said that he liked the 'aggressiveness' of the defender who 'will become one of the best centre-backs in England'. No pressure, then. But Sami Hyypiä – at 32 and with over 350 games played for Liverpool at No. 4 – had actually had a terrific season, blemished only by his illness-marred submission to Drogba at Anfield.

The Finn has many strengths: he passes well on both sides, has great control for a big man and wins most things in the air. But in the past he has said that he is probably too nice to be a footballer – he seldom fouls – although he has all the necessary determination and reading of the game to see out the remaining two years of his Anfield contract. When Benítez told his resident centre-backs that he was buying in competition for the position, Hyypiä said, typically, 'Fine with me.' Why should he worry? He still finds it difficult to accept that he has played at a level well beyond his Willem II days in the Netherlands: 'I wouldn't have believed I would go on to achieve what I have.' It's that niceness again. In a business full of sharks and poseurs, Sami Hyypiä is a straight man and a Liverpool rock. He has a shout for 'all time Anfield great' status and certainly deserves his Champions League medal. Young Daniel Agger, no matter his qualities, may yet have to await his chance at Liverpool Football Club.

GOING DOWN TO RIO

For pretty much the first time in 13 long years Manchester United looked a little vulnerable, no longer nailed-on title challengers. Chelsea's thunderous emergence was part of this story and so too was the departure of Roy Keane, the uncompromising United team leader. But the key thing was that the domestic core of United's dominant side in the 1990s – Gary Neville, Paul Scholes, Roy Keane, David Beckham and Ryan Giggs – was now thoroughly fragmented and too few suitable quality replacements had been recruited by Ferguson. United had an astonishing 19 players currently out on loan, as they searched for the new brigade. OK, the urchin Rooney would pick up well from the brilliant quiet man Scholes (a player, incidentally, with *no* agent), but Beckham and Keane had few obvious peers. Critically, too, Ryan Giggs – the most consistent and gifted forward in the history of the Premier League – was finally beginning to fade. Bizarrely, most United fans – glams to the last – would rather fête the half-career of the flawed 'genius' George Best than they would celebrate the huge contribution made to eight recent Premiership titles at Trafford Towers by the talented, loyal and perpetually frown-faced Welshman Giggs.

And with his core men dissolving around him, Alex Ferguson was apparently in deep crisis: United were already dumped out of the European Cup by Benfica, held by tiny Burton Albion in the FA Cup, losers in the Manchester derby and an insurmountable 16 points behind runaway leaders Chelsea. The fiercely loyal and often vicious local fanzine *Red Issue* even confirmed that Ferguson's reign was drawing to a close with an angry 'Time to Go, Fergie' piece on their hero manager's alleged progressive senility. *Red Issue* was also furious at Ferguson's recent praise of the 'excellent' US carpetbagger owners, the Glazers, and at the way the club was treating its most committed fans: 'Sometimes you wonder why we put up with it –

giving everything you've got when they need you, then once you've served your purpose they shit all over you.' This was a truly heart-warming sign for any Scouse intruder of telling Salford disharmony. So, the day's match was really about second place – but it was one that United *needed* to win or else Fergie might be liable for the rubbish skip at any time.

This was also an important moment for Rafa Benítez; it was his first meeting with United in which the balance of power had perceptively shifted to Anfield. But, for all their improvements and defensive solidity, Liverpool had failed to convince recently against the major powers in the league, and the Reds hadn't lowered United's colours since the departed Danny Murphy's OT heroics under Houllier. The question was whether the Liverpool manager now had the courage – and the resources – to attack United in Manchester when the hosts were at their lowest ebb for some time. We needed to know the answer. That was why we had wandered through the grizzly multi-national drinking parties outside Lou Macari's fish and chip emporium on Old Trafford Way and were now gathering on the apron outside the old Scoreboard End as the Merseyside coach fodder began to arrive, loudly, from just 25 miles to the west – but actually from another country.

This fixture is one of the few occasions left now for Liverpool fans in the brushed-up hooligan desert that is the Premier League, where drinking nearby or wearing club colours is strictly inadvisable – unless, of course, you travel in an official coach with the required police escort and with only 100 yards to negotiate to the away section. Or else you are a bona fide psycho or suicide case. (There were a few of those present that day.) There is still domestic Red contempt for benighted Evertonians, of course, bass ridicule (not to mention envy) for the upstarts from Chelsea, who 'have no history', and also a mystification at the unrequited loyal enthusiasm of the drink-addled Geordies. But these are nothing to the dark emotions still stirred at Old Trafford. There is still a sense of real visceral hatred between United and Liverpool: it may yet consume us all.

You could feel the animosity in the air outside the ground, an edgy electrical storm brewing. So it was best to get inside, free from local imbibing and any of the gentle pre-match ribbing we might exchange elsewhere, where we can relax and be amongst 'our own' and all those inflatable number 5s, floating European Cups and banners about our exclusive 'European Cup' enclosure – albeit surrounded by heathens and infidels on all sides.

Old Trafford shows all the marks of United's global reach: yet more seats in the stadium corners peer at us from behind plastic sheets, as if housing the future places of the dead. Soon, 75,000 supplicants will pledge their devotion here, mocking the 5,000 principled men and women who withdrew their fan labour and formed their own United club in protest once the Yankee dollar had moved in and seduced even the previously saintly Sir Alex. We wish them well in their search for community and 'authentic' sporting ties in the tin sheds and ploughed fields of local football in the northern counties. The plush executive boxes and electronic advertising boards – 1,000 angry Nike swooshes marching the touchlines like so many Dalí ducks – tells you that this is no provincial marketplace, no local pasture for settling mere regional disputes. This is a fully late-modern *European* football place, one marked by all the paraphernalia of the new sporting economies of signs and space.

After this piece of larceny, Ferguson would say that snatching this sort of late victory against the grain is a hallmark of Manchester United's great qualities. But it was more a sign of Liverpool's inherent weaknesses. Faced with a United team lacking both confidence and real guile – the inept Patrice Evra at left-back, and Ryan Giggs and John O'Shea in midfield with the unconvincing and inexperienced Kieran Richardson – the visitors controlled much of the game without ever really threatening: mediocrity rules. Liverpool looked tepid, and it was tempting to say something we had known to be true for some time: that the majority of Premier League teams had at least one forward more potent than any at this Liverpool. Against United the Frenchman Cissé plumbed new depths, even by his own miserable standards. Unable to stay consistently onside or to latch onto any of Gerrard's precision passes with anything remotely approaching determination or real skill, Cissé managed to rise unmarked from his arse in United's six-yard box to poke the ball over the bar with an open goal beckoning, an opportunity that seemed impossible to miss. 'Astonishing incompetence' the press later called it. We had other words for it – for our £14 million man. We could all guess at what would happen next. As Liverpool weakened late on – the natural cost of strikers failing to convert ample possession into goals – Rio Ferdinand's injury-time scoring header from a free-kick conceded because of new man Kromkamp's naivety had an air of awful inevitability about it.

To be honest, Gary Neville's little celebratory jig in front of the Liverpool section cut no ice with us. Let him have his day, no matter how the FA saw it. Ours would come. But in the darkness outside later we could hear all the familiar car-park sounds of this regional dispute angrily and violently continuing, even as Benítez was emptily contesting referee Mike Riley's decisions. He should have examined more closely his own, because the Spaniard's carefully chosen forwards – Crouch and Morientes, and his terrible bequest from Houllier, The Lord of the Manor of Frodsham, Cissé – were surely among the poorest ever to assemble for this proud football club. As a result of this fact, a feeble United now stretched four points clear of Liverpool in the battle for second place in the Premiership.

LOSING MY RESISTANCE: GOD'S BACK!

The Liverpool manager then acted in the only way imaginable (actually it was unimaginable) to the agonising farce we witnessed at United. Give him his dues: he signed the very best man available, responded immediately and well to our accusations. 'I could see the passion in him,' Benítez explained, no doubt making favourable mental comparisons with his current crop. 'He's a different kind of striker to what we have.' You bet he was: he found space, scored goals; he *cared*. Text messages ricocheted around the globe between Reds at the news of this signing, at the wonderful audacity, the romance, of it all. It was a future JFK football moment for all Liverpool fans everywhere: 'Where were you when . . . ?' It would almost certainly end in tears, of course, but frankly, just at that moment, who cared? We just accepted it for what is was, wallowing in its sheer rightness.

Benítez was bemused by it all and said later that he had never seen a player so excited about completing a move. Again, it was the clinical professional talking about an English player who had real feeling for a club and its supporters. It was Toxteth time. Because the millionaire property-owning, arse-baring, touchline-sniffing, docker-supporting, Manc-hating, one-time-Evertonian, greatest-goddamned left-footed striker this country had ever seen was coming home. Robbie Fowler was back at Liverpool Football Club.

Robbie had wasted what should have been the best years of his football career away from Liverpool – he was only 26 when he left, booted out four years previously by Gérard Houllier for Leeds United. As football writer Kevin McCarra said, Robbie was not so much sold as sent into exile by Houllier. The Frenchman claimed later that this £11 million sale was a good deal for Liverpool – but by what measure? The manager argued that Fowler's body was giving up. Houllier certainly hated the Robbie cult among the fans, despised the Liverpool man's popularity and his tabloid-like vulnerability in the city. Robbie played poorly for Leeds; he lacked both fitness and application. Reds might say that being forced to leave Anfield simply broke his spirit. In any case, few could argue that Houllier abjectly wasted the Fowler cash. Asking if you would prefer El Hadji Diouf to an even half-fit Robbie Fowler was a no-brainer. And it was Houllier, remember, who signed Djibril Cissé for £14 million. So how do you rate the French coach's judgement of strikers and his assessment of character?

Of course, the lumbering Robbie of today compared to the predator

Fowler at the age of 21 or 22 was a daft sleight of hand. No one on the Kop now expected him to return to those glory years: people were just happy that they had been alive to witness them. But this signing emphasised some of the emptiness and meaninglessness of some recent deals at Liverpool – guys coming in with only a fraction of Fowler's commitment, talent and belief. The sheer emotion of his return had also instantly put the manager in a better place with the club's supporters. It would also act as a shake-up to his current crop of failures. 'Benítez has shown he's one of us, by bringing Fowler back,' one Reds fan told *The Independent*. She spoke for many more. Through this deal Benítez had shown Liverpool fans that he actually did have some true Scouse blood running through his veins.

Robbie had six months on lowered wages to show that he was worth another season in Red. And now everyone at Anfield was just waiting for two things: to see Fowler in a Liverpool shirt once again and to see him score in front of the Kop. 'I'm so happy, it's frightening,' Liverpool's newest signing said. He was like a child in his joy, something which was to be celebrated: it *was* a fantastic story in a sport, let's face it, which was often too full of money-grabbing, shitty ones.

Portsmouth (away) in the FA Cup fourth round was beyond Robbie's reach – he had stuck a hat-trick past little Scunthorpe for Manchester City in the third round so was cup-tied. Seeing the European Cup (a $^3/_4$ copy, actually, produced by some fellah in West Derby) resting on a pool table in a Pompey pub was a pre-match confidence boost. The match should have been a real test, but Portsmouth under arch-fixer H. Redknapp were focused on Premiership survival only, and so Liverpool were expected to win with minimal resistance. Kromkamp started – and did OK on a pitch that was so newly laid that the seams poked through its dark, sandy top, making the ball bobble about drunkenly. Fratton Park sure had 'character' – which meant an end open to an icy wind and offering terrible toilets. It felt like the 1960s (or 1860s). Liverpool (in white socks, pop-pickers) started poorly but got a gift of an early penalty, which Gerrard scored. A Morientes flick to Riise – the Spaniard's one meaningful contribution – produced a flashing drive from the Norwegian past a startled Dean Kiely for 2–0. O'Neill headed a second-half reply for the home boys but neither the crowd nor the Pompey players wanted a replay in these circumstances, and so the game drifted to its conclusion with the Reds still alive in the FA Cup. Next round (gulp): Manchester United at Anfield.

Robbie finally came off the bench against a cussed ten-man Birmingham City in a night Premiership match at Anfield that was atypically packed to the rafters just for his homecoming. He was greeted by a banner that immodestly read 'Fowler God 11: welcome back to heaven'. This match actually felt more like the other place. Agger – a nervous start for the Dane – was fouled by Damien Johnson for a harsh red card, but a toothless Liverpool could not break City down. Fowler's touchline warming up on the hour mark roused the Kop and even seemed to help break the deadlock because a slick move between Gerrard, García and Morientes then ended with the Liverpool captain (who else?) scoring past Taylor.

Fowler's first steps back in red had a dreamlike quality about them: was it a ghost we were seeing? He was heavier in movement (and stature), but it was identifiably the no-backlift kid who still seemed to glide effortlessly into that most priceless real estate in sport: space in the opposing penalty area. But instead of speculating, Liverpool now dangerously tried to run down the clock, inviting late Birmingham hope, which horribly converted into a tangible return when Xabi Alonso spoiled Fowler's night – not to mention that of his huge supporting cast – by inexplicably chesting Emile Heskey's late header past his own goalkeeper. There was still time for Robbie to net an overhead kick that was so offside he might have scored it from on the Kop – but the crowd went wild anyway. God was back, all right – but he hadn't brought Liverpool three points against these bogeymen strugglers.

FEBRUARY IS THE CRUELLEST MONTH

Liverpool's next six matches included Chelsea (a), Arsenal (h), Manchester United in the FA Cup (h) and Benfica in the European Cup (a). You could have called this crunch time, and you would not have been contradicted by us. At Chelsea the previously lovely José Mourinho was now trying the nation's patience with his utter gracelessness. He seemed charming once, but now he looked only spoilt and nasty – a bully. He was a bad loser and a truculent interviewee, accusing his growing band of detractors of trying to kill his Chelsea project with envy. 'Envy,' he said mysteriously, aping the great Cantona, 'is the gun of the incompetent.' The Portuguese manager was already beginning to look a little bored with life in England, arguing later that Chelsea lacked sufficient competition in the Premiership to keep them honed. Press headlines told you why: 'Played 23, won 20, losses £140 million: the high price of success in the Premiership'. This gross Chelsea project reminded the British press that only a fool could fail at this game when his budget had no limits. And José Mourinho, let us say right here, is no fool.

In the end a disappointing Liverpool were beaten pretty comfortably at the Bridge, after looking secure for half an hour. Basic errors contributed. Riise lost William Gallas at a corner for the first goal, and then when Warnock failed to keep the defensive line (his regular fault), Reina was beaten by the played-onside Hernán Crespo from a tight angle for the second. Liverpool (as always it seemed) struggled to generate the pace to make decent chances, this time with Crouch as a lone striker. Mourinho was correct when he said, 'If we score before them, we have got conditions to do what we need to.' Rafa Benítez had no convincing plan B for this eventuality. None. But this defeat was not even the central story. In the tunnel before the game we got a TV preview of what was coming, a little vignette of the modern Chelsea. Steven Gerrard offered a friendly handshake to the Chelsea mascot, a five year old who had been instructed by his shit-for-brains father to make a fool of the Liverpool captain by thumbing his nose at him. When this happened, Stevie, to his credit, just gave a wry smile, rather than cuffing the little brat. This kid was Chelsea through and through.

On the pitch we got more of the same – more of this gimcrack disrespect for opposing players and the game itself. With ten minutes left and the contest effectively over, the usually placid Pepe Reina ploughed into Chelsea's Eidur Gudjohnsen on the touchline. What had gotten into the Liverpool keeper? Predictably, Chelsea's A-Team – William Gallas, John Terry, Claude Makélélé and Michael Essien – now gathered to make merry with the referee, but it was the Dutchman Arjen Robben who collapsed hysterically as Reina gently pushed the winger in the face as a response to some sly aside. Reina, now furious, had to walk for this gross piece of fiction. Rafa Benítez was angry enough in the TV interviews later to try to make a bitter little joke about how he couldn't stay to meet the press; that he had to rush off to visit the stricken Robben, who must surely be in the local hospital. It was hardly Woody Allen, but it was good. And it was the Liverpool manager's personal code of ethics that seemed most damaged. 'What kind of professional can you be if you leave a player banned for three games?' he asked his interviewers rhetorically. He was fuming – and frankly, just a little bit self-righteous.

Of course, we should have all respected the Liverpool manager's stand. Robben had acted disgracefully and should have been punished by the FA – who were indefensibly silent and spineless about the whole thing, as usual. But does Benítez really say the same things – about disrespect and unprofessional behaviour – to his own serial divers, to García and Cissé, for example? We doubt it – at least we never hear about it. Actually, the English game is now completely infected by this sort of pathetic stuff. Some of the foreigners have raised it to a fine art, sure, but some English guys were also experts at it years ago. Mourinho was typically agnostic. 'Why should I comment on Rafa's words?' he said coyly. This really meant that he was siding with his own man Robben, who had done his job well, suckering the opposition to ten men and thus absolutely ensuring victory for Chelsea.

Ironically, it is Mourinho who says that English football is 'full of hypocrites'. In fact, the truth is that in front of the cameras and the press they *all* avoid any sort of reasonable moral position on the unspoken 'c' word in football: on cheats. Wenger, Benítez, Ferguson, Allardyce – as well as the now-silent Mourinho – all of them hide behind this façade of non-committal innocence. They all publicly deplore opposing divers and play actors, naturally, but they also defend their own players totally, no matter what their public sins. And in doing so they think nothing of the sport they are despoiling. It is the new professionalism in football. And it stinks.

At least Reina's dismissal offered a disgracefully belated opportunity for the forgotten Jerzy Dudek in the Liverpool goal. Dudek said that Benítez had promised him some matches during this busy spell, but this was a manager's little deception. There were no signs at all of this happening, not with Reina in such good form. 'I'll do my best, and after that we will see,' said Jerzy glumly. He should have packed his bags because Dudek's return at Charlton, along with that of Djimi Traoré, another Istanbul survivor, was a disaster. The goalkeeper conceded a penalty (Darren Bent) and a poor near-post goal from Traoré's flank (Luke Young) in another abject Liverpool London defeat. At forwards-free Wigan Athletic things improved slightly for the Pole on a rugby-churned mud heap. Sami Hyypiä scored the winner for a dominant Liverpool in front of nearly more Reds than Blues. Here, deep in egg-chaser country, Robbie Fowler struck the sort of left-footed cross that Harry Kewell could only dream of. Not that the hapless Fernando Morientes could finish it off, of course. How could you even *imagine* it?

Jerzy Dudek's last outing in this little spell of three (his last-ever for Liverpool?) was against Arsenal at Anfield in the Premiership. It was surprisingly one-sided. The Londoners had been struggling away from Highbury, and sections of the press were stupidly beginning to write off Arsène Wenger, saying he had lost the belief of his players. But this contest was still even at 0–0 until little García threaded home a rebound from a shot from Hamann very late on.

On Jamie Carragher's 400th appearance for Liverpool – Carragher had already played 3,322 minutes for the club that season, 400 more than any other player in England – Steven Gerrard had a first-half penalty saved by the brave Jens Lehmann. In contrast, a decidedly unfocused Thierry Henry adopted a disinterested 'What am I doing here?' persona for the entire match. Just maybe he was still musing over the possibility of signing papers elsewhere.

Which brought Manchester United to Anfield on 18 February in the fifth round of the FA Cup. It should have been one of the high points of the season – Liverpool had failed to beat United in the FA Cup for 20 years and were thirsting for revenge after Ferdinand's recent last-minute steal. But instead of great drama and thrilling red-raw football, the sheer ugliness of the occasion really kicked in and took the encounter way beyond sport and banter, and even outside the traditionally intense visceral satisfactions of local tribalism that uneasily link the fans of these two great clubs. The much-hyped Gary Neville business from Old Trafford was partly to blame. 'He overstepped the mark,' said an unusually stern Jamie Carragher, and the gutter press had a field day as a result. But even Carragher might have found it difficult not to seek some little revenge for the ugly, humourless Liverpool chant about Neville that had him 'fucking' his mother and his brother. The non-season-ticketed Kop picked this ditty up and also howled its unexpurgated Manc hatred from beginning to end – and got the same back in return. This was no simple satisfying hostility for bitter enemies. After a while it was just numbing and soul-crushing to listen to this bile from Liverpool fans. Was anyone here actually *watching* the match any more?

On the pitch, Peter Crouch's first-half headed goal was enough to defeat a tired and ideas-free United. Later Ferguson gracelessly said, 'It seems Liverpool can play for five minutes and win.' But there was little else to say about the football, which was hugely competitive but, like too many in the Anfield crowd, largely thought-free. Didi Hamann ruled the midfield battleground for the home side until just before the close of play, when a terrible incident roused everyone. The spiky United man Alan Smith dislocated and broke an ankle in an innocent tussle with Riise. This injury was so grotesque that the players of both sides quickly turned away whilst summoning the hospital crew. If Smith were a stricken steeplechaser – no idle possibility, this – they would have been calling for the screens. Everyone could instantly see how serious and hideous this was – a possible career-ending accident. Normally this would be a moment for the crowd to withdraw in respectful silence for a stricken warrior – to wait to applaud off the fallen victim. Instead, parts of the Kop (the most knowledgeable football fans in the world) started celebrating Smith's terrible plight – in song. Later there were reports that his ambulance was attacked by local scallies. (Are they Liverpool fans?) Finally, to top it all, the Liverpool club had to apologise officially to their guests after excrement was tipped onto United fans as the visitors waited to leave the stadium. Showered in human shit – at the home of football.

In the fallout to all of this – which includes the usual pious press garbage – we also got familiar deconstructions in the local Reds fanzines about what 'really' happened on this shameful afternoon. (And, frankly, it *was* shameful.) Of course, getting the details right is always important – many Reds fans *did* eventually applaud Smith off on his stretcher, and the Liverpool Supporters Club later sent Smith a letter wishing him a full recovery (but no apology). But don't let this cloud the main picture. Forget, too, the alleged depravities of United fans and the familiar 'they did it to us first' rationalisations or the usual 'the media did it' banalities. We well know where this kind of denial leads. These events actually made us look too much like the people we are often accused of being by our enemies. And we know that there is a very different story to tell about Liverpool: about passion, humour, an appreciation of opponents and basic respect for the game;

about Istanbul and all those other foreign trips where we mixed with the locals and celebrated the game together as civilised people. You don't have to suck up to the opposition or buy into any of the Premier League's marketing guff about the football 'family audience' to see that what happened against United is not who we are or who we should want to be. Let's not stoop to the sort of barbarianism that actually threatens to kill football and the many decent reasons for watching it at all. So it was hard to celebrate fully this hard-fought win, even with the European Cup now beckoning once more.

After Anfield and United in the FA Cup it was Lisbon for Champions League action. Just before kick-off in the rebuilt Stadium of Light, after Benfica's real golden eagle had swooped spectacularly down through the floodlights, the local ultras behind Pepe Reina's goal unfurled a huge banner showing the Benfica players stealing the European Cup from Liverpool and sneaking it through the Shankly Gates. This was a cute opening gambit but also a slightly disarming one. Did they know something we didn't?

These big European matches are the ones especially relished by Benítez and his backroom team. The 'intellectual' qualities of the contest and the lack of familiarity of the Liverpool players with the systems, style and the players of Continental clubs mean that the coach and his staff become much more important figures in setting the agenda. This also means more work with the technological aids that are central to the modern coach's meticulous planning. 'I have always said that the computer doesn't score goals,' Benítez told Paco Cordobés of *Abfutbol*, 'but it helps to manage the information. It means that you can manage data more quickly, much faster and much more logically. Then you can use the data to train the players better. One can't say this is something that is indispensable, but it is a help that allows you to win some time.' This kind of work is definitely a collective effort at Liverpool. 'For me the key lies in the fact that I have always surrounded myself with people that help me manage that information,' said Benítez. 'I have always had a good team working with me so we can take advantage of that information. Because there is so much data that can be picked up – statistical, videos, computers that dissect strategies, counterattacks, etc. – one man alone cannot manage it. And I say again, a team is needed that can analyse this data and reach conclusions.' We are talking some serious IT time here.

And this central emphasis on data and planning also partly explains why Benítez finds strikers so perplexing and so difficult to judge or trust. He has had some of the same difficulties here that he did at Valencia. He feels uncomfortable with the individualist qualities of goal scorers that are tricky to quantify or comprehend. He finds it harder to accommodate them intellectually or to include them in his carefully laid out game plans. How does a coach improve a striker who prefers not to overanalyse what works? Strikers must also do a team job for Benítez – the instinctive occupation of scoring goals is somehow just not enough for this collective perfectionist.

Cordobés then posed the really critical question about planning and preparation to Benítez. He told the Spaniard that lots of coaches get scared with technology and that they believe that the essence of football – its spontaneity and creativity – can actually get lost when introducing a modern tool like this into sport. Benítez was commendably firm in his reply: 'The idea is, in fact, to take advantage of the technology without losing the essence of football. That is the key: to try to know more about the hidden aspects of the game and, later on, to give value to the most important aspects. You must always check that your team is organised, and you must be able to observe that your players know how to put into practice the systems you want to use.'

Boiled down, Benítez was arguing that, as a player, you must be flexible in your responses on the pitch, as well as highly organised and well prepared. Technology used badly can help turn players into unresponsive cogs when you really need thinking, acting contributors and good decision makers on the field, men who can change their approach depending upon the condition of the match and the opposition. That is the theory at least: that the able coach takes a real risk if he sends his team out in a straitjacket with only one set of instructions, one way of playing. Preparing a team defensively in this way is much easier than the opposite. But if too much of the coaching gets onto the field, a team can look rigid and be unable to take its opportunities to change the flow of a match. In Lisbon the Liverpool team made just this mistake. It proved incapable of responding to the context of the match, of stepping out of its negative mindset. It was a fateful error.

Fowler, Kewell, Morientes and García all started for Liverpool, so this was no wholly defensive (or especially potent or resilient) Reds line-up. But Crouch, Cissé and Gerrard were all on the bench. This selection meant that the visitors lacked real pace and goal threat, as well as dynamism and control through the middle. And it meant that an initially timid and watchful Benfica, a toothless side who looked like they were obediently waiting to be punished by the European champions, began to draw confidence from Liverpool's diffidence and patent lack of firepower, especially when Sissoko was forced to leave the field with a first-half eye injury. It was the defensive linchpin Hamann, rather than the progressive Gerrard, who came on as a replacement. Why be so conservative? (Gerrard got just 12 directionless minutes at the end.) Nuno Gomes said later how surprised and comforted Benfica were that their famous visitors had been so negative. As Liverpool retreated – palpably limiting their ambitions to not conceding – Benfica came on more strongly. Pepe Reina had barely had a save to make or a single uncertain moment, but the predictable sucker punch came with six minutes left: we could feel it coming, perhaps the visiting bench did too. It was a rerun of the recent Old Trafford defeat. A Hamann foul on Liverpool's left offered a free-kick to the home team, and the lanky centre-back Luisão – by a distance Benfica's best player (no difficult task) – was unaccountably allowed to steal in to head gently past Pepe Reina. Benítez slumped on the Liverpool bench, apparently astounded by this setback and the manner of its delivery. His computers had not predicted this. And his team had stuck cravenly to its limited game plan when a little more aggression and ambition – and possibly a different team selection – would have surely produced a win in what was, after all, Liverpool's most important match of the whole season. And 0–1 was so much worse than a scoreless draw that to even risk it happening was a gross mistake against such weak opposition. The second leg at Anfield, where the pressure to score would be on from the very start and with Liverpool hardly renowned for their firepower, would now be a real test. Call it straight: the Champions of Europe were already facing elimination by also-rans from the competition they fought so hard, in June 2005, to be a part of.

LAST DAYS OF HIGHBURY, THE END OF EUROPE AND 7 (SEVEN) AT ST ANDREWS

Back in the Premiership Harry Kewell, showing some form again at last, scored the only goal in yet another Liverpool match in which the opposition was reduced to ten men (an astonishing eleven times this had happened already that season). Joey Barton went this time for Manchester City, and the Reds eventually eased home, despite Benítez noting the obvious 'nervousness' in Liverpool. But a goal just wouldn't come against Charlton at Anfield, the game ending in a 0–0 Premiership frustration – which meant nine points lost by Liverpool to two clubs, Charlton and Birmingham City, for want of decent strikers and Chelsea already out of sight in the league. 'The lack of goals is worrying,' said a clearly worried Benítez. Robbie Fowler was still not really match fit, and the Liverpool manager pointed out that Morientes was scoring great goals in training. That is, when the pace was off and the physical challenge was limited – so what did that actually tell us? Morientes would have to return to Spain in 2006–07 to rediscover his best goal-scoring form, ironically with Rafa's old club Valencia CF. His time in England was an experiment that failed. Momo Sissoko now faced a long lay-off with retina damage. Liverpool would miss his energy and defensive acumen, but the young Malian would have to improve his ball retention and passing skills to be really useful to Liverpool.

To be honest, Momo may not have made the difference in the Champions League return leg against Benfica at Anfield. Because in Liverpool's previous twelve matches the Reds had managed to score more than one goal only once, away to Portsmouth in the FA Cup. Morientes had not scored in 956 minutes, Cissé in 649. Momo had no goals at all. Astonishingly, only four – out of twenty-four – Liverpool Champions League goals that season were scored by strikers who were still at the club. It was a poor return for £27 million spent. Calling on the Kop to help out, as Benítez did, could only take us so far. 'Crowds can't score,' as Benfica coach Ronald Koeman astutely put it.

On another European evening Liverpool might have scored the two goals they needed to proceed, but the weight of Istanbul and the team's incredible unbeaten run in Europe, plus the lack of striker confidence and the early start to the season, all seemed to catch up with the players at once. Two other problems emerged to shift the Red focus: Rafa Benítez was publicly linked before kick-off with a possible move to either Real Madrid or Inter Milan, and late injuries to Riise and Hyypiä so destabilised the starting left side of the Liverpool defence that even the usually dependable Carragher for once began to look like a man skating on a frozen lake.

On the managerial question, Benítez only said that he wanted to concentrate on the Benfica tie, but it seemed clear that without adequate finance for reinforcements next season he would have to 'consider his position'. He had the same disagreement at Valencia after his first Spanish title, so this was no idle threat. In the match itself Benítez relied on García, Morientes and Crouch for the goals he promised Liverpool would score. But part of Liverpool's problem – one the manager could not solve in January – was that neither of his wide players, García or Kewell, could get behind the Benfica defence. So the Liverpool pressure was constant – ten early chances – but always predictable. Crouch, sprung free for once by Gerrard and Morientes, shot weakly at Moretto in the Benfica goal after 25 minutes, bringing back uneasy memories of Emile Heskey's bad nights under Gérard Houllier. Then, 36 minutes into the match, Simão Sabrosa showed why Benítez tried to sign him for Liverpool. Admittedly, Traoré and Carragher combined their mistakes to present the winger with a chance 20 yards out, but his curling right-foot shot into the top left-hand corner of Reina's net was an unsaveable thing of some beauty. And, unlike Olympiakos in 2004, Benfica were no novices at holding onto a lead in Europe away from home, and the Liverpool crowd knew it. Fowler and Cissé came on but to no avail because three home goals were now quite impossible. Instead it was Fabrizio Miccoli who signed off with a second Benfica goal, completing a historic win for the Lisbon club. The wonderful Istanbul spell had finally been lifted from this parish.

The loss was painful, but it was easier to take after the past season's incredible European success. And the lack of depth in the Liverpool squad – Traoré and Warnock were not of this standard and nor were the Liverpool strike force – had only strengthened Benítez's hand with the Liverpool board. Though whether the Liverpool manager wanted to stay at Anfield, or David Moores and Rick Parry could come up with the serious cash he was demanding for reinforcements, remained to be seen. Finishing second in the Premiership was worth £5 million, so that was still worth fighting for. But playing away in your last-ever visit to Highbury was hardly the fixture one might have chosen to pick up the pieces of a broken European campaign. However, as Arsenal marched on in Europe, at least Mourinho had paid for his show of hubris and disrespect as Chelsea crashed out of Europe in disgrace to Barcelona.

In recent years visiting Highbury as an away fan – at least behind the goal – was no lavish day out. Low prices used to compensate somewhat for the suffering of the away supporter in this dilapidated stadium, but not any more. Arsenal's new venue would raise more from corporate guests alone than from the whole of the old Highbury, making it the biggest revenue-raising football stadium in the world. In Spain club members must be consulted on price increases, keeping prices within reach of the poorest socio. Here the new Emirates Stadium would be an extraordinary cash cow housing 60,000 fans and 150 executive boxes. In one year Arsenal's match-day income would hike from £33 million to £70 million, including the sale of 'club level' seats on the halfway line for four seasons at a cool £19,000 each. All had already sold. Arsenal was £153 million in debt for the project, but on these sorts of figures that could clear in six or seven years. And they would be striding away from Liverpool, competing with Chelsea for major signings. This seemed to confirm that a new stadium at Anfield was all the more pressing.

It was the location and the architectural style of the old stadium that would be missed most at Highbury, even though the stupid queuing and searches of away fans that day meant missing the first ten minutes of a lively encounter dominated by the home team. Henry scored a typical opener, threading his run between Carragher and Finnan before bending his shot around Reina. But when García headed Liverpool's equaliser in the second half after Lehmann had parried Gerrard's shot, it looked like a reasonable Red point stolen. Except that five-star referee Steve Bennett then failed to see that Xabi Alonso had slipped in a tackle with Flamini and sent the Liverpool man off for a second yellow card! This piece of high pantomime was swiftly followed by another: a blind Steven Gerrard pass-back which picked out Thierry Henry, who scored – unapologetically. So we left Highbury for the last time pointless and frustrated, an appropriate ending to a north London trip that had too often ended the self-same way. Bring on the new world order.

DON'T SAY ROBBIE FOWLER – SAY GOAL!

Benítez's Liverpool had now scored just nine goals in their last fourteen games. It was starting to hurt and looked like an irreversible problem with this squad of players. So who could explain when the next five matches produced a twenty-goal haul for Liverpool? Did the coach change anything? Not in this case. Nothing that he or his players had mentioned, at least. The Liverpool team that next defeated Fulham 5–1 at Anfield was no different from those selected before. Riise and Hyypiä were still missing, and Morientes and Fowler started up front. Frankly, Liverpool played quite poorly, but suddenly the goals started flying in – including the opener, a header from Robbie Fowler at the Anfield Road end, his first goal back in Liverpool's colours. In fact, it was the return to scoring form of the 'Toxteth Terror' that sparked this Liverpool goal glut. Morientes also scored to add to a Fulham own goal (the irascible Brown) and two more Reds goals in the last minute – from Warnock and Crouch – offered an undeserved gloss that quite dismayed the Fulham manager Chris Coleman. It also inspired an even better 3–1 Liverpool win at Newcastle United. Crouch and Gerrard combined brilliantly and Jean-Alain Boumsong got his marching orders (number 12), just when United were threatening a comeback. Luck? Maybe, but it worked.

Birmingham City (a) in the midweek sixth round of the FA Cup was so *not* a fixture wanted by the relegation-threatened and injury-hit Blues that they would probably have paid for Liverpool's safe passage, unopposed, into their 22nd FA Cup semi-final. Anything, in fact, to avoid the humiliation that happened here and which threatened to engulf City manager Steve Bruce. Plenty of travelling Reds missed the first two goals, headers by Hyypiä and Crouch (eleven goals now in twenty-four games), scored before even five minutes were up. Which meant that with roughly 5 per cent of the contest over, 100 per cent of the result was known, chiefly because City had no identifiable forwards and no belief or heart. And far from consolidating or conserving their lead, the Liverpool players, having been in a goals drought, were now desperate to drink at the scoring well in their 53rd match of the season. This was the glorious story of the Blues night: 3–0 at half-time and four more Liverpool goals plundered in the second half with no reply, the best by a returned John Arne Riise. Momo Sissoko was also back – wearing chic red eye-protectors that were soon discarded as if he needed to clear his disbelieving eyes. It ended an intoxicating, unprecedented 7–0 victory for Liverpool, with Steve Bruce on the Birmingham bench in need of intensive care. Chelsea now lay in wait for an Old Trafford semi-final showdown.

With Everton next up in the Premiership at Anfield – Liverpool's seventh fixture in March – the rush of Red scoring could seldom have come at a better time. For this collision both Beattie and Gerrard wore No. 08 shirts to mark the city's Capital of Culture status, but culture was far from the agenda in a rip-roaring, eleven-yellows-and-two-reds contest that typified the best of the British game and the continuing intensity of the Merseyside rivalry. Alan Stubbs later protested that it was foreign players who were now making trouble by demanding yellows for opponents – García was especially picked out – but this was simply the sort of raw-boned conflict that went back over a century of football and 202 previous football meetings in this city, irrespective of from where players were recruited. It was an Englishman, Steven Gerrard, who picked up his two first-half yellow cards within just forty seconds, referee Phil Dowd applying the letter of the law and forcing a Reds reshuffle as their captain slinked off. The Anfield leader immediately fell out of love with the Liverpool No. 08 theme.

If anything, Everton's game now diminished in front of the Liverpool ten, as though they suddenly became quite afraid of the possibility of a victory at Anfield at last. As if to confirm their uncertainty, on the stroke of half-time Phil Neville glided a header into his own net from a sharp Alonso corner. García added another immediately after the half-time break in front of a foaming Kop, lobbing the ludicrously positioned Richard Wright. Everton finally woke up, proving that zonal marking's greatest failure was that it could not ensure that the opposition's only major threat from set-pieces was given special attention. So Tim Cahill scored from an Everton corner, Carragher shoving Crouch angrily in his frustration at the lack of cover for the Australian pest. Now the Blues would surely come on strong in the remaining half hour: except that substitute Andy van der Meyde managed only five minutes before elbowing Alonso in the head to offer Mr Dowd the opportunity to even things up with a second red card. Before the end Harry Kewell received a pass from Finnan in front of a backing-off Everton defence and hit a no-back-lift scorcher past Wright to seal the points for Liverpool. 'I am delighted with the players, the supporters and the final score,' Benítez said later. We guessed that he meant he couldn't have been happier after experiencing the sort of bloodied theatre the coach might spend a career working in Spain without matching. Would you want to leave for Real Madrid and risk losing all *this*?

ENDING IT ALL IN STYLE

Now on a perceptible roll, Liverpool cleaned up in their remaining six Premiership matches, which meant a run of nine consecutive Premiership wins to close the season following the defeat at Arsenal – so much for flagging in the home straight. West Brom and West Ham both succumbed to the pace of Djibril Cissé, Blackburn Rovers to the Frenchman's strange interpretation of the offside law, which brought a winning Liverpool goal in controversial circumstances for Robbie Fowler. Fowler was also on the mark to beat Bolton Wanderers (1–0) and to open up the scoring at Portsmouth for a final-day Liverpool 3–1 win. Robbie looked set for a new Liverpool deal. Steven Gerrard trashed Aston Villa with two goals in the 3–1 final home league win, and thus finished the season as he started it – scoring goals. However, it was goals *conceded* by Liverpool at West Ham (2–1), at home to Aston Villa and away at Portsmouth that meant that the club record for clean sheets in a season (35) just agonisingly evaded Pepe Reina, Carra and their colleagues.

Liverpool finished the 2005–06 season with a hugely commendable eighty-two Premiership points, just one behind second-placed Manchester United and only nine behind champions Chelsea. It was a twenty-four point improvement on the first Benítez season – Liverpool had won eight more games than the seventeen they won in 2005. The Reds had also caught up 26 points on Chelsea compared to 2005 and 18 on Manchester United. Arsenal finished twenty-five points ahead of Liverpool in 2005 – now the Gunners were fifteen points adrift of the Reds, an astonishing forty-point turnaround for Wenger's European Cup finalists in just one season. Such improvements so soon were way beyond even Benítez's expectations. There was no league championship to claim for Benítez in 2006, as there was for him in Spain in both 2002 and 2004 – although 82 points was at least competitive again in the Premiership title race. There was even a feeling that it could be bettered in the new season. Benítez did seem to be working some of the same magic at Liverpool that he once performed for Valencia – before he left the Spanish club in tears. And he still had the 2006 FA Cup to contest – if, of course, he could overcome the semi-final challenge of a familiar opponent: José Mourinho's Chelsea. It would prove to be an Old Trafford battle of monumental proportions – and was one every bit as challenging in its own way as the one he had taken on to change both the culture and the structure of football at the Mestalla Stadium in Valencia.

9

Reigning in Spain:
Rafa Benítez at Valencia CF

The historic *doblete* for Valencia CF; the Benítez 'boot room'
at the Mestalla; running out of contract in Spain; why not
be a *manager*, rather than a coach? Benítez is wearied by the
Valencia board; heading for Merseyside – and freedom!

2004: RAFA RULES IN SPAIN AND EUROPE

It was May 2004, towards the end of Valencia CF's historic *doblete*
(Double triumph) of the 2003–04 season. Valencia had already
secured La Liga (again) and also the UEFA Cup, having beaten
Olympic Marseille in the final. But there were still tiresome league
fixtures in Spain to complete after a long season. Bob Paisley might
now have let his team off the leash, or else his players might have
taken the chance themselves, as they once famously did in a Teesside
bar before a season-closer in 1982 at Middlesbrough. But those were
different times and a different country. Instead, Rafa Benítez showed
that his ambitions for the Valencianistas and for attaining complete
professionalism had few limits. Three days after clinching the
Double he was already strongly focused on the remaining La Liga
matches. 'We want more,' he told reporters. 'We will try to reach
80 points and to score more goals to finish the season as top scorers,
as well as being the club with the best defensive record.' In fact, he
was already thinking about the *next* league season, about making a

statement of intent to the rest in Spain and to his own players. It was a performance both obsessive and impressive – part anorak, part football perfectionist.

In his first season at the club (2001–02) the untried, inexperienced Benítez had won La Liga for Valencia by seven clear points from Deportivo de La Coruña. It was a triumph based on organisation and defensive solidarity, and it was produced almost entirely by remotivating the squad that had been put together by Héctor Cúper. Valencia CF had scored only 51 goals in 38 matches, a record low for modern Spanish champions. They were coldly impressive – to match their coach – but this also made them a difficult team to love, based as they were around the defensive ruthlessness of goalkeeper Santiago Cañizares, defenders Amedeo Carboni, Fabian Ayala and Mauricio Pellegrino, protected in midfield by David Albelda and Rubén Baraja, and on the flanks by the prodigious defensive and attacking work of Francisco Rufete and Vicente. Goal scoring seemed to have been a wholly secondary concern to the young coach – or at least there was no room for a defined goal poacher in his team, a trait that Benítez brought with him later to Liverpool. The new coach, famously cautious and meticulously prepared, sometimes played with no recognised strikers at all. Instead he expected his midfielders and his more offensive players – Kily González, the brilliant Argentinian Pablo Aimar and Mista – to snatch goals when they could, and then he relied on the defensive solidarity of the whole Valencia CF team to see the thing through. It usually worked. The new champions scored more than two goals only twice in the league, and they managed only six goals in total in the six matches against the three relegated clubs – but it was still enough for thirteen priceless points. The philosophy of Benítez seemed to be 'never more than we need'. His top scorer, the midfielder Baraja, weighed in with just seven league goals. Some Valencia fans wondered if this approach was really any different to the style pursued by the discarded Cúper. But there was one key difference: Benítez was a winner and Valencia CF had the title to prove it.

Refused serious cash for reinforcements, the following season Valencia slipped to fifth place in La Liga (still struggling to score goals and now bound for the UEFA Cup) but taught Liverpool a painful lesson in the Champions League group stage, comfortably beating Houllier's side both home and away, the latter a 2–0 lesson. The Kop sucked in its breath at the economy and the efficiency of the Spaniards, who won only 1–0 at Anfield in the return but did so at a stroll. Valencia also put out Wenger's Arsenal in the second group stage, the giant Norwegian John Carew scoring the winning goal in a match the north Londoners looked in control of for long stretches. Ironically, Cúper's Inter Milan then demolished Benítez's hopes in a tight quarter-final, winning on away goals.

THE HISTORIC DOBLETE FOR VALENCIA CF

In 2003–04 Valencia were more impressive, and more likeable, La Liga champions. Mista, a more mature player now and given a more attacking brief, came up with 19 league goals, Vicente with 12. Benítez had just piloted Valencia CF to its best-ever season, losing only five matches in all competitions. There were just three defeats in La Liga, a 0–1 loss to Gençlerbirligi in Ankara in the UEFA Cup and a 0–3 setback against Real Madrid in the quarter-finals of the Spanish Cup. Valencia were generally solid at the fortress Mestalla and also conceded only 15 goals away from home in all competitions, an extraordinary defensive record – and still the Benítez signature today. But the big change from 2002 was the greater freedom to attack as Benítez's confidence grew: a 6–1 win at Malaga and a 5–1 drubbing of Mallorca, for example. Benítez had transformed the club into one of the most feared in Europe: strong at the back, penetrating in attack. In La Liga his team ended up fully seven points clear of Real Madrid and never faltered in the run-in despite an amazing second-half-of-the-season recovery by Frank Rijkaard's Barcelona, who had begun to show signs of the great team the Dutchman was building towards and that would win a La Liga and Champions League Double for the Camp Nou in 2005–06. The Valencia CF title win had actually involved a stunning 15-point turnaround for a stumbling Real Madrid. This was even more impressive because Real were desperate for title success in what was the club's centenary year. Benítez had built this Valencia side with huge mental strength designed for the long haul. 'When we were eight points behind [Real Madrid],' Benítez remarked, 'one could give it up for lost. But this team is a good long-distance runner and that allowed us to catch Real Madrid. So, everything has come out perfectly for us. The team was getting stronger, week after week. The quality of the footballers here is evident.' Quite.

This meant two La Liga titles in just three years for Benítez, something that was beyond even the great Valencia sides of the 1940s. And he had done it on a fraction of the budgets available at both Real Madrid and FC Barcelona. But he was also well aware that keeping things going at this level would require an even greater effort. 'None of us had hoped to arrive here so quickly,' he said. 'What has been achieved has been thanks to a great attitude. The difficult thing is to maintain it over a period of time. So this doesn't mean that we don't have to reinforce to face the future.'

Benítez was also beating other (more dubious) records at the Mestalla. In the thirteen previous years, no coach had managed to stay for even three consecutive seasons at the club. The last had been the Uruguayan Víctor Espárrago. Valencia CF had been in a period of real turmoil when the young and inexperienced Benítez had arrived to offer a new direction. In his three seasons in charge Benítez had now coached Valencia for one hundred and sixty-two matches: one hundred and fourteen in La Liga, nine in the Copa del Rey, two in the Super Cup and thirty-seven in European competitions, including the Champions League and UEFA Cup. This stint had produced 88 victories (55 per cent), 41 draws (25 per cent) and just 33 defeats (20 per cent). But the real measure of Benítez's achievements, as any Valencia fan would confirm, was in the trophies won in these three seasons. Silverware from home and abroad marked this as a football club – and a coach – going places.

A few days after his second title win a number of top European clubs started expressing an interest in recruiting Benítez, but to some potential suitors he still seemed the rather awkward perfectionist. After confirming that his main influence in the sport was the old AC Milan coach Arrigo Sacchi, Benítez declared to an *El País* journalist that he still had work to do at the Mestalla: that his team had not yet arrived at the pinnacle of Sacchi's teams. These teams could, said Benítez enviously, 'manage tactical concepts very well, they had players of the highest quality and they were also very competitive'. So these were the three components to drive Benítez's entire managerial career: tactics, competence and competitiveness. Not a bad trio – but difficult to get all three of them spot-on at the same time. This was to become the key challenge for the future.

Benítez was also a great competitor and had excellent concentration. Before the biggest matches he was much more centred in his work, mapping every single movement of his players in training. With notebook in hand he would write constantly between observations, later analysing his notes carefully before reaching his conclusions – and acting upon them. The meticulousness with which Benítez and his coaching team went about their work was one of the aspects that most impressed the Valencia players and fans. They learned that Benítez studied every tiny aspect of the game, and he always managed to exude a sense of security thanks to the fact that nothing was left to chance on the pitch. Benítez believed that going the extra millimetre was vital in gaining a competitive advantage in high-level sport.

According to the players from Valencia, Benítez believed everything had an explanation. This was why he talked so much in training, constantly challenging and correcting them. 'Benítez has no problem talking,' the players would smile – or wince. This incessant dialogue with the players was one of the key characteristics of Benítez's regime at Valencia in the three seasons he coached the blanquinegros. It was no coincidence that a fortnight after his arrival at Valencia the reserve goalkeeper Andrés Palop (now at UEFA Cup holders Sevilla) told the press that he had spoken more with Benítez in those two weeks than with the previous coach Héctor Cúper in two years.

Another feature of Benítez's reign was his capacity to raise himself and his players for the most important matches, an indispensable quality for guaranteeing success in cup tournaments. Valencia fans might also have found it illuminating to have checked the face of Benítez twenty-four hours before the final of the 2004 UEFA Cup and compared it with Héctor Cúper's before the final of the Champions League three years before in the San Siro. It was Benítez's first major final, but he was probably calmer than most of the Valencia fans. He was clearly at ease, confident and smiling. It might have been just another match he was contemplating rather than the biggest game of his short career as a top coach. His only concern was to 'read' the match effectively for his team. He affirmed this with the press. 'There is no fixed rule,' he told them, 'about how you see a match. Some [matches] will demand a stress more on attack, others on defence. But in the beginning we will do our usual things. We will see what sort of control we manage to establish in the match, and depending on if we are superior or not, we will make adjustments to our approach.' He made it sound very matter-of-fact, because his preparation had made it so. However, this sort of outward calmness and concentration didn't hide the deep excitement that the coach also felt on waking up on the morning of a major final. 'I feel very proud to be here,' he said before the 2004 UEFA Cup final. 'Not having been an elite player means that when you get chances like this the satisfaction is much greater.'

THE VALENCIA 'BOOT ROOM' AND THE MESTALLA FANS

When the staff at Valencia CF assembled to say 'goodbye' to the Mestalla crowd after their second championship season on 10 May 2004, the home players came onto the pitch one by one to receive their standing ovations. The practice has just been introduced in England for the Premiership title winners. Finally, Benítez's own moment arrived. He was called by the man on the Mestalla PA system to come onto the pitch to receive the adulation of the home fans. But he refused to take the field alone. Instead, he entered the Mestalla like a champion but alongside his backroom team: Antonio López, Paco Ayestaran, José Manuel Ochotorena, the club doctor Jorge Candel, Juan Angel Ballesteros and Manolo Maciá. It was a fitting ovation and a typical Benítez gesture because the relationship between Benítez and his technical team was central to Valencia's success – just as had been the case in Bob Paisley's time at Liverpool. Benítez had always stressed to the fans and to the Spanish media that his achievements were only the fruits of a large technical team, each of whom had their specific responsibilities. A few days before facing Olympic Marseille in Gothenburg Benítez had presented his core group of collaborators – the 'top table' of Antonio López, Paco Ayestaran and José Manuel Ochotorena – to *El País* in a story headlined '*La cocina de Benítez*' ('Benítez's kitchen'). It offered a real insight into how the Benítez coaching and training unit worked. The coach dealt with his key backroom men individually, starting with Antonio López: 'Antonio López is a first-class coach with experience in taking decisions, and he also has a tactical vision. He also has a good and trusting relationship with the players that I cannot have. We did the same coaching course together. We faced each other as opponents when I was in charge of the Real Madrid Under-19 team, and he was in charge of the Atlético [Madrid] side. I realised then that he was a really well-qualified guy. This year the strategies we have designed have come out better for us.

Antonio has had much more responsibility in designing these plays.'
López acted as a necessary buffer between Benítez and his players. His
role was to help maintain the authority of his boss without alienating
the players. He was the man who got close to the players, who dealt
with any personal issues or complaints they might have had about
their place in the team or how they were being treated by the coach.
López, like Joe Fagan at Liverpool, had the easy skills to appease
players who were dropped or reprimanded, helping them to overcome
their disappointments – and encouraging them to come back to prove
Benítez wrong. But he also worked on the playing style of the team.

'[Paco] Ayestaran has already been with me for eight years,' Benítez
continued. 'His teams are always in good physical condition, especially
at the end of the championship. And he is also a good coach; he
contributes useful tactical things. He is very dynamic and demanding.
He takes control of the training sessions. Before that we sit down,
and I tell him which are the key themes of today's work: what I have
identified from the videos of our opponents' play. Then we design the
week's work: the exercise load and the aims of the exercises, depending
upon whether the opponent plays more of a long-ball game or more
of a short passing game. Against Olympic Marseille we know that we
should try to dominate the match. We have already worked out so
many variants on this sort of approach that it won't be too complicated
this week. We will only need to change a few details.'

Paco Ayestaran was a key figure not just on the fitness side for
Benítez but also in putting into practice the manager's assessments of
opponents through the application of his boss's research in the week's
coaching. This was a major departure from some early approaches to
football coaching. Benítez and his team did *all* their coaching with
the club's immediate opponents absolutely uppermost in their mind.
Everything was tailored to meeting the specific challenge offered by
the team's next rivals. This meant that the players were always focused
on the week's problems and were seldom bored. Each week's training
offered a new challenge by matching the week's work directly to

the system and the individuals one would face at the weekend or in midweek. This kind of obsessive attention to preparation and detail – a far cry from the old Anfield adage of 'let the opposition worry about us' – was one of the reasons why Benítez became so frustrated when he first came to England and found his weeks so clogged up with fixtures. How matches got in the way! He claimed this sort of congestion meant that he simply had insufficient time to prepare properly for games.

On his goalkeeping coach, José Manuel Ochotorena, Benítez commented, 'Ochotorena contributes great calmness and common sense to the training. He has that sort of vision of the goalkeeper that we don't have among the other coaches. He was a great goalkeeper, and he is also up to date.' To sum up the roles of his coaching team, he said, 'In a few words, Ayestaran covers the physical capacity, Antonio López the improvisation and Ochotorena the serenity. Me, I am quite cold and analytical.' This last comment was especially telling, showing that Benítez recognised the importance of establishing a balance between the physical, emotional and analytical – between the needs of the minds and bodies of his players. He also recognised his own emotional detachment, relying largely, instead, on his carefully selected staff to offer both the imagination and warmth that any team of human beings in any line of work requires to make for a happy and successful environment. And this *is* work for Rafa Benítez, let's make no bones about that; football is a job, a serious business. But every ship also needs a captain, a man who offers direction and strong leadership. This was Rafa's key task.

Despite his own emotional reticence, Benítez connected well with the Valencia fans right from his arrival at the club in June 2001. He decided on the use of a clever piece of PR, a 'human' touch that was actually fully researched. In his initial presentation to the fans, Benítez greeted them in the distinctively local Valencian Catalan dialect. Predictably, this piece of measured localism went down a storm with the natives, an antidote to the monosyllabic misery suffered in the

Cúper years. It was designed, of course, to help buy Benítez and his staff some time with the Mestalla hard core, should he need it. He didn't.

After defeating Sevilla to win his second La Liga, in the 'dead' fixture that followed at the Mestalla and amid the wild celebrations that followed, one could clearly see Benítez singing the official club song. The coach thanked the crowd for their support and for his own recognition from the fans, and they replied with a then favourite song at a club not entirely noted for singing the praises of its coaches: 'Rafa Benítez, laralalalala, Rafa Benítez, laralalalala . . . !'.

And as they looked to the future the Mestalla fans began to protest loudly to the board of directors at Valencia CF that their favoured man, their new coaching hero, surely deserved an extended contract. Admittedly, this seemed a no-brainer in England: a man wins you two league titles, including your first for more than thirty years, as well as a European trophy, and you hesitate to offer a longer stay? You must shackle him right away, preferably on a five-year deal and congratulate yourself on your fortune and foresight. But not in Spain. Here it seemed that *no* board of directors wanted their coach to become too comfortable, too secure, no matter what his achievements. He may yet damage your own power base and influence within the club. He may become just *too* powerful – awkward, even. Coaches, after all, come and go. This team could be coached to more success by anyone. In this sort of climate, Benítez was, astonishingly, only offered an additional one year on his contract, which had just one more year to run. This was his 'reward' for three trophies won for Valencia CF. His contractual relationship with the club would actually expire in June 2005. It was a short-sighted, fateful mistake by the club's hierarchy – but one entirely in tune with the culture of the Spanish game.

RE-SIGN BENÍTEZ? THERE IS NO HURRY; HE STILL HAS A YEAR'S CONTRACT

May was nearly over, and Benítez's position was still unclear. Would he stay at the club? The fans began to fear the worst. What was his incentive to stay, having been made such a shabby offer by the board? Maybe he would prefer to look for new stimulation at another club – or even in another country? In a shock development, the national committee of coaches in Spain confirmed that Benítez could actually leave Valencia CF right away by simply presenting a letter explaining why he wanted to leave and agreeing to give up all his contractual payment rights. It would be so easy for Benítez to break away immediately from Valencia CF! Manuel Llorente, the general director of the club, finally recognised that the contract Benítez had with the Valencianistas might not even include any compensation clauses (although Liverpool FC would later have to pay around 400,000 euros for Benítez's release – still chickenfeed). This valued coach, the most successful in Spain and in the club's history, could leave Valencia CF instantly – apparently for free.

In an interview with *El País* on 24 May, Benítez was incredibly enigmatic about his future, giving free rein to all types of conjecture. 'I have one more year on my contract,' he said. 'I don't want to say another thing.' He wanted to continue at Valencia CF – but not at any price. He was seeking a solid sporting project, but the club seemed to be in a state of uncertainty, lacking real direction from the top. Benítez also knew that he was wanted at a number of other European clubs: Liverpool, Beşiktaş and Bayern Munich, as well as several Italian clubs, had been mentioned. Feelers had gone out. On 25 May Jaime Ortí, the president of Valencia, seemed unaware of the imminent contractual 'problem' with Benítez, saying that he had no plans to speak to the coach because '. . . we have time. He has one more year on his contract.' That same day, in an interview published in the sport newspaper *Superdeporte*, Benítez responded to questioning on his position in an extremely ambiguous way, allowing the gathering storm to stir more violently at the Mestalla. 'They [the Valencia board] have told me that they intend to speak to me,' he confided, before adding pointedly and with some menace, 'but the facts are always more important than words.'

This whole episode, of course, clearly demonstrated the mentality of Spanish football club administrations. The coach was simply someone hired to put into place the policy and selections of the sporting commission on the club board. The sport director would decide which players the club should sign, and the coach would then try to shape the team accordingly. The coach would act as a convenient scapegoat should such selections prove ill thought out or unsuitable. He could then be sacked with as little pain as possible and everyone could move on. No one at Valencia CF had ever contemplated the possibility that the club might actually want to *secure* the position of its coach over the long term. The club was geared, instead – like all Spanish clubs – to the moment when the coach would have to be sacked. This was usually sooner rather than later, as the history of Valencia CF confirmed. Rafa Benítez had produced a problem that Spanish football clubs were ill prepared to respond to: he was successful and wanted to stay. But García Pitarch, the sporting director, insisted on signing players Benítez didn't want, and it had even looked as though the board had on occasions intended to say 'goodbye' to him. The directors knew too little about the game, and they lacked respect for the coach, a crucial absence in his otherwise satisfying working environment. Something had to give. After the last training session of the season on 28 May 2004, when the gathered journalists asked Benítez about his future for the umpteenth time, he made a little joke – one that carried a chilling warning for all those who loved the club and who had ambitions about its direction. 'Yes, I will stay,' said Benítez, 'for a couple of weeks.'

THE AMBITIONS OF RAFA BENÍTEZ

Benítez's own mind was now swirling. He felt a debt to the club that had offered him the opportunity to work in the First Division of Spanish football when he was an unknown coach in the Spanish Second Division. He also valued the support and real warmth of the Valencia fans, and, not unnaturally, he felt a bond with his players despite his attempts to remain professionally detached from them. But Benítez also hated the organisation of the sporting side of the club. Like most Spanish clubs, Valencia CF had a clear delineation between the club's sport director, who was in charge of playing policy and transfer decisions, and the coach, who was basically a well-paid skivvy, hired to do the board's bidding. Benítez thought the two roles should be merged into one. He wanted to sign his own players and so shape everything on the playing side of the club. He knew that this was possible. He saw Irureta's improved position in Coruña, and he had noted the very different situation in England. There the coach did everything on the football side, short of sorting out the financial part of the players' contracts. Why not be the *manager* at Valencia CF, so cutting through all this disrespect, disagreement and unpleasantness?

Benítez had already raised this issue during the first renegotiation of his contract. But now – with another La Liga title and a UEFA Cup to his name – he saw himself with much more power to negotiate. This proposal would mean an end to the sporting *bicefalia* (two heads) inside Valencia CF, something that would solve, at a stroke, the lack of fluency and trust in his relationship with García Pitarch. (Pitarch was charged with delivering the club's new economic agenda, so he had his own internal problems to deal with.) Accusations had been constantly firing back and forward between these two men during the 2003–04 season. Benítez was effectively demanding some long-term security and trust at Valencia, and a situation that would give him complete responsibility for the sporting side of club affairs in a way that would more mirror the English situation. The creation of this position would also force a change in the traditional functions and power of the board of directors. These men would no longer be able to experiment with their own football theories and signings, whilst letting the poor coach cop the blame if things went belly up. Benítez was really asking for a radical shift in the whole club structure of the Spanish game.

Contact between Benítez's agent García Quilón and the general director Manuel Llorente had actually begun during March 2004. At that time the Valencianistas had been recovering from some poorish mid-season results, and the Spanish title had looked a long way off. So, without too much enthusiasm, Llorente had offered the Benítez camp a single season more. The parties could talk later, at the end of the campaign, but there was little optimism for a settlement that could satisfy both sides. The negotiations continued with little progress. After the season's end, Llorente reportedly told Benítez that despite his achievements a longer contract was still not possible because if the coach lost three matches in a row the following season, how could the club then sack him? This obviously callous indifference hurt the coach. A few days before the UEFA Cup final Benítez declared on Canal 9 TV that, 'It seems I am more valued outside than inside the club. I want to stay, but it is no longer clear that the leaders of Valencia CF want me to stay.' These were the words of somebody who felt he had given his all for a club that had not responded in kind. They were the words of somebody who was both offended and wounded. However, change *was* coming at Valencia CF. But would it arrive soon enough?

THE REMODELLING OF THE BOARD OF DIRECTORS OF VALENCIA CF

The deadlocked negotiations for Benítez's new contract coincided with another matter of major importance in the life of the club: the composition of the shareholders of Valencia CF. The Valencianistas had experienced a period of huge uncertainty – which had annoyed the coach – as a consequence of the temporary return to the position of club president of the majority shareholder Paco Roig. Roig had been sniping at the club from the outside, making policy decisions difficult to enact. Businessman Juan Bautista Soler then stepped in to offer a major investment, and *he* was able to take control of the board of directors. Roig sold all his shares at a large profit and disappeared from the scene. The removal of weaknesses that had characterised the board of directors under Jaime Ortí – and which had often drained and frustrated Benítez – would now open the way to a new era of greater stability. Or so it seemed.

Logically, these changes and the uncertainty involved must have affected the way in which Manuel Llorente acted during his negotiations with the Benítez camp. But a number of players' contracts had been renegotiated during this time, and the new agreement between Bautista Soler and Paco Roig actually took place three days *after* Benítez announced that he was leaving the club. This meant that the new majority shareholder had no time to renegotiate a deal to try to keep Rafa Benítez in Spain. Things had already gone too far.

Actually, by 27 May Valencia had already revised some of its initial positions, and it had even accepted some of the conditions demanded by Benítez. Benítez had also sought assurances that Valencia CF would make four signings at a cost of 6 million euros (£4 million), a very modest sum for a club that needed reinforcements and had just won La Liga and the UEFA Cup. After all, Benítez had won the doblete with pretty much the same players that two seasons earlier had won La Liga and had also played in the two Champions

League finals. He now wanted more than a promise, given that the club had already reneged on such agreements in the past. The club's transfer policy was, in fact, one of the fundamental aspects of the negotiations between the club and the young coach from Madrid. In the summer of 2003, for example, two players, Nestor Canobbio and Ricardo Oliveira, arrived at the club without the approval of the coach and his backroom team. Benítez wanted no more of this sort of puppeteering. Only by making signings identified by the coach, he argued, could Valencia CF maintain the competitive levels required by the demands of the Champions League. These requests were actually very coherent, given the difficult economic situation of the club. The coach hadn't asked for great stars but rather for young players with promise or players spotted by the Valencia coaching staff who still had their reputations to make. This was no case of a struggling club being held to ransom by an overly ambitious coach: Benítez was actually bending over backwards to make his player demands fit with the limited Valencia CF pocket.

Both sides now took some days to think matters over, and they committed themselves to speak again over the weekend. But Benítez was getting uneasy. This situation was absurd! Although his agent was now advising him that the club was coming round in Benítez's favour, on the night of Sunday, 30 May, the coach told his agent that his decision was clear: he was leaving Valencia CF. That same weekend the local press in Valencia published a story on how the club would make important structural changes to meet the demands of their unhappy coach. This appeared alongside another report that Liverpool Football Club was finalising details of an offer to recruit the same Rafael Benítez. On Monday, 31 May, García Quilón visited Benítez's home to try to persuade him to stay – or at least take more time to think about his decision. But Benítez was fixed. Beşiktaş had offered him the most money, and both Roma and Tottenham had made bids – but without the vital Champions League carrot. Liverpool had offered him a serious sporting project. He was headed for Merseyside. Then, a group of directors from Valencia CF, including the future president Juan Bautista Soler (who wanted to take charge of the negotiations), went to the home of Benítez. They met for more than four hours, with Bautista Soler accepting that Benítez had been badly treated: after all, as he pointed out to the disgruntled coach, he (Benítez) was the fundamental axis around which the entire Valencia project was now hung. But Benítez was not for budging.

The next day (1 June) Valencia called a press conference. More than 100 journalists and reporters turned up. The young coach was visibly moved. It was a side of Benítez not often – if ever – seen in public that was on show when he read a prepared statement: 'I have made possibly the most difficult decision of my sporting life: I won't continue at Valencia CF next season. I take as positive the intention of the club to reach an agreement with me, but I am weary because of the events of last season. I am weary, both personally and psychologically, so much so that it has made me reconsider my stay here. On the professional side of my life I will take a few days to analyse the alternatives and to make the most appropriate decision. On a personal front I want to thank the players and employees of the club, the media and especially the fans for all their support during these three years.'

At this point – when talking about the fans – Benítez began to cry, before departing from his written words to say, 'I have two daughters, one of them is Valencian and both are *falleras* [local girls involved in the traditional festivities of the city]. For that, Valencia and Valencia CF will always be in my thoughts and in my heart. Thanks to all of you, lots of luck and Amunt Valencia!'

In less than one minute Benítez had read the statement and was gone. Emotion had overcome this most analytical and detached of men. It had been an incredibly dramatic display, and Benítez had looked strained throughout, reflecting the tensions of the past few days. He then said goodbye to the employees of the club in the Paterna training base.

Minutes after Benítez had left the press room with tears in his eyes,

Jaime Ortí and Manuel Llorente appeared in front of the media. Both made it clear that only Benítez knew the real reasons for his departure, because the Valencia club had made it entirely possible for him to stay. It had been a long week in the life of the Spanish champions.

WHY DID BENÍTEZ LEAVE?

Initially, the Valencianistas were silent, stunned by the news of the departure of Benítez. But the Valencia fans soon began to ask why he had decided to leave. They mused that the coach had shown a certain distance from the club for much of the previous season. In several press conferences he had shown himself to be at odds with the sporting policy of the club outlined by the board of directors and by sport director García Pitarch. But after victories in La Liga and the UEFA Cup these differences had hardly seemed to matter. Now it was suddenly obvious that these were crucial divisions. And no one in the city could really say that the exit of Benítez was a huge surprise. The outcome was just the culmination of something that had probably been coming for a long time.

People close to Benítez certainly knew that the ex-Madridista felt unappreciated by the club. He had told close friends that he felt *ninguneado* (a Spanish expression that means to feel 'as nothing'), and Benítez thought that the club was always looking for ways to get rid of him, though these feelings receded following the Double success of 2003–04. In fact, at the end of the 2002–03 season some directors from Valencia CF had planned to sack Benítez, proposing either Roberto Fernandez or Carlos Bianchi as a replacement. Benítez had also been thinking of leaving the club for some time, and two months before he left, rumours had abounded that Valencia had approached other coaches, something that really gnawed at him. But the thing that probably really pushed him over the edge – *la gota que colmo el vaso* (the drop that filled the glass) – was the suggestion that the club was in negotiations again with a former coach, Claudio Ranieri.

Benítez was also very angry that he was one of the last people on the club staff to have his contract sorted out. The club had re-signed Ayala in September and Albelda in December 2003. Other players were lined up next to sign new contracts. Benítez had trouble working out how the club could effectively plan for its future without agreeing to his appointment on a long-term contract in the English mould. The policy of the club was in total conflict with his own views.

But it was also obvious that the offers that Benítez received at this troubling time were especially attractive. Within hours of his dramatic leaving speech it seemed clear that he had already completed a deal with Liverpool Football Club for just the sort of post he had so longed for in Spain. There would be no more football decisions made for him from an executive's armchair. Even at the beginning of his last season in Spain the Valencia board had told him that he must limit training, since the sports planning of the club should be in the hands of those who operated at an executive level. What madness was this? He was tired of this sort of abusive treatment, of being prodded by guys who knew nothing about the game. Rick Parry told Benítez that he would be revered on Merseyside and that he could decide everything on the football side. 'Everything?' asked the coach, leaving nothing to chance. 'No directors?'

'In the boardroom!' the Liverpool chief executive reassured him, smiling. Benítez's English was shaky, but they spoke each other's language, these two football men. They both thought they would get on together just fine.

10

Visions of Rafa

Chelsea – Paisley's Liverpool? Liverpool's young cup fighters
down City; José loses the plot at Old Trafford; Liverpool lose
their way in Cardiff – but win somehow.

BENÍTEZ VERSUS MOURINHO

In 2006 football writer David Lacey said, 'The more times Chelsea
play Liverpool, the more like Liverpool they become.' He meant that
in a very different era and a different context – global players, squad
system and unlimited cash – José Mourinho had built a team and an
approach to the game that had actually returned football to the very
traditional English values established under Bob Paisley at Liverpool
in the 1970s. Chelsea, like Liverpool before them, were built on
resolute defence and were efficient and professional rather than
especially exciting – though the 1979 Paisley side scored 85 goals, and
Chelsea scored an impressive 124 goals in Mourinho's first 63 games
in charge in the Premiership. These were hardly negative outfits. The
problem was that Paisley's Liverpool and Mourinho's Chelsea both
performed at such an incredibly high level of consistency, technical
proficiency and discipline that what was so special about these teams
was often missed by the casual viewer. The repetition of excellence
can often look boring.

If today, when Chelsea steamroller opponents, it is simply explained
in terms of 'all that money', then in Bob Paisley's day Liverpool's
repeated dominance was seen as a natural consequence of the club

recruiting, as if by magic, 'all the best players'. The 1979 Liverpool success was achieved with just 15 players, whereas Mourinho used 30 to secure his first title with Chelsea. Today's Chelsea certainly has no Kenny Dalglish, and the midfield powerhouse Michael Essien is still a (very) poor man's Graeme Souness. But Chelsea does have the limpet-like Claude Makélélé, and Wiliam Gallas and John Terry can look like an Alan Hansen and Phil Thompson partnership on good days. Goalkeeper Petr Cech is a match for any keeper, even Liverpool's Ray Clemence. Today's Chelsea may also have an advantage of pace and penetration on the flanks over Paisley's Reds because, after Steve Heighway finished, Paisley's teams relied largely on full-backs to deliver crosses. Of course, Bob Paisley won three European Cups for Liverpool, and Mourinho has yet to win one at Chelsea – though we already know from his FC Porto days that he *can* do it.

In the 1970s top British players wanted to join Liverpool because of the club's metronomic success in the title race and in Europe. You were guaranteed medals at Anfield. The same still applies at the current Chelsea, but the cash appeal has taken matters onto a different level entirely. There were players back then that Bob Paisley crossed out on his list of targets because wages were an issue – Liverpool Football Club were not brilliant payers. But if money *was* a problem to a potential recruit, then the Liverpool boot room would simply assert that this was, clearly, no authentic 'Liverpool player'.

No such difficulties seem to tie down Chelsea's Mourinho, and asking for outrageous money these days seems to be regarded as simply part of any decent professional's make-up. Mourinho identifies whom he wants to sign and then hands matters over to the lawyers and accountants. Most players will take the bait in the end, though once you start getting into the £5-million-a-year bracket, a couple million extra, one way or the other, will not always sway everybody. And top football players still seem to be able to show some club loyalty when push comes to shove. Liverpool still has Steven Gerrard – at least for now – and Manchester United and Arsenal appear to be able to hold on to their star assets, even in the face of Mourinho's blandishments and Chelsea's pretty purse. Mercifully, not everyone, it seems, sees themselves as a Chelsea player.

Although Chelsea's league dominance in 2005–06 had been clear once more, Mourinho had looked much less secure – often ill at ease. He had fallen out with the press and with rival managers, and he increasingly came over as arrogant and somehow 'in' but not 'of' the British game he once so charmed. Mourinho was also beginning to lose the trust of his patron at Chelsea, Roman Abramovich. By early 2007 the British media would be full of stories about the growing rifts between the pragmatic Chelsea manager and his impatient chairman. Chelsea had also looked occasionally vulnerable – a 0–3 Premiership loss at the Riverside and a chaotic defeat at neighbours Fulham – which meant that Liverpool's Old Trafford FA Cup semi-final against Chelsea was one that Rafa Benítez and his staff really believed they could win. Liverpool had the resources and the tactical know-how in a one-off contest to press Chelsea hard – the Benítez record in Europe against Mourinho was three draws and one win. Rafa also wanted to win this contest to make up for what he now called the 'bad moment' at Burnley in the FA Cup in 2005, but also because of Liverpool's collapses to Chelsea in the Premiership that season and the circumstances of those defeats. The 1–4 loss at Anfield and the 0–2 at Chelsea (where Reina was dismissed) had left a bad taste in the mouth. The press had been building up the Iberian coaching rivalry angle and the struggle between these two was now looking a little like that between Wenger and Ferguson a few years before – but without the same levels of personal enmity.

Rafa actually has some very interesting things to say about the relationship between coaching and the writings of the British press. It is almost as if he *wants* British reporters to examine his preparation so they can see the disparities between what he has carefully prepared his side to do and what sometimes happens on the field. This access might also 'fill in' for the interviews he hardly ever gives in English. He told Paco Cordobés of *Abfutbol* in November 2005, when talking about the media, that, 'In principle, everything is much calmer here [in England] and that helps when working. But, on the other hand, there is a danger when people make evaluations, because they [fans and the press] don't see what you are doing during the week. They don't see how you are preparing for matches.' Did Rafa think that his work and preparation was somehow hidden too much – that it needed more public exposure (and celebration)? He continued, 'Therefore, any decision you take is weighed up simply in terms of the result, more than for your intentions. Spanish journalists see your weekly work and that you are trying to do something in a particular way. On occasions they [the press] are condescending. But if you don't get the result, at least they have seen that you have worked hard during the week and they respect you more.' If the press *saw* the week's coaching work – as in Spain – and it was high quality, then it was easier to blame the players, not the coach, if things went wrong. You could see his point.

Meanwhile, that monkey Mourinho had now returned cheekily to the matter of the Robben-inspired sending off of Pepe Reina by arguing that somehow this equated morally to Liverpool accepting the García 'no goal' in the previous year's European Cup semi-final second leg! This claim seemed *so* outlandish that, in other circumstances, it could have been taken as a sign that the Portuguese manager might actually be cracking up. But it was probably more the twisted logic that came from Chelsea's current superiority and their coach's remarkable – and increasingly insufferable – self-belief.

YOUNG GUNS IN SPORT CITY

Before this showdown there was the early fruits of Liverpool's new youth policy under Benítez to consider: an FA Youth Cup final against Manchester City. It was Liverpool's first youth final for ten years: since David Thompson, Michael Owen and Jamie Carragher were among the first-ever Liverpool side to win the cup in 1996, eventually downing West Ham United 4–1 on aggregate, having attracted more than 20,000 fans to the home leg at Anfield. From a winning youth-cup side these days a top club can reasonably expect a few standout youngsters to make it as professionals and maybe even one or two (the 1996 Liverpool team was exceptional with three) to graduate to the highest levels of the Premiership. Today, for example, the first-team squads at both Middlesbrough and Aston Villa are benefiting from recent youth-cup triumphs, and one Wayne Rooney helped get Everton to the 2002 final.

In terms of young player development Liverpool FC must now see itself in a similar light to these outfits. Rafa Benítez knows that his club cannot compete with Abramovich or the Glazers in the global market to buy up some of the world's highest-ranked finished products. So a successful youth-development strategy is now a central feature of the new Spanish regime at Anfield. This new reality has also meant working hard at repairing the relationship between the Liverpool Academy director Steve Heighway and the club manager, a relationship that had become distant and unproductive under the stewardship of Gérard Houllier. The Frenchman, vastly experienced in this area in France, damagingly felt himself to be the Liverpool club 'expert' on the development of young players and soon alienated many of his Academy staff, including the sensitive Heighway. Benítez and his coaches had since built uneasy bridges and reasserted the importance of this side of Liverpool's affairs. This final was one of the results.

The Kop was full of pre-pubescent and wide-eyed Scousers – all of whom were waiting to see the Liverpool future – for the first leg, which attracted a healthy crowd of 11,000. They got what they came for. An effervescent Liverpool won 3–0 (Robbie Threlfall, Ryan Flynn and the classy Spaniard Miki Roque scoring) on the back of some thrilling, fast-paced football, led by wingers Adam Hammill and big first-team hopeful Paul Anderson, and backed up by the willing labour of Wirral-born striker Craig Lindfield. The cultured Reds midfielder Paul Barrett – rejected by City – looked like he should be in a boy band, while his more rustic centre-backs, the Ghanaian Godwin Antwi and Englishman Jack Hobbs, fought a sterling battle against a team of young Manchester City giants, including the much-coveted, powerful 16-year-old striker Daniel Sturridge. Despite some goalmouth frights, it was an unexpectedly easy first-leg Reds victory – City were big favourites – but it was also very clear to us that even at three goals down the Manchester side were by no means out of the contest, with the second leg to come, twenty-odd miles eastwards down the M62.

The return, at the City of Manchester Stadium in the Sport City complex at Eastfields, was on the evening before the FA Cup semi-final with Chelsea at Old Trafford, so there was no shortage of Reds fans in attendance. Steve Heighway said later that the siege and defeat that we were about to witness that night reminded him of Liverpool's very first European honour, the 1973 UEFA Cup, when Shankly's Liverpool took a three-goal lead to Mönchengladbach in the two-legged final and were absolutely slaughtered by the Germans in the away leg, losing 0–2. Sheepishly, they collected the trophy in front of hooting Germans, battered 3–2 aggregate winners. City – made up entirely of British youngsters – brought in the strapping first-teamer Micah Richards to add to their considerable muscle and to the tenacious skill of full-back Shaleum Logan. For much of the evening it looked, quite literally, like men against boys as the home team piled on the pressure to move into an ominous 2–0 second-half lead, both goals from the irresistible Sturridge. But in the siege that followed, Antwi stood firm at the back for the visitors and young substitute Roque contributed some much-needed second-half class and control in midfield, which, added to buckets of luck, was just about enough to see the junior Reds through. They would face no sterner test than this, even in an extended professional career.

This hard-won victory was a vindication of sorts for Rafa's vision to recruit players on a much wider basis at this level. (Though in 2007 when Liverpool remarkably retained the Youth Cup, they did so with a team made up of largely local talent.) But it was also a reminder of how precious little serious work Liverpool had done on the youth side even in the club's glory years; after all, this was only Liverpool's second youth title in 54 years of the competition. And when the Reds squad came to parade the cup right in front of us, aping celebrations they had seen many times on TV, what shone through was just how incredibly young and enthusiastic these guys looked at the start of their playing lives in this tough business. They probably all saw themselves in future FA Cup semi-finals – though, of course, most of them will quickly fall by the wayside. It is a heartless, Darwinian struggle in British football – the survival of the fittest and not always the best. But Benítez seems committed to giving young players a chance to show what they can do at Anfield, thus repairing a recent relative Liverpool failing. And maybe ten years from now we will see a couple of these lads doing what Carra and Michael have managed to do over the last decade – make a very good life for themselves in the game, mainly by bringing glory and success to Liverpool Football Club and to its ever-demanding supporters.

ALL DAY PERMANENT RED

Outside Old Trafford on the day of the Chelsea match any semblance of the innocence or sportsmanship of the crowd that had been on show at Eastfields the previous evening at the FA Youth Cup final (although, in all truth, it had actually been in quite short supply) was pretty much gone – the serious business was now at hand. The Liverpool fans really saw this battle as one that pitted authenticity and an organic culture and history against a rather dangerous, ersatz confection built on Ambramovich's millions and so much west London sand. 'In a country where people are interested only in points, coins and transfer fees,' said Mourinho pointedly, 'this is the worst club to be the manager of. Chelsea is always treated in a negative way.' He may have been right. The Red supporters' 'You ain't got no history' anti-Chelsea song was repeated ad nauseam around Old Trafford for hours before kick-off, shredding the nerves (and eardrums) of friends and foe alike. (We could hear it from our adjacent drinking spot in the hotel's yard.) Chelsea FC actually has *plenty* of history, of course, just very few trophies to adorn it – until now. They have bought their way into the football toffs' club. So the Chelsea fans simply shrugged and grinned and pointed to the champions tag on their replica shirts; meanwhile, a group of well-dressed, gold-braceleted fifty year olds in blue shirts swapped stories in our hotel bar about the 'good old' hooligan days down the Fulham Palace Road. How times had changed. Forty-one years previously, Liverpool had beaten Chelsea 2–0 in an FA Cup semi-final at Villa Park (Peter Thompson and Willie Stevenson) on the way to that very first FA Cup win. There could have been precious few times since when the Reds were such underdogs, and such national favourites, in a contest of this importance. We could almost feel football's silent majority calling us home to wipe that handsome smirk off José's designer-stubbled face.

And things suddenly looked much easier than we could ever have imagined, because the master tactician Mourinho selected what seemed to us to be close to a joke Chelsea line-up. Matt Dickenson later wrote in *The Independent* that the entire press box looked at Chelsea's team and asked, 'What on earth does he think he's playing at?' To begin with he had selected the Italian reserve Carlo Cudicini in goal instead of the near-impassable Cech. And where, exactly, were Chelsea's penetrating forward runners, their wingers? They had a whole roster of them. But there was no Damien Duff or Arjen Robben or Joe Cole – no pretensions at all to use width, usually Chelsea's trump card. (Riise said later that he heaved a huge sigh of relief when he saw Chelsea's team; there would be no chasing shadows for the afternoon.) And the dangerous Frank Lampard seemed to be playing on the left-hand side, with the more defensive Michael Essien the blunt head of the midfield diamond where young Frank should surely have been – goal-scoring Frank. How confusing was this? Geremi, a little-seen squad midfield player, had been shuffled in at right-back with (left) full-back Paulo

Ferreira in front of him – in midfield. It looked like more patching up. Chelsea Football Club had all of these players, all this cash, and yet here was a brilliant coach who was merrily screwing square pegs into round holes for a vital FA Cup semi-final. Was it that Mourinho was just so confident, so concerned to stress his coaching credentials, that he felt he could field just about *any* Chelsea team for this contest? This could be the only explanation. It was almost as if he was saying to Rafa, 'Look, I'll pick my worst possible side – and I'll *still* beat you.' (Benítez had no such problems or pretensions – his strongest team started: García supporting Crouch, Kewell wide left, Gerrard on the right and both Cissé and Morientes on the bench.) Or else Mourinho was trying to neuter Benítez's trump card, the Liverpool manager's painstaking preparations, because they must also have been out of the window once these team sheets were in view.

Who would adapt best? We soon saw the answer. After 20 minutes of sparring – punctured by two glaring Drogba misses – and with Chelsea looking mainly uncomfortable and disjointed, as you might expect, Terry raised his studs high with García to win the ball cleanly on the edge of the Chelsea box. Mourinho would complain later that this was no free-kick, certainly not in England. But the World Cup was coming, and referees had been given clear instructions on just this kind of 'dangerous' play; so the free-kick was reasonably given. John Arne Riise stepped up to play a simple little set-up with Steven Gerrard before *passing* the ball through the Chelsea wall and beyond the unsighted Cudicini. Riise said later that he purposely placed his shot through the gap, but this seemed hard to believe – the wall appeared to open up, involuntarily, after the ball had been struck. No matter – Liverpool had a crucial lead in a match they could surely only win from the front.

Drawing confidence from this lead and from Chelsea's stumblings, both García, on the right against the awful Del Horno, and Harry Kewell, on Liverpool's left against the ponderous Geremi, suddenly began to traumatise their opponents. This was exactly the reverse of the pattern we had feared: Chelsea's wingers getting behind Liverpool's full-backs. Crouch was fighting for everything with Terry, and Gerrard was making chances, not always best accepted. When half-time came, Liverpool were still intact and seemingly not at serious risk. We just hoped that José would stick with his vanity project and trust his strange formation to claw the goal back. Of course, he made changes, one immediately: Robben came on to replace Del Horno with Ferreira moving to left-back.

Before we had a real chance to see if this adjustment could really affect things – though there had already been signs – Liverpool scored a second goal. It was both ugly and beautiful. A Finnan throw-in was *twice* misheaded backwards by the Chelsea rearguard, putting García through on goal 40 yards out but being chased furiously by blue-shirted defenders. There is a lot this Spaniard cannot do well on a football field – defend, keep the ball, take sensible options under pressure – but there are also things he can do brilliantly, such as lob volleys from distance on his left side. And this was what we got; he struck the ball gloriously with the outside of his left boot and beyond the helpless Cudicini. The Red half of Old Trafford exploded.

Soon both Cole and Duff were required to join the fray; the match was slipping away from Chelsea. Mourinho basically threw all his fancy strategies out of the window and told his side to plough forward – what did they have to lose? And it brought a goal after 70 minutes. It was a terrible time for Liverpool to concede when even another five scoreless minutes might have broken Chelsea's resolve. Riise, in trying to head clear from a near-horizontal position, somehow squirted the ball up in the air in the centre of the penalty area and towards the lurking shape of Didier Drogba. There was still no real danger: the ball was looping high with little pace, Hyypiä was getting back and Drogba could not possibly score from that position. Unless, of course, Pepe Reina, excited by the opportunity to show his defensive mettle, committed himself fully to the challenge – and didn't make it. But the chances of that happening were nil. Absolutely zero. And then a figure in green hurtled from Liverpool's goal line, followed by the object of his desire dropping gently behind him – and into Liverpool's unguarded net.

The Red stands were now filled with mortal fear, balanced by hysterical bawling. Chelsea were pouring forward, and Mourinho's side went to three at the back, a move that was countered (countered?) by Benítez bringing on Cissé for the tiring Crouch. You could see the manager's thinking: use Cissé's energy and pace to relieve pressure and keep Chelsea's defence on its guard. The problem was that the Frenchman's performance was so poor, so lacking in even the basic tenets of the striker's arts and defensive responsibilities, that it was suddenly like Chelsea were playing against no Liverpool attackers *at all*. John Terry strolled forward with the ball, Cissé watching on in admiration. Gallas no longer defended at all – until Morientes arrived from the Liverpool bench to pull him back. Benítez was doing his nut on the touchline, urging the bemused Cissé to close down defenders. 'Moi?' This little exchange was almost comical, and was reminiscent of a man carrying a trainer's bucket on a parks touchline on a Sunday morning trying to explain to his fledgling Under-10s the critical importance of the team ethic. And still Chelsea swarmed forward, threatening to kill Liverpool's hopes at any second.

But as the clock ticked agonisingly down it seemed as if Liverpool were finally safe. From behind us someone shouted out the same: 'We've fucking won it!' But at this very moment Robben squeezed the ball through to Joe Cole, onside and alone on the left-hand side of Liverpool's penalty area. He *had* to score. After all, he had a record to keep up against Benítez's Liverpool – we were his personal bitch. The ball sat up invitingly, and Reina simply spread himself across his goal, hoping against hope that the shot would somehow hit his body and, defying geometry, career over the bar as Shevchenko's had done off Jerzy Dudek in the final minutes in Istanbul. But actually this incident was more like Gudjohnsen's missing moment at Anfield in the closing minutes of the European Cup semi-final in 2005. Because our man Pepe was not required to make a save at all. Instead, he turned to retrieve the ball from the wailing, head-in-hands Blue wall behind his goal. Joe Cole, for once, had not scored for Chelsea against Liverpool. And Rafa Benítez, not José Mourinho, was in his first English FA Cup final.

UNDER THE HAMMER?

What should we say about the 2006 FA Cup final? Liverpool stole the first FA Cup final in Wales in 2001 when Michael Owen scored twice late on to defy Arsenal, and they just as surely stole what might be the last one in Wales in 2006, Steven Gerrard's extraordinary last-minute reprieve setting up penalties, a Liverpool Football Club speciality. Apart from Gerrard and possibly Hamann – who gave another imposing substitute's display, if not quite matching the heights of Istanbul – most of the decent performances on the day came from a despairing West Ham: Dean Ashton showed Sven what he might be missing; Nigel Reo-Coker, Yossi Benayoun and Matthew Etherington all impressed in midfield; and Danny Gabbidon was a picture of calm serenity for the Londoners at the back. For Liverpool, Cissé scored a stunning – and very necessary – goal to get the Reds back into the contest before half-time, Reina had another wobbly match, conceding a mishit second-half cross by Paul Konchesky, and Kewell succumbed to his customary final injury: he managed to make it into the second half but hardly touched the ball. All of this was secondary, however, to Steven Gerrard's match-defining performance: two stunning goals scored and one made (for Cissé) to lift a stuttering Liverpool to an unlikely win and end an uneven but ultimately satisfying season.

Gerrard top-scored for Liverpool, bagging twenty-three goals in fifty-two matches in all competitions – but only ten goals came in Premiership games. This 'conversion' of Steven to a direct attacking threat to complement and feed off the organisational talents of Xabi Alonso had been one of the coach's major achievements in 2006. For all his (many) faults, Djibril Cissé still ended up with nineteen Liverpool goals, nine in the Premiership. The Frenchman made 52 appearances for Liverpool, but the vast majority were as a substitute. Only Hyypiä, Carragher, Reina and Gerrard appeared in more games than Cissé – but they played many more minutes and were much more reliable. Sami Hyypiä, especially, had risen to the challenge of a crowded programme and little experienced back-up by playing 58 times that season, all but a handful from the start. Most fans – and probably the Finn himself – had thought he might play about half that number in 2005–06. Sami is a true Red.

Rafa Benítez could look back on a season of real progress. Liverpool looked stronger and better balanced, more like the strange old piano analogy often used by Bill Shankly: you need eight men to carry the thing and three (why *three*?) people to play it. Benítez had brought in a few more useful piano carriers – Zenden, Kromkamp and especially Sissoko – and away performances in the Premiership improved accordingly. Further forward, things were still more uncertain. Cissé and Morientes both looked at risk in a summer cull, and Kewell remained injury prone and inconsistent, vying between brilliance one minute and anonymity the next. Finnan, Carragher and Hyypiä had all been outstanding, but defensive reserve strength was still lacking. New man Agger – injured for a spell – would have to prove his worth.

As we now looked forward to the World Cup finals – with both England and Spain in contention and both boasting Liverpool players – Benítez was looking to strengthen his squad for a 2007 championship challenge. Earlier in 2005 *El País* had asked the Spaniard whether he felt the pressure of a big club like Liverpool demanding success after some years in the wilderness. He answered no: 'I feel it as a motivational factor. You observe people's pride, and far from feeling it as a weight, it cheers me up as I try to return Liverpool to the summit. It is a pleasant load. I see it this way, because it demands from yourself more responsibility, and the only thing that you want is to return with victories – just to pay back the support that the team receives at all times.' These were sweet words from a man we barely heard from out of his own language. He had, of course, both the respect – and the thanks – of all Liverpool football fans for 2005 and 2006.

What could we expect Benítez to deliver in 2007? It would be a season of early disappointments and then marvellous surprises but ultimately one of despair. There would be no silverware in the Spaniard's third season in England. Indeed, although Liverpool and Rafa Benítez would go close to conquering Europe once more, his club seemed as far away from winning the Premiership title in 2007 – another Manchester United triumph – as it had been during the reign at Liverpool of either Roy Evans or Gérard Houllier.

11

For Club – *and* Country?

Didi Hamann – German or Scouser? Houllier's troubled way
replaced by Benítez's new positive outlook; Wayne, Michael
and Steven – club men and national heroes; the new Liverpool
under Benítez for 2006–07.

'WE KNEW HE WAS RIGHT FOR LIVERPOOL'

As Rafa Benítez's second season at Liverpool, one crowned with an
FA Cup triumph, began to fade from view, the public in Liverpool and
other centres of football excellence around the globe were left facing
a World Cup summer of key football questions. One of these was: in
the global era, where exactly should the allegiance of football fans lie
– firmly with their club or region, or with the national side? This may
sound like a stupid question to most people. After all, your club never
has to *play* the national side, so what's the problem? But recently this
'club or country' wrangle has also raised some interesting controversies,
not to mention strained allegiances. Rafa Benítez had often talked about
the tensions in England between club loyalty and national ambition,
especially as some of his own key players would now be facing nearly
two years of near-continuous play, from August 2004 to July 2006.

In some ways support for national teams might have been expected to
become more solid and distinctive in the new cosmopolitan, international
era for the larger European clubs. After all, fans of top football clubs in
England and Spain today spend their supporter lives calling for greater
investment in players, and they often hanker after global recruits
to add exotic touches to the unleavened mash of the stock domestic

game. Which means that urging on African, French, Spanish and even German recruits has become a very new dimension of supporting a club in the modern era in England. Notwithstanding the emotional ties to clubs felt by fans, this inevitably becomes a matter of shouting home these well-paid 'mercenaries' for the private businesses they temporarily represent. For example, as Reds fans had 100 per cent focus on Istanbul in May 2005, Milan Baroš was already excited by an arranged move to Juventus (which eventually fell through) that had been agreed just before the Champions League final. Business is business. Moves away from Anfield had also already been arranged for other Liverpool players who were in the squad and on the field on that May night in Turkey. All this sort of personal and occupational uncertainty might be expected to signal, for fans, rather more intense support for national teams in the global era. After all, these teams are traditionally linked to their followers by somewhat stronger ties of blood and soil rather than by large cheques. Not so – or at least, not necessarily.

For one thing, by hiring Sven-Göran Eriksson, a dull Swede, as England manager the FA rather blew out of the water all that precious 'money can't buy' extolling of patriotic national affiliation that was supposed to be such an important and distinctive feature of coaching, playing and supporting international football. The FA then chased the Portugal-based Brazilian Phil Scolari before World Cup 2006 on a hugely embarrassing abortive mission to find Sven's successor, eventually settling for an Englishman after all, Middlesbrough's Steve McClaren. The note-taking McClaren, for all his strengths, looks all over a keen No. 2 rather than the top man for the England job. In this case the marketplace seemed to be as active in international football – at least in recruiting a manager – as it clearly was in the club game.

Although Liverpool chief executive Rick Parry confirmed that the Reds had looked at other managerial options – including British ones – before appointing Rafa Benítez in 2004, there was no 'pendulum swing' inside the Liverpool club for a British coach after the ultimately failed foreign shift under Gérard Houllier. The Frenchman's Anfield difficulties had been undermined by heart problems, changing his whole approach to the job and to the pressures he faced. 'Finishing fourth, as we had eventually done under Gérard in 2004, was the minimum requirement for Liverpool,' Parry confirmed. 'We were getting no closer to being real title contenders, and Gérard had definitely changed since his illness. He was much more insecure; he was constantly worried by media coverage, especially the kind he was getting in the local press. The atmosphere inside the club and at Melwood was not as buoyant as it should have been. So we eventually told Houllier we needed a change, which he accepted. Because we were struggling to make even the fourth-place spot in 2004, it was impossible to start looking for a new manager before we announced Gérard's departure. This would have caused instability, and, anyway, it is not the Liverpool way. We were fortunate that the Valencia situation developed as quickly as it did, because we didn't have much time to make an appointment. We knew all about Rafa, of course, and he satisfied completely the two criteria we had laid down: the new manager had to be young, hungry and ambitious – not looking for a pension plan, as Rafa likes to put it – and he had to be someone with a proven ability to win the league. So this was a pretty small field. He laid down no conditions at all when we talked – that is not Rafa's style – and we agreed terms right away. Making an appointment in this way may seem ludicrous from the outside. You have no detailed recruitment process or interviews, and he didn't even come to the city to look around. But recruiting a football manager is not like appointing a bank manager or a professor. These things have to be done very quickly, usually on instinct or feel and often in the full media glare. We knew he was right for Liverpool.'

But for fans of clubs like Liverpool, today's global smorgasbord of player and managerial recruits for their clubs has made some national team issues more, rather than less, difficult to resolve. Because, in the new global era for football, 'foreign-ness' is no longer a function just of where a player – or a manager – comes from, or where he was born. It has much more to do with how they identify with and perform at your football club. In recent years at Anfield, for example, imports such as the Benítez recruit Antonio Núñez and Houllier's El Hadji Diouf were immediately and identifiably 'foreign' players, in the negative sense, for most fans at Liverpool – but then so, in the end, was the Leicester-born trundler Emile Heskey. All these recruits seemed somehow transient, passionless and unattached – not at all the right Liverpool stuff. Sadly, Djibril Cissé has some of the necessary traits to join this largely unloved camp.

But ask any Liverpool fan about a Didi Hamman or a Sami Hyypiä, for example, and most of them would tell you that, after Fowler, Carragher and Gerrard, Hamann is currently the biggest 'Scouser' at the club. A German? Who cares? He plays as if his life depends on the outcome of each Liverpool game; his performance never drops, and so he is now 'one of us'. Hamann's kids probably have Merseyside accents by now (like his), and their dad favours the betting shop in the same way that Bob Paisley and Terry Mac did in a different era. Didi even has a cute nervous facial tick that we like to think has a local origin. It is just an accident that he wasn't born here (and people in Liverpool were enraged that he was left out of the *German* 2006 World Cup squad). Hamann is a nailed-on Liverpool player *first*, a player from another country (as if anyone in L4 ever thinks about that) a very distant second.

At the managerial level, the calm Spaniard Rafa Benítez already has some of the vital Hamann traits in the eyes of Liverpool followers: it feels as if he *belongs* in Liverpool 4, even if he maintains a keen interest in the fortunes of his old club Valencia, and he may even be tempted, on occasions, to consider a return to Spain. 'Why would he *not* go to Real Madrid?' asks a bemused Rick Parry, rhetorically. 'Real is a huge challenge and Rafa's home club, and we had a real scare over the Madrid interest in him in 2006. But Rafa knows he would not have full control in Spain, and he is also a man of honour. And he genuinely really likes it here [in Liverpool]. He has a real bond with the fans and the club, though there is none of that nonsense that he had always been a Liverpool fan. He loves the passion of the place and is wedded to the job: he prefers to spend his time watching football videos rather than socialising. He also has a tremendous coaching pedigree, ambition, enthusiasm, single-mindedness and an absolute determination to succeed. He was very unhappy and frustrated with the Spanish system, where the whole process of buying and selling players is an art form. We couldn't offer him a blank cheque at Liverpool to make signings, of course, but when I look back at the list of players he first asked for, most of them are now here.'

This points to the strange contradiction once more: the detached, ultra-professional Spanish coach who is apparently seduced by the sheer emotionality of an Irish–English football club, something that probably both enthrals and confuses him. But what had Benítez specifically brought to Liverpool that was *different* from the last days of the Houllier era? 'At the end,' Parry said, 'Gérard had begun to get obsessive about things that were actually out of his control: press coverage, fixture congestion, it all became a huge drama and a crisis. Now, if we have a problem with fixtures, Rafa will say, "Are these things already fixed? Can we do anything about it? No? OK, let's move on." He is much more decisive, more positive. He doesn't get caught up or distracted by things we simply can't change. He is very focused in that way.'

One of the more recent Benítez signings, the Malian Momo Sissoko, also seemed to be authentic 'Merseyside' stock: didn't the young midfielder bust a gut and risk his eyesight playing for Liverpool in 2005–06? For Rick Parry, Sissoko was indeed a signature Benítez recruit, one that had to be made after a difficult beginning for the Spaniard in the English game: 'It was certainly a steep learning curve for the manager and his staff for that first season in the Premiership. We knew it would be difficult, that it would take time. And the day Rafa arrived was the very day in 2004 that Steven Gerrard first said he wanted to leave for Chelsea, so none of it was easy.

'In the first season in England Rafa was always keen to monitor, scientifically, the performance of the players, so he wanted to rest them whenever he could. This caused problems on occasions. Jamie Carragher was actually due to play in the postponed FA Cup tie at Burnley, but by the time we played that match Rafa had decided that Carragher also needed a rest – and, of course, we lost the tie. This caused a lot of negative publicity, but we were convinced it was just a blip. And would we have won the Champions League in 2005 with a lengthy FA Cup run? I don't think so. But Rafa knew he needed to strengthen the defensive side of the team, because we were also losing at places like Middlesbrough, Birmingham and Southampton in that first season. With respect, you don't easily lose at these sorts of places now – not with Momo in your side. The players here are also much fitter and stronger under Rafa – look how strongly we finished this last season.'

Liverpool players would need this extra fitness in the summer of 2006 as they faced new World Cup challenges in searing heat. In the finals Liverpool fans were now faced with the very real prospect that some of their favourite club players would eventually end up in direct opposition to the England national team. What would they do then? What if García, Xabi Alonso and Pepe Reina all lined up for Spain against an England side in Germany that had no Gerrard, Crouch or Carra in it? Would it really be that easy to get behind Gary Neville, John Terry, Frank Lampard, Joe Cole and the rest of the 'lads' in white playing against these blood-Red men from Anfield? (One Liverpool fan in Germany, perversely, wore Neville's No. 2 England shirt with the word 'wanker' defiantly replacing the Mancunian's name.)

As the 2006 league and cup season in England came to a close and the World Cup loomed, the British press increasingly filled up with pieces about the fitness of key England players for Germany. Rafa Benítez had even spoken publicly on a number of occasions about the importance of the authorities *protecting* players at club level in order to ensure their well-being for international duty in the summer. What he meant was that Liverpool football club needed an easier club programme. He was seeking a definite club advantage. Rafa never once thought about resting any of his international players to protect their World Cup places. How could he? He would have been vilified in Liverpool if he had even tried.

The response at a Chelsea or a West Ham to the same problem might have been slightly different on this and other connected fronts – though Mourinho and Pardew are hard-headed enough to put their own jobs first. However, the supporter flags and banners at these clubs are usually merely adapted Cross of St George England flags, or, worse, Union Jacks. We had seen that much in two recent cup finals in Cardiff, in 2005 and 2006. Were these London guys essentially *England* fans who filled their time in between international fixtures by following the local stiffs? Throughout the season, and again immediately after the FA Cup final of 2006, Liverpool's own Steven Gerrard was at pains to assure British journalists that, yes, he was fit and, yes, he was looking forward to England duty. At these moments most Anfield fans probably still wanted to hear rather more about the anticipation of pulling on the red shirt of Liverpool rather than the white of England, though it was intriguing that Gerrard – like Michael Owen before him – was now occasionally being applauded by fans of other clubs at Liverpool away games *because* of his England status. It was as if these onlookers also felt that they owned a part of Gerrard – or that they wanted to. Mercifully, Liverpool's Jamie Carragher was rather less forthcoming than Stevie on this England score. For Carra (like most Reds, we would bargain), the next Liverpool match was usually all that mattered, and he always said as much when asked about England issues. For Carra, most Reds fans assumed, the very suggestion that the World Cup final itself might be more important than, say, gubbing United at Old Trafford was simply preposterous. At Liverpool, the fans' banners carried no signs of English affiliation, no compromising Cross of St George: they carried, instead, words and pictures about players like Bootle's own Jamie Carragher.

Unsurprisingly, Carragher had soon become one of Benítez's favourite players at Anfield. Carra is, of course, a team player first and last, an absolute requirement under the new Spanish regime. 'The idea of building a team "around" certain players is completely anathema to Rafa,' confirmed Rick Parry. 'He has no time at all for so-called football "stars". He thinks only about building a team.' This approach – the idea that all players are made equal – probably contributed in no small measure to what Parry describes as the 'misunderstandings' that precipitated both Michael Owen's departure from Liverpool in 2004 and also almost led to Steven Gerrard leaving the club a year later. 'Rafa had told Steven he could help improve his game: that he didn't have to be this *Roy of the Rovers* character who was trying to do everyone's job,' Parry said. 'Steven had been carrying the Liverpool side for some time, but this had to change under Benítez for the benefit of the player and the team.' And what did Parry recall about Steven's night of 'should-I-leave?' torment after Istanbul? 'We had quite a torrid time that evening because, effectively, it was all done; Steven had absolutely decided he was going to Chelsea. Then we started getting phone calls from him: "Would you still have me back if I changed my mind?" "How soon could you announce it if I changed my mind and wanted to stay?" Steven's a good lad, a Liverpool boy, and sometimes you don't realise what you have at a place like this until you are actually faced with leaving. But Rafa wasn't fazed by any of this. Part of him probably thought, "Why do I have to spend my time telling a guy as talented as Steven Gerrard what a good player he is?"'

WAYNE'S WORLD AND MICHAEL'S ENGLAND

Benítez was almost certainly prepared to let Steven Gerrard leave Anfield if that was what the Liverpool man had decided – remember, you have to be positive and deal only in things you can control. And despite his resolutely Scouse roots, Gerrard was already a disturbingly national football property, an England star. The signs of where these sorts of club v. country tensions in England might lead were already being strikingly played out in the spring of 2006 in the cases of two other Merseyside products, Michael Owen and Wayne Rooney.

Rooney, by now the tabloids' national football saviour, had actually been quite badly injured – metatarsal time again – during the league match between Chelsea and Manchester United at Stamford Bridge in May that finally confirmed the title for the Abramovich franchise. But the TV faces of many Chelsea fans – England devotees, of course – soon contorted from delight (Chelsea won 3–0) to horror as they saw Rooney being carted off on a stretcher with the World Cup finals a matter of weeks away. Rooney's departure from Portugal in 2004 through injury had shaped a seductive fiction, encouraged by Sven, that England were on track to actually *win* Euro 2004 before this minor catastrophe struck. With England now painted as potential (if improbable) World Champions in the making, we were faced with more agonising weeks of 'will he, won't he?' suspense and daily bulletins from the urchin's fast-healer oxygen tent (we kid you not).

If this little West London soap opera had been played out at Anfield, of course, the stricken Rooney would almost certainly have been smugly serenaded all the way to the treatment table, World Cup or no World Cup. By contrast, a Chelsea fan later actually rang up a BBC phone-in show to say that she was proud to be an England fan *first*, Chelsea only second. And that Rooney's injury took priority, somehow, over her own club's second title win! Sven even talked about flying out a 'half-fit' Rooney to Germany, and Theo Walcott, a teenage kid not ready enough for even one minute's pitch time in Arsenal's first team in 2006, was now selected by the hapless Swede to 'replace' Rooney at the World Cup finals in case the United man lapsed. Tragedy was rapidly being replaced by farce.

Michael Owen's 'club or country' conundrum seemed even more bizarre than the injured Rooney's. Michael had cost his new employers Newcastle United a pretty packet, of course, and the little master had started well in the North East, firing in the goals. But yet another metatarsal injury meant a long lay-off for Michael, with Newcastle's season already in dire straits. The big national question, and the key question it seemed for 'Michael Owen, Inc.', became: would the striker be fit for Germany? Even his own manager, Glenn Roeder, seemed to offer bulletins only on his striker's England chances, rather than Michael's prospects of ever lining up in stripes alongside the fast-fading Alan Shearer. Maybe Owen could fit in a few games for the floundering Geordies – just to prove his fitness for England? Sven's brow lightened at the thought of it. Michael actually ended up playing just 32 more minutes for Newcastle United before the end of the league season, a miserly return even given the England man's notoriously cautious approach to matters of his own fitness. Owen seemed carelessly oblivious to his responsibilities to his new employers and also to the Newcastle bar-code army. His priorities – as they had been since his return from Real Madrid – appeared to centre entirely on him regaining his England place and playing in Germany. The reasons why Rafa Benítez seemed happy to let Michael leave Anfield in 2004 were now much clearer: could Owen ever be fully focused on his team responsibilities at Liverpool with all this England stuff to contend with? In fact, a half-fit Wayne Rooney imploded in Germany, getting sent off in England's deciding fixture, and the ex-Liverpool man Owen was badly injured, meaning another long period out of the game. Michael was beginning to look like a very poor £17 million investment for his new club – and not such a serious loss for Liverpool FC.

BENÍTEZ AND THE LIVERPOOL FUTURE

Rafa Benítez, like most top European club managers, would have watched the 2006 World Cup finals with interest for two reasons: first, to check that he had not missed any rising young players or potential signings he might still consider for Liverpool. And second, to witness whether his own club players managed to survive the tournament without suffering complete exhaustion and/or serious injury. The relatively early departure of both Spain and England from the finals offered some relief in these last respects; it also offered some much-needed rest for Gerrard, Carragher, Alonso and Luis Garcia, all veterans of the 2004–06 Liverpool playing marathon. So Rafa Benítez could start his third season at Anfield with both a sense of stability and reasonable optimism. 'We knew the key thing for Rafa after Valencia,' Rick Parry said, 'was that he needed a project in which he could be sure that everyone was pulling in the same direction. We had no doubts that Rafa could manage in England. He didn't have much knowledge of the British game when he arrived, but he was a student of the game, very adaptable and a quick learner with plenty of European experience. We may not match Chelsea in 2006–07 – their spending power is enormous – but at least we know that under Rafa we are definitely in contention again.'

With Chelsea's recent emergence under Abramovich and Mourinho, with a hungry young Arsenal team in their lucrative new home – Liverpool will not be in theirs until 2009 at the earliest, by which time the original Anfield design may already be out of date judging by the new generation of World Cup stadiums in Germany – and with Manchester United desperate to challenge again, winning the Premiership title in England in 2007 is probably as difficult as it has ever been. Nevertheless, Rafa Benítez seems to be up for the challenge.

Liverpool FC has still to field a team in its history with no British players – but it was always a possibility during the 2006–07 season under their 'global' Spanish manager. The 20-year-old Argentine defender Gabriel Paletta (from Club Atlético Banfield) and the experienced left-sided Brazilian defender/midfielder Fabio Aurelio (from Valencia) were snapped up by Benítez in the summer of 2006. The exciting Chilean winger Mark González was also finally granted a work permit for his new club in early July. The new Liverpool campaign for 2006–07 was beginning to take shape – and with a decidedly Hispanic flavour. But will the Kop notice more the heritage or the quality of these imports?

As the new arrivals began to assemble – and more would soon follow – some key Liverpool figures from Istanbul and the 2005–06 campaign would prepare to move out of Anfield. The most significant of these was, without question, Dietmar Hamann, a master defensive midfielder in an era when the position was becoming the very fulcrum of general team strategy. He had been a vital Liverpool presence wisely recruited by Gérard Houllier, and he had also, uncomplainingly and unforgettably, rescued Liverpool at their lowest ebb in Istanbul. His new adventure, at Manchester City, would soon fizzle out. Djibril Cissé would leave on loan for Marseille, a man plagued by serious injury and terrible hairstyles who never really found his feet in England. The same might be said of Fernando Morientes, who was quickly returning to Spain, his English ambitions unfulfilled. Leaving too was French defender Djimi Traoré, for Portsmouth, another Istanbul survivor who would always have his 2005 European Cup medal to show to his many doubters. Later, local hopeful and fellow left-back Steven Warnock would also move, this time to Blackburn Rovers, though Liverpool would never quite solve the problem of the left side in 2006–07 after these departures and a serious injury to the Brazilian Fabio Aurelio.

Benítez, like Arsène Wenger and the other technocrats in European football, no longer sees the passports of players, only what they can bring to his team. And the fans? Well, they will continue to argue that local passion and commitment ideally needs to be fused with global talent. They will want to see both quality global signings *and* local kids given a chance – as in Liverpool's successful 2006 Youth Cup-winning side. And they will also continue to rail chauvinistically that any perceived lack of commitment on the pitch can still be directly linked with the arrival of 'foreign mercenaries'. But in the end – as with the great German Liverpudlian Didi Hamann – being a 'Scouser' in the new global era (or even a 'Basque' or a 'Catalan') is increasingly more an attitude of mind than it is an accident of birth (is Thierry Henry any less the icon of modern Arsenal for being French?). So, in the summer of 2006, as fans of Liverpool, Barça and Bilbao, and all the other 'sub-national' communities around the world, grazed around the World Cup finals in Germany, their thoughts would soon return to the bigger, more important tests that lie ahead – in European club-football land. As Rafa himself might say, 'Amunt Liverpool!'

Epilogue

The One and Only? Rafa Benítez, US Dollars and the Road to Athens 2007

World Cup failure; Liverpool title favourites in 2007; new
signings and raised expectations; the sad end in the beginning;
the Liverpool Americans – over here and in charge; the bumpy
road to Athens.

WORLD CUP WIPEOUT

As Rafa Benítez considered his transfer options ahead of a new
English season and Liverpool Football Club moved ever closer
to securing the kind of investment the Spaniard now demanded
for league success, there was only summer football misery to
contemplate in Germany in 2006. In a blaze of national flag
waving and extraordinary fan support, there was more England
international failure – which finally meant adios to Swedish Sven,
his pockets stuffed with FA sterling. Even before this, there was a
charmless managerial chase around Europe for the men from Soho
Square, before they stumbled back to the UK to hire a very familiar
face: Steve McClaren (*Steve McClaren!*). The new England man
was an almost uniformly unpopular replacement for the reviled
Sven; a resignation or (more likely) a future sacking just waiting to
happen. Rarely could Spain's Jesús Gil's words on a new managerial
appointment in football have seemed more appropriate: 'It may be
that he is not the right man, but when all the other trains have left

the station you can only take the one that is left.' Or else go for the time-serving stationmaster.

Both Sven and McClaren had been let down in Germany by their 'Golden Generation' of players, of course – another set of very ordinary England outings for Liverpool's Steven Gerrard among them – but the real failing here was in squad selection and a lack of inspiration and imagination from the bench and on the coaching ground. McClaren, for his part, had 'led' Middlesbrough to the UEFA Cup final in 2006 mainly on the back of a couple of unlikely home revivals from the dead against very ordinary European opposition, including familiar Liverpool foes FC Basle. In the final in Eindhoven, the Spanish club Sevilla proved to have no such soft centre. They ran out embarrassingly comfortable 4–0 winners. The Brazilian Daniel Alves, a long-time Liverpool transfer target, looked like an uncompromisingly talented if unstable presence on the Spanish right-hand side. Word seeped out of Anfield later that Rafa Benítez had been furious at being held up by the Liverpool board in 2006 when offered Alves for £12 million – the midfield man was probably worth double that amount by 2007. This guy could still have fun in the Premiership if, that is, he could manage to stay upright for more than five minutes at a time. But Barcelona and Real Madrid were now also said to be interested, and the new Alves price tag was climbing daily. He would stay in Spain as Benítez fumed.

This unconvincing progress to the UEFA Cup final – and then the abject collapse which followed – and his anonymously loyal work alongside the gloomy, failing Sven, got McClaren the top England job. It was awarded to him by staunch Reds fan and caught-in-the-headlights new FA chief executive Brian Barwick. How could it come to this? Even the rudimentary Sam Allardyce was preferable to a sort of slow national death. But bumbling Sam, and his shoal of football nutritionists, scientists and statisticians, was rejected by the FA. As was Martin O'Neill, who looked on, bemused like the rest of us, as McClaren cosily settled in at Soho Square. Big Sam would very soon become the subject of some clumsy (and largely unsubstantiated) BBC TV allegations about Premiership bungs – a very nasty business. For his part, the Northern Irishman O'Neill would eventually join Aston Villa as manager, lured by new US cash and Doug Ellis's timely departure. Martin could make even the Villa play and would certainly assure that they would be difficult to beat from then on. Could anyone really say the same of McClaren's England?

LIVERPOOL – 2007 TITLE FAVOURITES!

For many Liverpool fans, and naturally for Rafa Benítez himself, the summer exploits in Germany were briefly diverting. Especially interesting perhaps was a satisfyingly spiteful World Cup fallout to savour. It was between England's Wayne Rooney and Cristiano Ronaldo, Portugal's talented winger, in Gelsenkirchen – both men domestic employees of Manchester United, of course. A steaming Rooney got his marching orders for a spot of disorderly stamping in a dull quarter-final meeting. His United teammate Ronaldo later winked conspiratorially to camera, implying he had suckered poor Wayne and possibly the referee. This piece of high drama was not the stuff of training-ground harmony back in Manchester. In fact, this violent, angry tiff, and the deception which followed it, might just be enough to further destabilise what seemed like an already tottering project at Trafford Towers when a new season approached in England. Sir Alex Ferguson and his coaching staff had to fly, post-haste, to Germany to reassure the Portugal man that he would be accepted and loved again, everything forgotten, back in the Manchester fold. Real Madrid looked on with undisguised avarice as young Wayne busily texted make-up notes to his new-found (and cunning) buddy.

Meanwhile, the ageless Ryan Giggs, a man never distracted by the World Cup but one now seeking to overtake Liverpool's Phil Neal in the English club medal count, would be searching for a record ninth league title in 2007. He was surely United's greatest-ever player.

But even Giggs would miss the Madrid-bound Van Nistelrooy, and Roy Keane had not yet been effectively replaced at Old Trafford. The brilliant Paul Scholes was another long-term injury worry for Sir Alex. Replacement midfielder Michael Carrick looked seriously undercooked at £17 million from Spurs. All round, United looked a little uneasy and potentially vulnerable, no question. Reds fans, west along the M62 – and their equivalents at Arsenal and Chelsea – could only sit and hope as the men from Manchester visibly creaked in their pre-season outings.

Arsenal's Arsène Wenger also seemed damaged by events in 2006, but this time by the Champions League final defeat in Paris. His main man and 2006 World Cup finalist Thierry Henry seemed fatally unsure about whether to stay with the club or join the European Cup winners, the multi-talented Catalans from Barcelona. He eventually stayed in London for the 2006–07 season but, perhaps predictably, not to much purpose. Sure, there were impressive new signings to fear at Arsenal – the Czech Tomas Rosicky and William Gallas from Chelsea among them – but Ashley Cole and especially Sol Campbell were gone from the Arsenal rearguard and would be missed. And the club's brilliant Dutch muse Dennis Bergkamp had finally retired. Eric Cantona excepted, Bergkamp had probably been the most influential foreign player in the history of the British game: the Highbury Dalglish. All this meant that Arsenal – powerful, graceful Arsenal – suddenly looked callow and transitional, rebuilding for a new era. The Gunners were also moving into a cavernous new arena in August 2006, a sure sign of uneven home form to come. A frustrated Wenger would eye up Europe rather than stake all his chips on a serious league challenge in 2007.

Across town at 2006 champions Chelsea, things were also thrillingly uncertain. Even the previously cherubic José Mourinho was beginning to look a little less like the avuncular and winsome pin-up he had seemed when he first breezed into the British game as the self-proclaimed Special One in the summer of 2004. At Porto, he had reminded us that it was a case of 'God, and after God, me.' Not any more. The Portuguese manager was still ruthlessly, cleverly funny in a sport that often seemed to lack real brains and to have had a humour bypass – though José's labelling of Arsène Wenger as a 'voyeur' was to hit a new bum note. Mourinho was now routinely whining in press conferences – about referees, about penalties, about crowds, about injuries – and he looked increasingly like a captain without a crew as new players arrived at Stamford Bridge either by the back door (Ashley Cole) or, seemingly, without the coach's knowledge (the hulking Dutchman Boulahrouz) or approval (the German World Cup captain Michael Ballack). Mind you, one of these unsolicited new arrivals in west London in 2006 made everyone in the English game sit up: in rolled the Ukrainian master striker Andriy Shevchenko, lately seduced for megabucks from AC Milan.

If someone else other than the Special One was now doing the player recruitment at Chelsea – the Dane Frank Arnesen, by all accounts – he was buying at European football's equivalent of Harrods, not the local corner shop. José still complained and moaned, of course. The Ukraine man was not *his* pick, no matter what his supposed qualities. Like Rafa Benítez, José Mourinho had not come to England to be second guessed by some backroom bureaucrat, and he also had no truck with star players who might bridle at the Chelsea work ethic that he had carefully built around Drogba, Makélélé and Essien. Inevitably, Shevchenko and his wife were rumoured to be close to Roman Abramovich and his Russian entourage. It was also rumoured that the arch-pragmatist Mourinho was now frustrating his Russian boss, a man who must have reasoned that he had spent enough money in west London to demand his victories with style as well as substance.

So the previously invulnerable two-times Premiership title holders looked slightly shaken and disunited for 2006–07, their coach at odds with his owner. The new men at Chelsea, who had been brought in to secure Champions League success, would also take time to settle, especially under the glowering eye of the Special One. But Chelsea still had Cech, Lampard and Terry as well as their other battle-hardened and focused warriors to contest the Premiership at home. And the fearsome Drogba was now teamed up with a new striking mate, the deadly Shevchenko, a man with something to prove to his new boss. It was not all bad news at Chelsea.

With three of the big four in England apparently in some turmoil – or at least promising to be initially unsettled and fixated on Europe – the British sports press was now full of a Premiership title challenge that would surely come from another direction. Improbably, the new 2007 Premiership title favourites were not from Manchester or west or north London but, instead, from Liverpool. The reasoning for this slightly zany choice went something like this: first, three seasons into his new life at Anfield, the Spaniard Benítez had now become fully acclimatised to the battering brutality of English football. A slightly fortunate European Cup win in 2005 coupled with wretched away league form had been followed by a much improved and more consistent showing in the league and an FA Cup win in 2006. In his first two seasons in England, the Liverpool manager had already secured two of the three key football trophies available to him. OK, the missing pot was the hardest of them all to grasp – the Premiership title – but Benítez had recognised his failings in 2004–05, part rectified them with good signings in 2005–06 and could now fully focus on a positive domestic league challenge in 2006–07. He might also soon have the cash to buy players he really wanted, rather than opt for those he could afford. Liverpool as champions seemed an obvious and simple choice, a no-brainer – to British sports journalists, that is.

Second, Wenger, Ferguson and Mourinho all seemed to be more likely to be focused on Europe, rather than on domestic silverware in 2007, if all for different reasons. The 2006 defeat in Paris had at last made winning the European Cup seem realistically within Arsenal's grasp, and Wenger's side obviously lacked the fortitude and experience to win the Premiership in 2007. At Chelsea, Roman Abramovich already seemed bored with reeling off Premiership titles and domestic cup wins – he now demanded the big prize for Chelsea, or his scowling manager might be shown the door. Finally, it was widely assumed that pensioner Sir Alex was only hanging on at Manchester United for that defining second Champions League win: a European legacy of sorts to go with United's domestic dominance in the 1990s. Which left Rafael Benítez and Liverpool.

Benítez, already a European Cup winner at Anfield in 2005, was now visibly bridling at suggestions (mainly from the mischievous Mourinho, of course) that he would never build a serious title-challenging side at Anfield. A successful 'cup' team, sure, but his Liverpool had only history for comfort and now lacked the mettle and the steely consistency – the necessary seriousness – required to compete in the league. This was incendiary stuff, and it left a furious Benítez mumbling on about the missing millions that supposedly kept Liverpool out of the title reckoning. Which all meant that, even more so than his chief rivals – or so this opaque reasoning went – Rafa Benítez wanted the Premiership title very badly indeed in 2007. Steven Gerrard confirmed as much. He reported that the message that came every day from his global fan mailbox was no longer about Europe. It simply said, 'Get the league for us.'

The third reason why the pundits backed Liverpool in the league in 2007 seemed the most improbable of all: it was the supposed quality and statement of intent provided by Rafa Benítez's new signings for 2006–07. The focus was all width and attack – feeding time for the lanky Peter Crouch. The South African-born 22-year-old Chilean left-winger Mark González, for example, had certainly impressed in Spain, and Benítez had been indulging him for some time, positively hounding the British immigration services for the work permit that would allow his long-purchased new star to show exactly what he could do in England. Frankly, no Liverpool fan was yet convinced. The guy was fast, sure, but he had never faced the kind of physical pounding and work ethic that would now confront him weekly in the Premiership. He had a lot to prove.

On the right-hand side it was potentially worse news, because in came relegated Birmingham City's Jermaine Pennant, an ex-con and a player once released by Arsène Wenger because of his determined waywardness. Pennant seemed alarmingly inconsistent and lacking in the sort of discipline, real pace and quality – possibly another El Hadji Diouf – to be part of any serious title-chasing team. Did this new man (with *no* senior international caps to his name) really have the technique, brains and maturity required to be a key player in a Liverpool 2007 league title challenge? This seemed doubtful to say the least; unless, of course, the crafty Benítez had seen more than most seasoned observers of the English game.

And to provide balance for Pennant on the right, in came another unstable influence on the *other* side of the field in the shape of Blackburn Rovers' left-sided striker Craig Bellamy. The recommendation here was Bellamy's 13 league goals for Blackburn in 2005–06 (but from how many chances?) and also his authentic aggression and pace. And perhaps, too, his cut price £6 million fee and 'lifelong Liverpool fan' credentials. But Bellamy's close control and crossing ability seemed much less assured than even that of his Rovers teammate Morten Gamst Pedersen. And now Liverpool fans would be pressed to compare the limited Welshman to the Robbens, Ronaldos and Rooneys of this world. It seemed a tough ask. Bellamy's other notable quality was his unerring capacity to fall out with pretty much every dressing-room (and there were many) he had ever played in; he was a sort of Taffy Stan Collymore. He also had some of Stan's least attractive tendencies *off* the pitch, including a mouth and general approach to life that meant he found it difficult not to respond to the routine nightclub goading and the dangerous temptations that now faced all senior British professional footballers in England. He needed to grow up fast. Like Pennant, he looked more like trouble rather than a potential source of salvation for Liverpool in the Premiership.

Finally, in a rather more inspired move – or at least a more solid one – Benítez eventually returned to Continental Europe for a striker Liverpool had been associated with in despatches for some time: Feyenoord's Dirk Kuyt. The sturdy Kuyt had good touch and intelligence, and the credentials of a reliable finisher. His record was a goal every two matches in Holland, a true striker's tariff. He was also robust, missing only five matches in seven seasons in Holland. He was a willing worker, a man who could be reasonably relied upon to keep the ball when all else was falling apart around you – a team player who soon impressed Steven Gerrard and the other Reds' seniors with both his application and technique. The crucial question about Kuyt – the only one answered in the case of the other major Benítez signings in the summer of 2006 – was: did he have the basic cruising speed to survive in the Premiership? Did he also have real dynamism and invention? We would have to wait and see.

So, for around £25 million spent – less than on one Wayne Rooney, certainly – and none of it on really proven Premiership quality, Rafa Benítez was widely supposed to have converted his failing league side into authentic title contenders. None of it really added up, not even the theory of it. To be fair to him, the Liverpool manager was slow to voice his own view that this kind of bargain-basement transfer work would make Liverpool truly competitive at this level. And as we closed in on the 25th anniversary of Bill Shankly's death, it was also pertinent to return in this context to the great Liverpool man's philosophy for the game as expressed in his 1970 autobiography. Successful teams, argued Shankly, needed, above all, courage. 'Courage is more than being able to stand up to buffeting on the field of play,' he said. '[It is] to have principles, be they of fitness or morality and stick by them; to do what you feel you must do, not because it is the popular thing to do but because it is the right thing to do. Courage is skill, plus dedication, plus fitness, plus honesty, plus fearlessness. It is a big word.' And a typically brilliant analysis from the Glenbuck sage that still had resonance almost 40 years later. Did *this* Liverpool, under *this* manager, have *this* kind of courage, as the British press guys now suggested?

But there it was, in grubby newsprint: it was Liverpool that was now the popular choice to unseat the incumbent English champions in the 2007 Premiership as Chelsea Arsenal and United all scrapped it out for European glory. Meanwhile, Rick Parry and the Anfield backroom men continued to try to tie down a takeover deal with either Dubai investors DIC or unknown American entrepreneurs to provide an impatient Rafa with the sort of backing the Spaniard claimed he *really* needed to win the title. Benítez at least had a close season clear of conjecture and unrest among his own players for once. He could remain focused on league business, on making that vital fast start in domestic competition. But, as is often the case with football, the 2006–07 Liverpool story didn't quite play out like that. Shankly's 'courage' was often hard to trace. In fact, after just two months of the new league season, no one at Anfield even bothered with the Premiership title theory any more.

LIVERPOOL'S 12-MATCH PREMIERSHIP TITLE CHALLENGE

OK, no bullshitting. No one could doubt that Liverpool's first six away fixtures in the 2006–07 Premiership season were daunting tests: at promoted Sheffield United and then at Everton, Chelsea, Bolton Wanderers, Manchester United and Arsenal – five deadly away trips in a row. Who was on the computer keyboard at the Premier League? If we could stay in touch with the top two after these trials, the title might even be on. This was the new theory. Even some losses with, say, seven points gained from a run of these six early ball-breakers might be a decent return. But Benítez's Liverpool managed just one, from a Robbie Fowler equalising penalty at Sheffield. It was the only Liverpool goal scored in the six matches. At Everton, Bolton, United and Arsenal the defeats were comprehensive: ten goals against; none scored. Even Chelsea beat Liverpool playing with ten men for a half. Was this rank bad luck, a tough run of fixtures that simply offered no respite, or a return to the familiar Benítez away-match failings of 2004–05?

This 'new' Liverpool certainly looked cautious and toothless away from Anfield, and also vulnerable at the back, with Reina and young Daniel Agger struggling for a foothold and the new Reds wingers predictably failing to keep the ball, make it consistently to the byline or put in anything resembling a convincing defensive shift away from the comforts of home. The Dutchman Dirk Kuyt seemed confident and lively at Anfield, but near anonymous in hostile territory. Benítez, meanwhile, just kept messing around with his forward players, seeking a formula, but actually sowing seeds of doubt. After 12 games in 2006–07, Peter Crouch, Liverpool's leading scorer, had started and finished precisely one match – as had the much trumpeted Mark González. From February 2005, Benítez had famously fielded 99 different Liverpool teams in 99 consecutive fixtures. Where was the consistency, the inner certainty about Liverpool's best XI? It all looked rather messy and disjointed – and terrifyingly lacking in ambition – especially on the road. In October veteran Liverpool director Noel White said as much and was eventually forced to resign for publicly criticising the coach. But the facts did not lie. In winning the Premiership title in 2006 Chelsea had lost a total of five games; Liverpool had already lost five matches (out of twelve) by 12 November 2006, the latest an abject 0–3 submission to Arsenal at the Emirates. Whatever the reason, there would be no league title for Benítez in 2007. Even the dogs in the street knew it.

In Europe the story was different, if not exactly inspiring. After uncertainly seeing off Maccabi Haifa in the qualifier, Liverpool drew a reassuringly weak Champions League group that included PSV, Galatasaray and Bordeaux, and proceeded to deal with these rivals with some efficiency, if hardly with great flair or anything approaching real style. A 0–0 draw in Eindhoven, when the hosts seemed cowed, smacked especially of a wasted opportunity rather than a job well done. It spoke of the brand of Benítez pragmatism and technocracy at its least attractive. Nevertheless, as December approached, and with three European wins secured at Anfield, Liverpool could even afford a Keystone Cops defeat in the final fixture in Turkey and still qualify at the top of the group. But this time there was little reward for sweeping away the early opposition: it was European champions Barcelona that now awaited Liverpool in the last 16 of the Champions League in February.

Before then it was a case of picking up the Reds league form, and things did indeed improve as the opposition diminished. From 25 November to New Year's Day 2007, against moderate rivals, there were seven Liverpool league wins, one draw and only one defeat, a 0–1 Boxing Day robbery away to Blackburn Rovers. But Liverpool were still well adrift in the Premiership, and a possibly season defining week loomed next for Benítez in early January 2007: two meetings with Arsenal in the domestic cups, both of them at Anfield, which was by then something of a fortress. Two victories and a slick Liverpool limo could power on with the season still stretching invitingly ahead, both at home and abroad. Two defeats and the wheels might just come off the unreliable Liverpool jalopy, and with the Nou Camp looming. We got the defeats – alarming ones.

In the first meeting, the FA Cup tie on 9 January, all Kopites willingly gave up the first six minutes of the contest in favour of an astonishing protest made up of continuous chanting and a fan mosaic for justice for the Hillsborough 96. Bill Shankly himself would have marvelled at this collective show of courage – at the power of popular protest, the sheer gritty politics of the Liverpool crowd. But as the placards came down it was Arsenal that sparkled with Tomas Rosicky positively mocking Benítez's purchase of Pennant for around the same price by scoring and generally tormenting his hosts with authoritative touches of real vision and quality. Even the Bootle colossus Jamie Carragher gifted Wenger's men a second-half goal, thus sealing a stunning 1–3 reverse. The League Cup tie with Arsenal just three days later at least offered potential balm for this deep Liverpool wound, especially as Arsène Wenger was determined to use his youngsters for the re-engagement. It looked like an inviting offer of an easy Liverpool victory, but a stubborn Benítez predictably refused the bait and the relative security of an extended League Cup run. Instead, he fielded Steven Gerrard amidst a raw mixture of his own untried and uncertain squad players in front of a packed and raucous Anfield congregation who had bought the cheap tickets on offer. The outcome was devastation.

Coupling the hapless and flat-footed young Argentinian centre-back Gabriel Paletta (a £2 million Benítez gamble) with a slowing Sami Hyypiä and Lee Peltier, a raw local right-back, in front of the nervous Jerzy Dudek was sufficient encouragement for the inexperienced Arsenal youngsters, who on this night were crucially supplemented by Cesc Fabragas and the burly Brazilian striker Baptista. Paletta, especially, managed to make the Arsenal reserve centre-forward, the young Frenchman Jérémie Aliadière, look like a fleet-footed world beater as Arsenal tore through the callow Liverpool rearguard almost at will. Baptista ended the evening with an unprecedented four goals, Arsenal with six and Liverpool three. Statisticians reached for their record books. Later, Benítez tetchily stuck to his guns about selecting a Liverpool team he thought was capable of winning the match. Some critics thought he simply had no time for this competition, seeing it as a distraction to his 2007 Champions League ambitions. They may well have been correct. Benítez even managed to try to turn this embarrassing surrender to his advantage by suggesting that the result simply revealed the acute quality gap he had warned about that was growing between Liverpool's academy and the global youth system now in place at Arsenal. To keep pace, Liverpool needed to spend and recruit globally, he argued, even at schoolboy ages. This opened up another can of worms and a particular Rafa bête noire.

Later Benítez would again call for reserve teams from the Premiership clubs to be allowed to play in the Football League (as in Spain) and for a complete revamp of the academy system in England. Here he fell out badly with both fans of smaller league clubs in England and with Liverpool academy director Steve Heighway's holistic – and fiercely local – approach to producing young talent. This clearly hurt.

In 2007 Heighway was proudly on the road to coaching Liverpool's second youth-cup-winning squad in two years. He bridled at Benítez's implied criticisms of the Liverpool way at youth level, saying, 'In our current youth team, nine of the starting eleven I brought here at nine years old. To me, that's a youth policy. Buying players at 16 to put them in the academy is not really a youth policy, is it? Not truly, not for me.' This seemed like an impasse: a case of the 'new' football world meeting the old; a clash of hard professional Continental values set against the careful and warm nurturing of precious local hopes in Britain. 'That dream [of playing for Liverpool] has to exist for Scouse kids,' said Heighway bluntly and not unreasonably. Most fans would probably agree with him, at least on an emotional level. The coach Benítez, more coldly perhaps, wanted only winners from anywhere and by any route. There is no room for politics or sentiment in the Rafa school: he exists only to coach winning football teams. It was Heighway who resigned, leaving with a bitter rejoinder to Benítez at the season's end. And it was the Liverpool manager who would soon be sustained in his globally focused, cold-eyed view of the business of elite sport – albeit from a rather unexpected source.

FISTFULS OF DOLLARS

After negotiations lasting months, even to the point of verbal agreements and handshakes, a potential £450-million investment in Liverpool FC from the Middle East consortium Dubai Investment Capital – a bid fronted for the Maktoums by proclaimed Liverpool fan Sameer Al Ansari – was formally withdrawn on 31 January 2007. DIC was furious at the collapse in negotiations, describing the Liverpool board as 'dishonourable' and the club as 'a shambles'. Claim and counter claims followed, with further recriminations and real anger. American sports and property tycoon George Gillett had also been in talks with Liverpool for some months, but he had seemed unwilling or unable to raise the necessary capital to cover a share buy out,

Liverpool's existing £80-million debt or the cash required to build the new Liverpool stadium. He also seemed reluctant to fund player recruitment on the scale now demanded by Benítez. The DIC group sneered that the soccer-phobic Gillett would not know Liverpool FC from a 'hole in the ground'. But Gillett had now done some homework, and he returned to the Liverpool board with a big-money partner, the Texan sports and property man, and staunch George Bush supporter, Tom Hicks.

Hicks had made his fortune from raising private equity to fund multibillion dollar corporate takeovers. He also owned US sports franchises. Together these hard-nosed Americans now tabled a joint bid worth £5,000 a Liverpool share – a reported £174 million – more than that offered by DIC and raising the value of David Moores's shares to a reported £88 million. They also cleverly promised Reds shareholders that they could keep all their existing rights for priority tickets if they sold up. It was hard to resist. Gillett had also shelved his preference for a shared stadium on Stanley Park and was willing to guarantee the other necessary investment at Liverpool, which brought the total to a reported £450 million – or just under ten times the current reported paper valuation of Everton. At the very last second Liverpool accepted the US offer over the DIC proposals. But there was a price tag. Most of this money – £298 million of it – would be raised in loans, with Liverpool FC paying off some, if not all, of the £21.5 million annual interest involved. The Americans planned to register the club in a holding company, Kop Investment LLC located in the tax havens of the Cayman Islands and the US state of Delaware. Hey, these guys are businessmen, remember.

It was a lot to take in. After 115 years of transparency, local ownership and patrician values – and even a spell of self-ordained football socialism under Bill Shankly – LFC was now in the hands of the sort of global capitalists who made no secret of their ignorance of the sport or of their deep commercial interest in the Premiership. They openly highlighted the attractions of the booming TV monies, growing internet income for football, expanding markets for the club in South East Asia and South America, and even their plans for introducing American-style 'bunker suites' into the new Liverpool stadium: underground living rooms where the corporate elite could dine in plush splendour and watch banks of TV sets before taking an elevator ride to their match seats. The new stadium would also be put up for naming rights to the highest bidder: Anfield was old hat, apparently – spent symbolism. Major changes were clearly afoot. It all seemed so foreign, so commercially sterile – so *American*.

Local resistance to this corporate smash and grab of a world famous sporting institution – just two months in completion – was surprisingly muted on Merseyside in many people's eyes. But then the cosmopolitan city of Liverpool is no stranger to American cultural and commercial penetration, and it was also becoming increasingly clear that there was no benign British investor willing to stump up the sort of money that was now required. Hard realism was at work – what was the alternative? Rafa Benítez was also a central figure in driving this deal on, even if he stayed mainly in the background. He had certainly become frustrated at Rick Parry's difficulties in getting the 'right sort of people' to invest in the club. Benítez had heard promises from the Liverpool board that a deal was 'only weeks away' virtually since he had arrived at Anfield in the summer of 2004. By 2007, and despite the Miracle of Istanbul, Liverpool FC seemed no nearer to being competitive in the Premiership and had slipped to 10th in the European football club money league. Real Madrid was now making louder and louder noises about coming back to reclaim Rafa from Liverpool. Even with a newly purchased £4-million home on the Wirral, it seemed that an investment deal needed to be done, and done now, in order for the Spaniard to commit to Liverpool in the longer term.

The new men from the USA were also very well managed in their attempts to sell this remarkable takeover to Liverpool supporters. They showed little of the arrogance of the Glazers, for example, who thought that money was its own explanation and who had made no attempt at all to engage with Manchester United fans or to attend United matches. 'They are very private people,' said Hicks of the Glazers. 'I have owned sports teams for 13 years. I gave up my privacy a long time ago, and it is easier for me to be open about these things.' That was clear. The Liverpool Americans were soon in the directors' box at Anfield and were also paraded in front of the British press and to Liverpool supporters. They seemed to enjoy the public exposure, and they handled it well. They came to their first meeting armed with all the right notes about the traditions of the club, the famous Kop, the passion of the fans, the 18 titles, and even the bleak years of the 1930s and '40s and the Liverpool tragedies of the 1980s. They had swotted up more on their purchase than many Liverpool supporters might have done. Their transatlantic slips showed only occasionally: the use of the terms 'franchises', 'defence men' and the 'Liverpool Reds', for example, emphasised uneasily the surreal and distancing feel to these events. Were they really talking about *us*, these avuncular but icily determined baseball and ice-hockey magnates? And what were they doing posing cockily under the 'This is Anfield' sign, as if they owned the goddam place?

The rhetoric skilfully employed by the new men about 'the Liverpool family', mainly in an attempt to try to hide aspects of the bleak economics, also worked well for the them. The Moores family dynasty would now be seamlessly replaced by Gilletts and Hicks. This was the message, reinforced in a commemorative booklet issued by Liverpool Football Club as if the organisation had been acquired through marriage by some august royal family from a superior and distant culture. It was business, sure, but with a fun face and with deep 'respect' for the institution and for 'family values'. Frankly, some of this sounded like straight Bush-speak, but it was also carefully measured and clearly well meant. Gillett's son Foster even came over to work on a day-to-day basis on an executive level with Rick Parry. This last bit of news was a little left-field; Liverpool had once briefly had two managers (Evans and Houllier) to disastrous effect and two men in charge of administration when Rick Parry had first joined the club and found Peter Robinson reluctant to leave his office. Now it would have two chief executives, one steeped in the English game and its values and commercial systems, the other trying to apply the hot breath of the US approach to mixing corporate profits with sport. And it would also have two owners. How, exactly, would this arrangement pan out, because it seemed potentially full of tensions and conflict. By the end of the season there were reports that, realising who now held the purse strings, Rafa Benítez had started to by-pass Parry and was talking directly to Foster Gillett in order to expedite transfers and other matters. The Liverpool chief executive and committed fan Parry was already starting to look increasingly and disturbingly isolated in the new Liverpool ownership structure.

Finally, what could also be said of the new American owners – for good or ill – was that, unlike the Glazers, they would be hands-on proprietors and that they would at least be *engaged* by the sporting side of the business they had bought. These guys did seem to like sport and to understand its cultural importance, the role of the fans and the more 'earthy' side to the English game. They soon found out about the latter. After attending the Reds away match at Upton Park on 30 January (a 2–1 win) they were both alarmed and impressed by the informality and the foul language of a typical English football crowd. Their Anfield debut came in the home Champions League match against Barcelona, whence they faced something even more bemusing to American sports fans than this or the 'zero–zero tie': a match lost on the night but, with the home crowd widely celebrating, a Champions League tie gloriously won. These Limeys and their sporting ways, and such glorious confusions: a home defeat but still we win! 'We are custodians not owners of the franchise,' Gillett said, thus simultaneously reassuring and alarming Liverpool supporters. This would be a steep learning curve for both Liverpool fans and their new American friends. The new deal would clearly not be without its traumas.

THE ROAD TO ATHENS

After the terrible home cup defeats to Arsenal, redemption of sorts followed for Benítez with a comfortable home win against an injury-ravaged Chelsea and Jermaine Pennant on the score sheet at last. Peter Crouch, who still seemed like Liverpool's only really reliable goal scorer, was by now mysteriously rooted on the bench as Benítez sought the magic formula up front. It was not found for the visit of Everton, who clung on grimly to a 0–0 draw at Anfield, prompting the Liverpool manager to remark casually to the media on how 'little' clubs coming to L4 often packed their defence and hoped for a point. Take a deep breath. Was this insult calculated? Was it connected to the expected impact of the new US investment at Anfield? It certainly had David Moyes and Bill Kenwright spluttering away, and it was also a welcome rejoinder for Kopites to all the premeditated 'People's Club' propaganda dreamed up by Moyes for Goodison Park at the start of his five-year plan for the revival of the Blues.

Nor was the Benítez magic much in evidence for the trip to Newcastle United (a 1–2 loss) or the visit to Anfield of table-topping Manchester United on 3 March 2007, though Liverpool did produce their best display against United in some years, before unluckily falling to a late, late Ronaldo free-kick forced in by John O'Shea in front of the Kop. The United players and crowd celebrated as if they had actually won the Premiership title. It may well, indeed, have been the crucial result of the whole campaign. In the middle of all this league action – which, for Liverpool, was now simply about fighting off the Premiership also-rans like Everton and Bolton in order to secure another top-four finish – the Reds played what could have been their last meaningful match of a disappointing season, away to Barcelona in the Champions League. And what a night it was.

Rafa had been convinced, perversely, that having one's domestic cup ambitions ended in three days in January by Arsenal had its compensations. This point was raised later by José Mourinho. Chelsea eventually won both domestic cups in England in 2007 and challenged for the league to the last – but failed, perhaps as a consequence, in the Champions League. Liverpool, with no such Premiership or cup distractions, could focus solely on Europe. God knows, this Benítez Liverpool side continued to look woeful away from home in the Premiership in 2007. The coach seemed obsessed with always trying to 'work out' the opposition when just playing with freedom would probably have sufficed. Nil–nil draws at both Aston Villa and Manchester City revealed the real poverty of his tinkering. But this lack of focus in home competitions also meant that the arch Continental tactician Benítez now had his vital preparation time – a full ten days between fixtures – in which he could meticulously plot the downfall of Barcelona in the Nou Camp. This arrangement played exactly to the Spaniard's strengths: setting a solid defensive base on the training ground against stronger, more fancied, Continental opponents and thus winning the tactical exercise – and the match – in Catalonia. Thirty-one years before, John Toshack had scored there in a famous 1–0 Liverpool win in the UEFA Cup semi-final. Could this Liverpool side repeat that extraordinary result, or at least stay competitive for the return leg at Anfield?

Initially, the prospects did not look good. The 2007 Liverpool Nou Camp project started badly, actually reminding observers of the dominant British player cultures of the 1970s when Toshack was at his peak. Benítez took his squad on an extended acclimatising and bonding session to Portugal – but some of the team got to know each other rather too well. A players' night out culminated in Craig Bellamy allegedly assaulting John Arne Riise with a golf club after the Norway man had refused to take part in a karaoke session. Paradoxically, the resulting press outcry may have pulled the Liverpool camp together, and having given the entire party a public dressing down Benítez slyly selected the key perpetrators for the match. Astonishingly, each of them scored as Liverpool came back after falling behind to a Deco header to win 2–1 against a ragged looking Barcelona side in which Ronaldinho seemed disengaged. The Malian Momo Sissoko looked back to the suffocating defensive form he had shown in the previous campaign for Liverpool; perhaps the presence on the bench of a new signing from West Ham, the Argentinian defensive midfielder Javier Mascherano, had stirred him? Benítez's real tactical masterstroke, however, was to play Liverpool's new Spanish right-back Álvaro Arbeloa at *left-back*, behind Riise, to counter Lionel Messi's habit of cutting in on his left side. After a very shaky start, the plan worked to perfection. Messi soon became isolated and ineffective, and Craig Bellamy celebrated his equalising goal, a weak header just before half-time fumbled into the net by Victor Valdés, by miming a golf swing. You really could not make it up.

The return leg at Anfield saw a half-fit Samuel Eto'o restored to the Barcelona ranks and a single late Eidur Gudjohnsen goal (after substitute Pennant criminally failed to track back) momentarily stir home anxiety. But Liverpool won through in a 0–1 defeat in front of their delighted and confused new owners and a wild Anfield crowd. Mascherano showed in this contest why Benítez had bust a gut to sign him: he was immense. A quarter-final meeting with group rivals PSV – minus their injured inspirational Brazilian defender Alex – now beckoned and proved no barrier at all to Benítez, Liverpool winning 3–0 in Holland. Peter Crouch was now back in favour and scoring, having recently claimed a consummate hat-trick in front of the Kop against Arsenal in the league (4–1). Crouch continued to puzzle; he was a man who could veer between the sublime and the toweringly anonymous. But this Liverpool win in Eindhoven was not the most impressive Champions League performance in the last eight: an exultant Manchester United provided that when they destroyed Roma 7–1 at Old Trafford, having trailed from the first leg. All this meant a destiny-defining rematch for Liverpool with Mourinho's Chelsea in the semi-final, with Manchester United meeting AC Milan in the other half of the draw. All sorts of intriguing possibilities now raised themselves: another United v. Chelsea climax (the most likely outcome) to cap a season of intense domestic rivalry between the two clubs; a Liverpool v. United final, meaning a potential policing nightmare for the Greek organisers and for the clubs and the English game; or a Liverpool v. Milan repeat from 2005, which was the least likely final, but the most appealing in terms of an obvious 'revenge' story for the press.

After the first legs both semi-finals hung deliciously in the balance, though Chelsea undoubtedly held sway over Liverpool. A single Joe Cole goal after poor work by Abeloa and a torrid night for Daniel Agger from Didier Drogba, meant that any away goal scored at Anfield would almost certainly win the tie for Mourinho. Chelsea deserved to have scored more, but Liverpool were still breathing somehow. In Manchester, meanwhile, the brilliant Brazilian Kaká had threatened to destroy United, but Ferguson's men clawed their way back to an uncertain 3–2 victory in the second half after some bizarre goalkeeping from Dida and following injuries to both Rino Gattuso and Paolo Maldini.

The return legs were contrasting specimens. On a rain swept night in Milan, weakened prospective Premiership champions Manchester United were simply blown away by their hosts, losing 3–0. Maybe the Italians *were* fated after all to gain revenge for 2005? They looked powerful and focused, though also flattered by United's surprisingly flaccid show. At Anfield, after the usual mind games – mainly sparked by Mourinho but sustained by Benítez's near constant references in the build up to Chelsea's disappearing title challenge and the vital role of his '12th man', the Liverpool crowd – came the Spaniard's selection bombshell. It was that Xabi Alonso, Benítez's 'son' on the pitch, a hero of Istanbul and resolute Benítez first choice ever since, would sit this one out. Javier Mascherano, now holding the Liverpool midfield with Steven Gerrard, who played in the centre for once, routinely gave the ball away early on in the match, but he also effectively stemmed Chelsea's attacking flow. The Anfield crowd could produce nothing like the cacophony of 2005 when the early 'phantom goal' from Luis García gave the Reds and their fans something tangible to cling onto. In 2007, even after Daniel Agger's coolly swept in left-footed first-half finish from a Gerrard free-kick, Liverpool still needed more to survive: another goal or perhaps even penalty kicks. The home crowd had to *concentrate*.

Of course, we knew that this was his signature – that Rafa Benítez misses out nothing in his preparations. That his great strength was in the details of such matters. He had almost certainly calculated in the prospects of penalties on the night – and he welcomed them. Tagging back two goals on Chelsea was asking a lot, so he would settle for 1–0 if he had to. His penalty takers were experienced and honed at this level – he trusted their professionalism. He even had Toxteth's Robbie Fowler to bring on from the bench to sink the stomach-churning fifth kick, if needed, with Anfield ablaze. Liverpool's own record in penalty shoot-outs was astonishingly good – just one defeat. But Benítez's real trump card was not history, or even the men in red who approached the penalty spot on the night: it was his goalkeeper Pepe Reina.

Reina had developed into arguably the Premiership's most reliable goalkeeper in 2007, and he had a remarkable record for having saved penalties in Spain. At Villarreal he saved seven out of nine spot kicks in 2004–05, and in the 2006 FA Cup final he had saved three out of four West Ham efforts. Reina's father Miguel, also a goalkeeper, had played for Atlético Madrid in the 1974 European Cup final in the Heysel Stadium, eventually losing to Bayern Munich in a one-sided replay. Because of nerves shredded by the unique stresses of standing between the posts, Miguel had only watched his son play six or seven times in Pepe's entire professional career. His son was made of sterner stuff. Reina had had worked intensely hard with the Liverpool goalkeeping coach José Ochotorena for exactly this moment, studying opponents and best guessing their preferences. This was his time.

So, when the rest of Anfield was living on its nerve ends as Reina saved two out of three kicks from experienced Chelsea internationals at the Anfield Road end, and while the Liverpool men confidently and calmly stepped up and drove their penalty kicks, one after the other, one, two, three, past the stringy, scrum-capped Petr Cech, Rafa Benítez was sitting bizarrely cross-legged on the touchline, serene and almost Buddha-like. He knew his goalkeeper well, and he now recalled the Spanish phrase he had used with journalists to summarise his response to Mourinho's pre-match jibes: *'No ofende quien quiere sino quien puedo'* (You can talk, but it is not offensive to me). By whatever means at his disposal, Benítez had once more defeated José in a major match where it really mattered – on the pitch. It was the suddenly unemployed Robbie Fowler in his last match for Liverpool at Anfield who now looked across from the centre circle to Benítez, even as Dirk Kuyt stroked in the clinching fourth penalty, before bedlam ensued. 'Fuck Pepe Reina,' he possibly muttered. It was Liverpool FC who were bound for Athens to meet AC Milan in the 2007 Champions League final.

Bibliography

BOOKS

Aldridge, J. *My Story* (Hodder and Stoughton, 1999)

Allt, N. *The Boys From the Mersey: The Story of the Annie Road End Crew, Football's First Clobbered-up Mob* (Milo Books, 2004)

Bahamonde, A. *El Real Madrid en la Historia de España* (Taurus, 2000)

Balague, G. *A Season on the Brink: Rafael Benítez, Liverpool and the Path to European Glory* (Weidenfield and Nicolson, 2005)

Ball, P. *Morbo: The Story of Spanish Football* (WSC Books, 2001)

Ball, P. *An Englishman Abroad: Beckham's Spanish Adventure* (Ebury Press, 2004)

Belchem, J. *Merseypride: Essays in Liverpool Exceptionalism* (University of Liverpool Press, 2000)

Borrell, J. *Todos los Hombres del Murciélago. Diccionario del Valencia CF* (Editorial Agua Clara, 2000)

Burns, J. *Barça: A People's Passion* (Bloomsbury, 1999)

Burns, J. *When Beckham Went to Spain: Power, Stardom and Real Madrid* (Penguin Books, 2004)

Carlin, J. *Los Ángeles Blancos. El Real Madrid y el Nuevo Fútbol* (Seix Barral, 2004)

Connolly, K. & McWilliam, R. *Fields of Glory, Paths of Gold: The History of European Football* (Mainstream Publishing, 2005)

Corbett, J. *Everton: The School of Science* (Macmillan, 2003)

Egea, A. & Gil, A. *Un siglo de fútbol en la Comunidad Valenciana* (Fundación Bancaja, 1998)

Gil, A. *XXV Anys Fent Penya* (Carena Editors, 2005)

Godsell, A. *Europe United: A History of the European Cup / Champions League* (Sports Books Ltd, 2005)

Hale, S. & Ponting, I. *Liverpool in Europe* (Carlton Books, 2001)

Hernández Perpiñá, J. *La gran Historia del Valencia CF* (Editorial Prensa Valenciana SA, 1994)

Hughes, C. *Toshack: FourFourTwo Great Footballers* (Virgin Books, 2002)

Inglis, S. *Engineering Archie: Archibald Leitch – Football Ground Designer* (English Heritage, 2005)

Keith, J. *Dixie Dean: The Inside Story of a Football Icon* (Robson Books, 2001)

Keith, J. *Billy Liddell: The Legend Who Carried the Kop* (Robson Books, 2003)

Kennedy, A. & Williams, J. *Kennedy's Way: Inside Bob Paisley's Liverpool* (Mainstream Publishing, 2004)

Lloret, P. *Camp de Mestalla* (Fundación Bancaja, 2001)

Lloret, P. *Rafa Benítez: The Authorised Biography* (Dewi Lewis Media, 2005)

Martialay, F. *Amberes: Allí Nació la Furia Española* (RFEF, 2000)

Munck, R. *Reinventing the City? Liverpool in Comparative Perspective* (Liverpool University Press, 2003)

Nicholls, A. *Scally: Confessions of a Category C Football Hooligan* (Milo Books, 2002)

Pead, B. *Liverpool: A Complete Record, 1892–1986* (Breedon Books, 1990)

Shaw, D. *Fútbol y franquismo* (Alianza Editorial, 1987)

St John, I. *The Saint: My Autobiography* (Hodder and Stoughton, 2005)

Williams, J. & Hopkins, S. *The Miracle of Istanbul: Liverpool FC From Paisley to Benítez* (Mainstream Publishing, 2005)

Young, P. *Football on Merseyside* (Stanley Paul, 1963)

JOURNAL ARTICLES

Ascari, G. & Gagnepain, P. 'Spanish football', *Journal of Sports Economics* 7:1 (February 2006)

Farred, G. 'God's team: the painful pleasure of the miracle on the Bosphorus', *The South Atlantic Quarterly* 105:2 (Spring 2006)

Giulianotti, R. 'Celtic, the UEFA Cup and the condition of Scottish club football: notes and recommendations from Seville, Spain', *Journal of Sport and Social Issues* 27:3 (August 2003)

Hand, D. & Crolley, L. 'Spanish identities in the European press: the case of football writing', *The International Journal of the History of Sport* 22:2 (March 2005)

Jones, P. & Willks-Heeg, S. 'Capitalising culture: Liverpool 2008', *Local Economy* 19:4 (2004)

Kennedy, D. 'Locality and professional football club development: the demographics of football club support in late Victorian Liverpool', *Soccer and Society* 5:3 (Autumn 2004)

Kennedy, D. 'Class, ethnicity and civil governance: a social profile of football club directors on Merseyside in the late-nineteenth century', *The International Journal of the History of Sport* 22:5 (September 2005)

McFarland, A. 'Ricardo Zamora: the first Spanish football idol', *Soccer and Society* 7:1 (January 2006)

Marne, P. 'Whose public space is it anyway? Class, gender and ethnicity in the creation of the Sefton and Stanley Parks, Liverpool: 1858–1872', *Social & Cultural Geography* 2:4 (2001)